24B
$1.50

AF696494

Northeast Asian Perspectives on International Law

Northeast Asian Perspectives on International Law

Contemporary Issues and Challenges

Edited by

Seokwoo Lee and Hee Eun Lee

LIBRARY OF CONGRESS
SURPLUS
DUPLICATE

MARTINUS
NIJHOFF
PUBLISHERS

LEIDEN • BOSTON
2013

Northeast Asian perspectives on international law : contemporary issues and challenges / edited by Seokwoo Lee & Hee Eun Lee.
pages cm.
Includes index.
ISBN 978-90-04-25708-5 (hardback : alk. paper) — ISBN 978-90-04-25709-2 (e-book)
1. International law—East Asia. 2. ASEAN. I. Yi, Sog-u, 1967– editor of compilation.
II. Lee, Hee Eun, editor of compilation.

KZ4335.N67 2013
341.095—dc23

2013023688

This publication has been typeset in the multilingual "Brill" typeface. With over 5,100 characters covering Latin, IPA, Greek, and Cyrillic, this typeface is especially suitable for use in the humanities. For more information, please see www.brill.com/brill-typeface.

ISBN 978-90-04-25708-5 (hardback)
ISBN 978-90-04-25709-2 (e-book)

Copyright 2013 by Koninklijke Brill NV, Leiden, The Netherlands.
Koninklijke Brill NV incorporates the imprints Brill, Global Oriental, Hotei Publishing, IDC Publishers and Martinus Nijhoff Publishers.

All rights reserved. No part of this publication may be reproduced, translated, stored in a retrieval system, or transmitted in any form or by any means, electronic, mechanical, photocopying, recording or otherwise, without prior written permission from the publisher.

Authorization to photocopy items for internal or personal use is granted by Koninklijke Brill NV provided that the appropriate fees are paid directly to The Copyright Clearance Center, 222 Rosewood Drive, Suite 910, Danvers, MA 01923, USA.
Fees are subject to change.

This book is printed on acid-free paper.

FSC www.fsc.org MIX Paper from responsible sources FSC® C109576

Printed by Printforce, the Netherlands

To my mentor, the late Professor Jon M. Van Dyke who shed his light on me.
—Seokwoo Lee

To my loving parents, who taught me to seek first his kingdom and
his righteousness.
—Hee Eun Lee

CONTENTS

ACKNOWLEDGEMENTS

The editors would like to thank Megan Webb of Notre Dame Law School (Class of 2014) for her valuable assistance with editing of the papers in preparation for the publication of this volume. Hee Eun Lee would also like to extend his gratitude to Professor John Witte, Jr., Director of the Center for the Study of Law and Religion at Emory University Law School, for enabling him to spend time at the Center during the fall of 2011 when a portion of this volume was edited. He would also like to thank Handong Global University for providing a sabbatical leave grant in 2011 to support the contributions he made to this volume.

IN MEMORIAM

During the editing of this volume, Professor Jon M. Van Dyke of The William S. Richardson School of Law at the University of Hawai'i at Manoa passed away on November 29, 2011. Professor Van Dyke, a contributor to this book, was a renowned expert on international law and maritime issues. He will be remembered as a dear friend and mentor who devoted his life trying to resolve difficult international conflicts in Asia and beyond. He will be dearly missed.

PREFACE

This book is based largely on selected papers from the first joint international academic conference of international lawyers from the Chinese Society of International Law, Japanese Society of International Law, and Korean Society of International Law that took place in Seoul, Korea on July 3, 2010. The conference was the first of its kind that brought together these three societies of international law and was entitled "Northeast Asia and International Law." Prominent international legal scholars delivered papers that covered topics such as Northeast Asian Perspectives on International Law, International Law on Foreign Policy-Making, Role of International Law in Promoting Cooperation and Resolving Conflicts in Northeast Asia, International Legal Education in Northeast Asia, and Northeast Asian Perspectives on International Adjudication. Professor Seokwoo Lee of Inha University Law School (Incheon, Korea) and Hee Eun Lee of Handong International Law School (Pohang, Korea) co-edited this volume.

CHAPTER ONE

OVERVIEW—"NORTHEAST ASIAN PERSPECTIVES ON INTERNATIONAL LAW: CONTEMPORARY ISSUES AND CHALLENGES"

Seokwoo Lee* and Hee Eun Lee**

Since the end of the Cold War, Northeast Asia has been one of the most dynamic and dangerous parts of the world. Encompassing the People's Republic of China, North and South Korea, and Japan, the region has undoubtedly taken on greater global geopolitical and economic significance. The region is now home to two of the three largest economies (China and Japan) in the world and with the inclusion of South Korea, accounts for about 20 percent of global gross domestic product.[1] With the exception of North Korea, all of the countries in the region experienced, or in the case of China currently experiencing, rapid economic development that has resulted in Northeast Asia accounting for one-fifth of world production, one-sixth of world trade, and about one-half of the world's foreign currency reserves. This great economic transformation is accompanied by the tremendous political forces that animate the region. During the early part of the 21st century, Northeast Asia has seen China's ascendancy from regional hegemon to a global power challenging the United States and the European Union. The region has experienced tensions over nuclear weapons on the Korean peninsula. There is more open talk about the possibility of Korean unification and its prospects for the region. Japan has made clear that it desires to validate itself as a legitimate international leader with a permanent seat on the UN Security Council, yet there continues to be the lingering impact of old conflicts between Japan and her neighbors that continue to shape the character and volatility of the relations between Northeast Asian countries.

Consequently, the popular narratives of contemporary Northeast Asia are often described in the context of the political economy of rapid industrialization

* Professor of International Law and Director of the Inha International Ocean Law Centre, Inha University.

** Associate Dean and Associate Professor of Law, Handong International Law School.

1 *Momentum Building for Northeast Asia Trade Deal*, KOREA HERALD, Nov. 1, 2011, *available at* http://www.koreaherald.com/national/Detail.jsp?newsMLId=20111101000818.

or from the point of view of international relations in light of the global balance of power and Cold War fault lines between the actors in the region. The dramatic economic growth of Japan and Korea during the latter half of the 20th century and the Chinese economy's meteoric rise in this century has been well documented and researched. Northeast Asia has also been the focus of much study in relation to the geopolitical climate of the Cold War in the context of the conflict between the United States and the Soviet Union. While economists and political scientists have made great contributions to study of the region and its modern history, a frequently overlooked area of study is the function and impact of international law on the relations of the countries in the region. Indeed, the argument that is being made in the pages of this volume is that international law has had an important, if somewhat muted role since it was introduced to the region by the West in the 19th century up through the period of the Cold War. It has taken on a more significant role in the post-Cold War era reflecting the dynamism of the region and the prospects for establishing an order based upon international legal principles.

The growing importance of international law in Northeast Asia can be attributed in large part to the forces of globalization that has brought about fundamental changes in the economic, political, and cultural spheres. Broadly defined, the phenomenon of globalization describes a process of integration that has come to dominate the latter half of the 20th century and continues to shape the world today. Although globalization encompasses both political and cultural activities, it is most well-defined in the popular discourse of what is commonly known as the "global economy." This economic globalization is identified by: global production, as demonstrated by multinational corporations having the capacity to locate and relocate modes of production to different parts of the world in the search for markets and lower costs; trade liberalization, as states have come together to embrace free trade through multilateral agreements like the General Agreement on Tariffs and Trade; and finally, through the relative free movement of finance capital where the global economic landscape is dotted by global capital markets as world financial centers like New York and London and those in Northeast Asia such as Tokyo, Hong Kong, and Seoul are becoming principal players in a new supranational order.[2]

As economic globalization has progressed, national boundaries have become more permeable to the influx and outflow of capital as well as to goods and services. In the case of capital, it has flowed more freely due to liberalization of national and international financial markets and the introduction of novel financial products and services, as well as the facilitation of financial investments in foreign markets through upgraded technological innovations and the presence of powerful new investors. For goods and services, the push for the successful

---

[2] Saskia Sassen, *Global Financial Centers*, FOREIGN AFFAIRS (1999).

completion of the Uruguay Round resulting in the ratification of the GATT and GATS and the eventual creation of the World Trade Organization has brought about momentous changes in the way trade is conducted between states. Borders are becoming more porous to non-domestic products and services.

In Northeast Asia, the depth and breadth of globalization's impact in the region can be seen through the growing and deepening economic linkages between all three countries. While the United States was Japan and South Korea's largest trading partner at the end of the 20th century, it has now been replaced by China. Recently, China, Japan, and South Korea have made increasing efforts to bring about the creation of a free trade bloc and have openly called for the drafting of a free trade agreement that would bring about a new legal order in the region. It is under these conditions that international law is poised to take on a greater role in bringing about greater regional cooperation and integration through a formal institutionalization of these trade and investment relationships. However, despite movements towards greater interdependence and the creation of a regional economic bloc, the region is also the source of serious political tensions that have their roots in ancient and recent history.

In contrast to the European Westphalian system of state sovereignty, interstate relations in Northeast Asia trace their origins to the tributary system established and maintained by various Chinese empires in which power was centered in imperial China and where tributary states in Japan and Korea took part in ritual obeisance to the "Celestial Empire." While it is understood that tributary states maintained relative independence in relation to the Chinese empire, it was clear that interstate relations were viewed in the context of Chinese imperial and cultural hegemony. With the wane and the eventual collapse of the Chinese empire and the epochal events that marked the West's engagement with Northeast Asia, the passing of the old order gave rise to Japan's rise and eventual recognition of Japan by the West as a legitimate sovereign power. The region then experienced a Communist revolution in China and Japanese expansion into the Asian continent through Korea and into parts of China and Southeast Asia in the first half of the 20th century. With Japan's defeat in World War II, there was a reordering of the Northeast Asian order which saw the establishment of independent states under the influence of both the United States and the Soviet Union which was exemplified by the division of the Korean peninsula into North and South marking the beginning of the Cold War. Due to the regional balance of power configuration during the Cold War, there was very limited official contact between Japan and South Korea with China and North Korea.[3] Northeast Asian relations were

[3] After the establishment of the People's Republic of China in 1949, China did not have any formal relations with Japan or South Korea until 1978, when Japan and China signed and ratified their Treaty of Peace and Friendship while South Korea normalized relations with China in 1992. Japan and South Korea have no formal diplomatic relations with North Korea.

defined in terms of the broader tension between the United States and the Soviet Union. Historically then, interstate relations in Northeast Asia were based not on international legal principles of state sovereignty and sovereign equality but were rather largely subject to the politics of hegemony in the form of either the Chinese tributary system, Japanese imperialism, or Cold War politics.

Thus, it was not until the end of the Cold War and the flourishing of globalization that the countries in the region engaged each other on common issues of interest and have interacted with each other on the basis of modern principles of international law. As a result, regional problems that lay dormant during the Cold War such as human rights concerns and law of the sea issues of maritime delimitation and access to ocean resources like fisheries and other non-security matters have raised the profile of international law. While geopolitical factors continue to be relevant in understanding interstate relations in the region, international law and its attendant principles have become the basis through which most Northeast Asian states engage each other. The increasingly important role of international law in Northeast Asia cannot be ignored in attempting to paint a complete picture of the international relations of the region.

Indeed, it is hoped by international lawyers in Northeast Asia that international law will bring about greater regional cooperation and integration as seen in other regions of the world. Thus, it is not surprising then that the inspiration for this volume comes from the first joint international academic conference of international lawyers from the Chinese Society of International Law, Japanese Society of International Law, and Korean Society of International Law that took place in Seoul, Korea on July 3, 2010. Many of the contributors of this volume participated in this landmark conference that brought the three societies together for the first time to examine the ways in which international law could help promote peace and justice in Northeast Asia. It is in that spirit that Kak-Soo Shin, South Korean Ambassador to Japan, in the second chapter offers his comments about the importance of international law in promoting regional peace, prosperity, and justice.

Ambassador Shin notes that formal interactions between China, Japan, and South Korea toward regional cooperation and integration have been on the rise. Despite significant obstacles such as a historical legacy of tensions, strong nationalist sentiments in each country, and differing political systems and states of economic development, the countries are engaged in fifty consultative bodies and more than one hundred joint cooperation projects and have also declared their intention to establish a permanent secretariat in Korea to strengthen and promote trilateral cooperation. He adds that there has been movement towards the drafting of a trilateral investment treaty along with nascent efforts to establish a free trade agreement. While regional interdependence can be readily found in the economic sector, he is confident that this will spill over into other areas such as the environment, human rights, maritime affairs including piracy, and other issues of common concern. Given this growing importance of international law in

Northeast Asia, Ambassador Shin observes that Korea faces a number of challenges when it comes to fully engaging international law. For one, Korea's recent shift to a graduate, professional law school model has precipitated a drop in enrollment in public international law courses, and he worries about the ability of future Korean lawyers to handle such matters domestically. As a second observation, he notes that Korea, outside of the WTO dispute resolution system, is generally reluctant to engage in third party adjudication because of a lack of experience. In the effort to further peace and prosperity in the region, international law should not be limited to rhetoric, but it should be put into practice and believes it is time for the region to have its own Court of Justice.

In Chapter III, Professor Toshiya Ueki of Tohoku University School of Law follows with a depiction of Northeast Asia's encounter with "European" international law and traces its use and application in the region up through the present day. Among the powers within the traditional East Asian system, he describes the relations between them as being unequal with the Japanese and Korean rulers paying tribute to the Chinese emperor. He observes that the relations between them could not be thought of as being "international" in the sense that there was a conception of sovereign equality. In contrast, in terms of relations with the West, Professor Ueki notes that while engagement between Northeast Asia and the outside world began from a "long time ago," he acknowledges that it is difficult to determine on what basis Asian and European powers dealt with each other. Nevertheless, he imagines that there could have been a *jus gentium*, a common set of rules for both sides. Thus, unlike Europe's relationship with the South American continent in the 15th and 16th centuries, there were no colonies in East Asia during the same period.

According to Professor Ueki, by the 19th century, the European understanding of its relationship with Northeast Asia was mixed. In Europe, there was recognition that there were distinct sovereign states in Northeast Asia, however, European dealings with the region where characterized by a series of unequal treaties through which European states opened Qing China and the Japanese Shogunate to trade and commerce with Europe. From this experience with Europe within the same century, Northeast Asian states began to adopt the substance and character of European international law. China, Japan, and Korea began to transform their engagement with each other into interstate relations that resembled Europe as bilateral treaties were concluded between them. With this embrace of international law, China and Japan saw an extensive engagement in the international legal system during the early part of the 20th century in the League of Nations system. However, as Professor Ueki notes, this participation came to an end in the years preceding World War II which continued to impact the region after the War and during the Cold War period where the countries in the region maintained relatively low profiles in utilizing international law. However, the 21st century has seen a dramatic change for Northeast Asia as individuals from the region have attained positions at the highest levels in international political and legal circles from the Secretary-General of the United Nations to the President of the International Court of Justice (ICJ). Given these contributions and the growing commitment of government officials and the legal academy in the region, he claims that East Asia will become an important hub for international law.

Embracing this observation of the growing significance of international law in Northeast Asia, the following chapters either provide perspectives on a number of contemporary international legal issues that are important to the countries in the region or provide a context to understand the significance of international law in historical or educational terms. Beginning in Chapter IV, Dr. Yann-huei Song from Academia Sinica in Taipei, Taiwan assesses the challenges of resolving present disputes over the South China Sea (SCS). He begins by detailing the rising tensions in the SCS, especially concerning the disputed claims of sovereignty over the Paracel and Spratly Islands by China, Taiwan, Vietnam, Malaysia, and the Philippines. Dr. Song argues that these persistent tensions (1) evince the ineffectiveness of the Declaration of the Conduct of Parties in the South China Sea (DOC), and (2) point to the necessity of a regional Code of Conduct (COC) concerning the SCS. He details the process by which the DOC was concluded between the Association of Southeast Asian Nations (ASEAN) and China, which was concluded in 2002 after three years of negotiations. While the DOC included several confidence-building and cooperative measures, Dr. Song stipulates that the final product was not legally binding and was not favored by countries like Vietnam.

Dr. Song goes on to describe the various country dynamics at work in ASEAN and China concerning the SCS. For example, the governments of Vietnam and the Philippines want to continue negotiations with China as an ASEAN bloc in order to counterbalance China's assertions of power in the SCS. On the other side, countries with close relations to China like Cambodia, Laos, and Thailand are not as concerned about the SCS and are more reluctant to put the issue on ASEAN's agenda. Dr. Song concludes by detailing ASEAN's recent activities in dealing with the SCS. He posits that with Vietnam assuming the chair of ASEAN, the rising tensions between China and its neighbors in the SCS will be addressed more directly by ASEAN. He also argues that the increasing involvement of the United States, particularly related to commercial activity in the SCS, will boost the confidence of Southeast Asian nations in standing up to the aggressive stance of China. Meanwhile, he points out that China is attempting to address the issues through direct bilateral negotiations rather than through multilateral or international means. He notes that ASEAN and China have reached agreement on the guidelines for implementing the DOC and the countries are actively engaged in following through with their goal of greater regional cooperation.

Chapter V continues the discussion on the topic of the South China Sea as Professor Kuan-Hsiung Wang from National Taiwan Normal University addresses the issue of regional cooperation concerning high seas fisheries. Professor Wang begins by outlining the crisis concerning fish stock depletion. He finds that, while the total amount of fish available for worldwide human consumption has increased, the problem of overfishing has led to the significant depletion of several species and impacted future fish stocks. He then goes on to describe three ongoing processes for managing fishery resources: international instruments, international organizations, and the actions of states. International instruments, like UNCLOS and UNFSA, set forth the duties of states to cooperate in conserving straddling and highly migratory fish stocks on the high seas. In the event that nations decline to participate in international instruments, Professor Wang asserts that Regional Fishery Management Organizations (RMFO) can also help to overcome collective action problems with overfishing. He cites as an example the Inter-American Tropical Tuna Commission which was able to strengthen conservation efforts by the parties through its 2003 Antigua Convention.

Professor Wang continues his discussion of the importance of regional cooperation by discussing in detail the case of the semi-enclosed South China Sea. He asserts that the combination of exclusive economic zones and highly migratory fish species creates the problem of maintaining a delicate ecosystem. As he points out, the complex boundary disagreements in the South China Sea do not need to be resolved before an agreement on the fishery issue is reached. In fact, Wang asserts that cooperation around fishery preservation might be a feasible way to begin the process toward broader regional cooperation in the South China Sea. He concludes by emphasizing sustainability and the precautionary principle as the foundational principles of regional ocean policy.

In Chapter VI, Professor Bing Bing Jia of Tsinghua University Law School explores the legal doctrine of *non liquet* and its impact in the realm of international law. He first addresses whether the gaps in the law that evince *non liquet* ought to be avoided in the international legal system. In answering this question, he begins by discussing the notion of *non liquet* in depth, comparing the views of Hersch Lauterpacht and Julius Stone. He goes on to highlight three instances in international law that can manifest *non liquet*: (1) a simple gap in the law; (2) incorrect formulation of the dispute by the parties; and (3) a dispute over a matter that one party deems non-justiciable. In this section, Professor Jia also addresses the tension between positivism and naturalism and the respective roles of the judicial and legislative bodies in the international legal system.

He goes on to describe two cases before the ICJ in which the doctrine of *non liquet* was employed. The first case was a 1996 advisory opinion on the *Legality of the Use or Threat of Nuclear Weapons*, in response to a question posed by the U.N. General Assembly. In its opinion, the Court stated that it could not definitively conclude whether the use of nuclear weapons would be lawful or unlawful under extreme circumstances involving self-defense. The second case concerns Kosovo's declaration of independence in 2008. The ICJ issued an advisory opinion concerning the legality of Kosovo's secession. While Japan and China took opposing views on the matter (the former invoking the doctrine of *non liquet*; the latter invoking the doctrine of state sovereignty and territorial integrity), the ICJ found that international law did not prohibit declarations of independence and upheld Kosovo's declaration. In this case, the existence of *non liquet* did not prevent the Court from making a judgment. Ultimately, a court invoking *non liquet* must still consider whether the absence of a prohibition in international law should be interpreted as implicit permission or as merely a gap in the law.

The next two chapter focus primarily on Japan's experience with international law in the past, and in the present context with respect to U.N. peacekeeping operations. In Chapter VII, the late Jon M. Van Dyke who taught at the University of Hawaii School of Law, discusses the introduction of Western international law into Japan. He asserts that concepts like the "rule of law" were not common in Japan prior to its participation in Western international law. Instead, Japan's legal system had operated based on hierarchy and relationships. He argues that what came to be known as "international" law was basically a Western construct based on the principles of reciprocity and self-interest. These principles of international law came out of the Treaty of Westphalia in 1648 and the Final Act of the Congress of Vienna in 1815, including the supremacy of treaties and the sovereign equality of states. Conversely, according to Professor Van Dyke, the international system in East Asia at the time was based around China as the central authority. He goes on to discuss the history of Japanese law in the early 19th century, with its feudalistic structures that placed emphasis on the Neo-Confucian concepts of obligation and hierarchy rather than "rights."

Professor Van Dyke continues by describing the westernization of law in Japan, beginning in the mid-19th century with unequal treaties imposed upon Japan by the U.S., through the late 19th century when Japan became a full-fledged member of the "family of nations." He explains how Japanese scholars justified the use of international legal principles in Japan, from the relation between natural law and Neo-Confucianism to the use of international law as a purely analytical process. He continues with a survey of international law development in the West at the turn of the 20th century as legal positivism came into tension with natural law theory. He then discusses the process by which the West applied international law to "uncivilized" nations. While there was no set criteria by which the West admitted countries into the "family of nations," he posits that the "Christian nation" requirement eventually had to give way to the realities of colonization and the increasing power of nations like China, Japan, Turkey, and Persia. Professor Van Dyke concludes his analysis with the development of international law in the 20th century in its evolution from a narrow focus on maritime and military rules to economic relations and human rights.

In Chapter VIII, Professor Osamu Yoshida of the University of Tsukuba follows with an analysis of Japan's role in United Nations peacekeeping operations. He begins by reviewing the guiding principles under both the U.N. Charter and Japanese law. Under Japan's International Peace Cooperation Bill, the Diet enabled the Special-Defense Forces to participate in international peacekeeping in accordance with its "Five Principles." These principles largely mirror the U.N.'s guiding principles for peacekeeping operations and include impartiality, consent, and limited use of weapons. Although the latest amendment to the bill allows Japanese forces to assist with election monitoring and humanitarian relief, Professor Yoshida points out that Japan still ranks 84th among U.N. member states in total participants in peacekeeping operations.

Professor Yoshida continues by examining the compatibility between Japan's peacekeeping law and U.N. practice, especially concerning the principle of self-defense. He notes that the United Nations' conception of self-defense has become increasingly broad. As a result, he asserts that it will soon become incompatible with the self-defense parameters set by the Japanese government. He goes on to discuss the challenges that this incompatibility presents to the overall control dynamics between the United Nations and the governments of the peacekeepers themselves. Professor Yoshida concludes by outlining Japan's present outlook on foreign policy and international cooperation. Japan's recent efforts indicate a desire to assert a greater role in international peacekeeping while remaining consistent with its core principles.

The last three chapters cover a number of important developments on the Korean peninsula in relation to international law. In Chapter IX, we, the editors, follow with a chapter that discusses the challenges facing South Korea in response to the sinking of the South Korean naval corvette, *Cheonan*. The vessel sank near the Northern Limit Line (NLL), the disputed maritime border between the two countries in the West Sea (Yellow Sea) on the South Korean side. While it was largely assumed at the time and later confirmed by a South Korean led commission that North Korea was responsibility for the sinking of the vessel that resulted in the deaths of 46 South Korean sailors, there were attempts by the South Korean government to attribute state responsibility for the act to North Korea. However, given a number of mistakes, missed opportunities, and miscalculations about how to confront the North, South Korea was only able to obtain a vaguely worded presidential statement from the U.N. Security Council that made no mention of North Korea. We propose a way forward for the South to engage the North more on its own terms.

The problem of dealing with North Korea in the complex international legal and political environment of the Northeast Asian region is further discussed in Chapter X, as Professor Jae-Chun Won of Handong International Law School addresses the legal challenges attendant to North Korea human rights abuses. Specifically, he assesses the effectiveness of regional and international responses when North Koreans flee across the border. He begins by outlining three elements that contribute to the wretched human rights situation in North Korea: (1) the personality cult designed to control the minds of the population; (2) harsh discrimination based on a politically determined classification system; and (3) lack of judicial due process. Professor Won then shifts the focus to China's poor human rights record concerning North Koreans. He details China's efforts to detain, exploit, and forcibly repatriate North Koreans who flee across the border into the Liaoning and Jilin provinces.

The remainder of the chapter focuses on the rights of North Koreans as refugees and asylum-seekers in third countries. Professor Won first discusses the protections afforded North Koreans by the domestic laws of South Korea, including the Constitution, the Nationality Act, and the Protection Act. Under the Constitution, the entire Korean peninsula is a single territory. As such, North Koreans acquire South Korean nationality at birth and are not subject to the naturalization process. Under the Protection Act, the South Korean government may protect any externally displaced North Koreans, provided they are not international criminal offenders. Despite these domestic laws, Professor Won asserts that South Korea has failed to adequately protect North Koreans who flee to third countries, citing China, Vietnam, and Cambodia as examples. He continues his assessment with the international protections afforded to North Koreans. In spite of the various treaties signed concerning refugees and asylum-seekers, he argues that the international community (most notably, UNHCR) has also failed to protect North Koreans, particularly in China. Professor Won goes on to discuss the international legal issues surrounding the refugee status of North Koreans, along with the solution offered by the U.S. North Korean Human Rights Act. He concludes by calling for a stronger international response to the situation facing North Korean refugees and asylum-seekers.

In the final chapter, Professor Hee Moon Jo of Hankuk University of Foreign Studies Law School outlines the changes in Korea's international legal education under the new law school system that was formally implemented in 2010. Korea's new legal education system is based on the model found in the United States that places greater emphasis on practical training of professional lawyers. However, as Professor Jo points out, Korea has adopted the U.S. model for legal education while maintaining the Japanese model for the bar exam. Under the Japanese model, the bar exam is more akin to a civil service exam, requiring elaborate legal knowledge. Conversely, the U.S. bar exam is designed to test for minimum competence as a lawyer.

Professor Jo goes on to discuss the current state of international legal education in Korea in light of the shift in the law school system. He points to two factors that influence the way international law is taught in Korean law schools: (1) the consideration of international law as a bar examination subject; and (2) Korea's position in international society. He posits that, as long as international law continues to be tested in such a comprehensive way, students will choose not to take international law in order to avoid facing it as an elective subject on the bar exam. Nevertheless, while at the same time that the bar exam is discouraging students from taking international law, the growing influence of globalization on Korea has made the subject more popular among students. In order to adapt to these changes, Professor Jo discusses how the teaching of international law has been evolving. He examines four basic teaching methods:

the traditional theory-based lecturing method, the case method, the problem-solving method, and the seminar. While theory-based lectures have been most common in law schools, Professor Jo advocates for an expansion in legal education to include more internships and clinical experiences. Ultimately, according to him, the bar exam model must be changed to reflect the increased emphasis on practical legal education in Korea.

As seen in the pages of this volume, we, the editors, believe that international law will play a more significant role in the international relations of Northeast Asia and that international lawyers from the region will give greater voice in offering a path towards managing and resolving some of the grave challenges our region faces. It is our hope that our modest contribution will be of some benefit towards the promotion of Northeast Asian perspectives on international law.

Seokwoo Lee & Hee Eun Lee

CHAPTER TWO

IN PURSUIT OF PEACE AND PROSPERITY THROUGH JUSTICE IN NORTHEAST ASIA

Kak-Soo Shin*

I. Introduction

As an ardent student and practitioner of international law, I often reflect upon the relevance of international law in the context of Northeast Asia. In light of the increasing interaction among three of the countries in this region, it is high time for international jurists of Korea, Japan, and China to seriously reflect on the role international law has played in creating a predictable and reliable environment for ensuring peace and prosperity in Northeast Asia, and to further canvass what the future prospect of the legal order in this region should be like.

It is well recognized that the twenty-first century will be the Asian era as the Pacific has already replaced the Atlantic as the center stage for the world. As the growth engine of the world economy, Asia is destined to emerge as one of the pillars of the international order. In particular, the Northeast Asian region is at the core of the rising Asian impact on the world, accounting for one-fifth of the world's population, one-fifth of the world's production, one-sixth of world trade, and one-half of the world's foreign currency reserve. Its economic size is third in the world next to NAFTA and the EU. In this regard, regional cooperation and integration in Northeast Asia assumes a growing importance. It is thus encouraging that among these three countries, there are currently about 50 consultative bodies and more than 100 joint cooperation projects underway at various levels each year that encompass a wide array of issues with regional implications.

In 2010, the leaders of the three countries were gathered on Jeju Island in Korea to attend the Third Summit Meeting in which they agreed to adopt Vision 2020 that aimed at joint efforts to accelerate regional cooperation and to set up a permanent secretariat in Korea. In Northeast Asia, the steady progress of regional cooperation, despite several significant barriers such as historical legacy, the

* Ambassador to Japan, Republic of Korea.

strong trait of nationalism, different political systems, and different states of economic growth, will build up mutual trust essential for the creation of a regional architecture that will bolster sustainable peace and common prosperity.

I would like to focus on peace and prosperity through justice in Northeast Asia in the sense that seeking justice and rule of law in this region will offer the region a valuable catalyst to shore up common efforts to make Northeast Asia more peaceful, prosperous, and progressive. Having gone through the tumultuous period of colonialism, war, poverty, and injustice in the last century, these three countries in Northeast Asia have always yearned for peace, prosperity, and justice, and also came to realize that these cannot be achieved without mutual cooperation based upon a holistic approach to these three core values. Just as prosperity is hard to attain without peace, peace is hard to keep without prosperity. Yet, it should be emphasized that peace and prosperity are hard to sustain without a foundation of justice. Indeed, this highlights the important role of international law in bolstering our joint endeavors to make Northeast Asia a region of peace, prosperity, and justice.

II. Northeast Asian Perspectives on International Law

At the outset, there is no denying that the traditional international legal system originated in the West from the time when the Treaty of Westphalia established an order based on sovereign equality in Europe in 1648. Later, North and South America had been incorporated into the "club of civilized nations" that could enjoy entitlements under international law. Yet, Northeast Asia remained nearly outside the purview of international law until the mid-nineteenth century when the region was forced to open up to the West. From then on, Korea, China, and Japan were awakened to the importance of international law in international transactions and have developed their own perspectives on international law. It is very interesting to note many comparative studies on how these three countries received international law in the context of their modernization drives during the nineteenth century.

At the present time, these countries in the region have emerged as major players on the international stage. No longer are these states merely passive participants in the international legal process. Rather, they have been taking an active role in formulating new norms in international law. This prominent profile in the international community gives these countries ample opportunities to project their values onto the creation and progressive development of international law.

International law does not exist in a vacuum. It is constantly interpreted, applied, and enforced by the "subjects of international law" often within different regional contexts. Without any intention to rekindle the controversy of Asian versus universal values, I believe that, with its cultural richness and historical legacy, Northeast Asia is well poised to contribute towards the development of international law. While interacting with each other for several millennia, these countries have acquired a rich cultural heritage replete with wisdom and practice that may also be helpful to the rest of the world. Additionally, geopolitical and economic dynamism in Northeast Asia has compelled us to formulate solutions to unprecedented challenges. In order to meet these challenges, the nations of Northeast Asia can combine Asian wisdom with Western knowledge in international law. Furthermore, these three countries can develop a set of common rules and standards applicable to them or even regional international law based on their unique culture and perspective.

III. International Law in Foreign Policy-Making

The Constitution of the Republic of Korea stipulates that treaties and international customs are part of its domestic law. Article 6 of the Constitution[1] embodies a comprehensive commitment for the government inclusive of the administrative, judiciary, and legislative branches to comply with international law. In keeping with this constitutional requirement, the Korean government has faithfully lived up to treaties it has concluded as well as customary international law. It is also the established judgment of the domestic courts, especially the Constitutional Court, that such compliance is the legal obligation of the government.

Likewise, the Korean government has consistently regarded international law as an essential element to be considered in conducting foreign affairs. In this regard, the Bureau of International Legal Affairs in the Ministry of Foreign Affairs and Trade is mandated to review all the diplomatic activities of the government to make sure that they are carried out in compliance with the rules of international law.

In 2008, the Lee Myung-bak administration espoused the slogan of "Global Korea" as its diplomatic platform. This is a multi-pronged policy intended to upgrade the nation's profile and broaden its network by riding on the wave of globalization. One of the ramifications under "Global Korea" implies that Korea must observe global standards in its diplomatic posture and acts. In my view, what forms the very core of these "global standards" is none other than international law. The Korean government is fully committed to the position that foreign policy based on international norms ensures its legitimacy, acceptability, and predictability.

IV. Role of International Law in Promoting Cooperation and Resolving Conflicts in Northeast Asia

Interdependence among the three nations, if not complete "integration," has been rapidly increasing as of late. As close neighbors with a regional and global

---

1 Article 6, Paragraph 1 of the Constitution of the Republic of Korea provides that "Treaties duly concluded and promulgated under the Constitution and the generally recognized rule of international law have the same effect as the domestic laws of the Republic of Korea."

partnership, Korea, China, and Japan have woven a dense web of cooperative networks in various areas. Not only have these three nations been discussing a trilateral investment treaty, but have also held the first joint study meeting in Seoul in May of 2009 for the purpose of concluding a free trade agreement. Until recently, major developments in regional interdependence have taken root primarily in trade and the economy. However, it is anticipated that there will eventually be further developments in other areas as well. Employing the tool of international law, there can be a common ground and the building up of a normative framework in diverse fields such as the environment, human rights, maritime affairs, narcotics, piracy, desertification, and transnational crime, to name a few.

In this context, one example of success in this regard occurred in the mid-2000s when Japan took the initiative to draw up a regional convention to combat piracy in the sea off the Strait of Malacca. Korea hosted several meetings to nail down the final text of the convention on the basis of the Japanese draft. Thanks to these strenuous joint efforts undertaken by Korea and Japan, fourteen Asian nations finally adopted the Regional Cooperation Agreement on Combating Piracy and Armed Robbery against Ships in Asia in 2004 and brought it into implementation in 2006. This regional initiative made great contributions towards the facilitation of close cooperation among the parties in the region that led to a drastic reduction of piracy in the Strait of Malacca.

By the same token, further efforts need to be sought in the field of maritime matters. Rough waters along the landmass of the Asian continent call for a regime that ensures peaceful development to prevent any flare-ups and resolve conflicts. International law will be an indispensable means to make this difficult quest a possibility. The Korea-Japan agreement of 1978 on the joint development of the continental shelf adjacent to the two countries is another good example for an amicable solution to the delimitation problem.

All in all, international law has an important role to play in forging a stable, predictable, and reasonable framework for these three nations and Asia. International law provides a set of agreed rules, by which these countries can manage amicable relations and promote mutual cooperation for peace and prosperity. It also helps to prevent any potential dispute by rendering guidance on what course of action a state should take. In this light, the governments of these three countries should endeavor to increase recourse to international law in their quest for closer and better ties among them.

V. International Legal Education

For international jurists, the important role international law assumes in the conduct of foreign affairs is crystal clear. However, the situation is totally different when it comes to the public that has little knowledge about international law. Even those who have received a regular legal education in Korea tend to focus their study on domestic law, as most law students are expected to be in private practice or become a judge or a prosecutor. In such an environment, few people who have a legal background have an interest in studying international law. Especially with the start of the law school system in Korea, there is little likelihood for law school students to focus their studies in international law which in turn only offers a narrow window of job opportunities.

For this reason, international legal education pertains to the realm of public goods like peace and security. If it is left to the private sector, no one will take care of it. Instead, the government and academia must make concerted efforts to promote international law or there will be a crisis in international legal education. It is common to hear law professors voice concern over the dwindling number of students who want to enroll in international law classes and major in international law. This has led to a lack of domestic litigation with the implications for international law due to the reluctance of practitioners to bring such suits because of their poor knowledge of international law.

Taking this problem seriously, the Ministry of Foreign Affairs and Trade of Korea, in cooperation with the Korean Society of International Law, has conducted several programs to promote awareness within the Korean legal community about the significance of international law. For instance, the Ministry launched a moot court competition for university students in 2009, while holding an annual thesis contest on international law for several years. These programs serve as a strong incentive for young students to get exposed to international law, helping them appreciate how international law relates to their legal service. Korea, China, and Japan have much to share and learn from each other in the area of international legal education.

VI. Northeast Asian Perspectives on International Adjudication

Although it has appeared in a couple of dozen cases before the World Trade Organization,[2] Korea has never been a party to third-party settlement in the area of international law. Korea has accepted the compulsory jurisdiction of the ICJ and arbitration in the form of a clause to that effect under bilateral and multilateral treaties, but has never had recourse to it. Lack of experience in inter-state litigation makes it more difficult for Korea to utilize third-party dispute settlement mechanisms.

Given its extensive engagement arising from its heavy dependence on overseas markets, capital, and resources, Korea needs to pay due attention to the usefulness of international adjudication as a means to settle disputes amicably and secure its interests. As a mid-term strategy to adapt itself to international

[2] As of June 28, 2010, Korea has had 26 cases before the World Trade Organization either as a complainant or a respondent.

adjudication, it is desirable for the Korean government to begin submitting non-political and technical issues to third-party settlement, and as it gains confidence and experience, to move on to issues of a political nature.

Peaceful dispute settlement should be firmly established as an integral part of the culture of the region and not merely just an idea discussed in textbooks. The old sages of Northeast Asia attached an importance to practicing principles, as opposed to merely preaching them. Similarly, principles of international law are meaningful only when they are put into actual practice.

A potential impediment to the establishment of such a practice is the excessive measure of nationalism that often engulfs the region and endangers the stability of the region. In such a situation, no state would dare to submit a dispute to international adjudication in fear of the backlash that an adverse judgment would provoke. The rule of law and reason should prevail over emotional whims. It is the duty of international lawyers to disseminate international law that can protect against such extremism.

Considering that international law constitutes the core of global standards, there must be the development of mutual trust through close cooperation. This endeavor must be made in tandem with efforts to increase a wider domestic appreciation of international law.

Conspicuously absent in Northeast Asia is a regional framework for dispute settlement when compared with the European Union or the Association of Southeast Asian Nations. As cooperation and integration advance, the time may come for the region to consider a comprehensive framework for dispute settlement including a possible Asian Tribunal of Justice or an Asian Court of Arbitration.

VII. Conclusion

Just as freedom is not free, there should be constant and conscious efforts to ensure peace and prosperity at the regional and global levels. It cannot be emphasized enough as to the significance of international justice in these endeavors. International law is indispensable for sustainable peace and prosperity, and this holds valid especially in the dynamic and volatile region of Northeast Asia. In this regard, it is important that the principles of international law, including peaceful dispute settlement, should not only be widely disseminated but also vigorously put into practice. International lawyers should not shirk their responsibility in making international law widely appreciated in the region.

CHAPTER THREE

HISTORICAL ANALYSIS ON THE IMPACTS AND INFLUENCES OF INTERNATIONAL LAW IN EAST ASIA AND ITS FUTURE

Toshiya Ueki*

I. Impacts and Influences of European International Law in East Asia before the 19th Century

A. *East Asia's Encounter with the Outside World before the 18th Century*

1. East Asia's Approach to the Outside World

It seems very difficult in the history of the world to define accurately from an academic point of view when the East Asian peoples encountered the outside world and some kind of "international" rules might have come into being. For example, in the middle of the 8th century, the Tang Empire's territories had been expanded, along with the "Silk Road," not only to Xinjiang, for instance in Turfan and Kashgar, but also to the present territory of Kyrghyzstan, Kazakhstan, Uzbekistan, and even to Afghanistan. In 751, the famous battle on the Talas River in Ferghana between Tang and Arab soldiers occurred, but it is not clear for us at all what rules of war were applied between them on the battlefield in central Eurasia. During the Mongol's Yuan Dynasty, in the latter half of the 13th century, Kubilai Khan received and entertained the Venetian merchant Marco Polo. Of course, Marco Polo was not a diplomat or on any kind of diplomatic mission in the context of the diplomatic law of modern international law. However, it is worth noting that such kind of intercourse between East Asia and the outside world had actually existed from a long time ago. It should also be noted that, between the East Asian countries themselves, there had been a long history of "international" intercourse, if we could say so, for instance, Japan's mission to the Sui and Tan Dynasties in China and between Korea and China.

These relations were mainly sustained within the original and traditional framework of East Asia, namely by the tribute to the Chinese emperors. These

* Executive Vice-President and Professor of International Law, Tohoku University.

traditional East Asian systems were based upon an egocentric and universalistic world image with a strong sense of the superiority of Chinese emperors. Under these systems, Chinese emperors were regarded as embodying virtue and spreading it throughout under Heaven. Therefore, there should be no "equal" relationship between Chinese emperors and other rulers in East Asia, and the latter were expected to send a mission to the Chinese emperor and to pay tribute to him in accordance with Chinese rules and rituals.[1] In this regard, these traditional systems within the East Asian region were not regarded as an "international" system in the sense of modern international law because these systems were not constructed on the basis of the "equality" of nation-states.

However, even in this period, we can find some examples of East Asia's encounter beyond the region. Here, the following two historical episodes of East Asia's encounter with the outside world should be mentioned. One is from China and the other is from Japan. The first episode is Zheng He's voyage to Southeast Asia and the Indian Ocean during the Ming Dynasty in the beginning of the 15th century. Zheng He was a Chinese Muslim, and he made seven voyages from China to Vietnam, Malacca, Bengal, Calicut, and even to Hormuz, Aden, and Mogadishu and Malindi on the east African coast in accordance with the Emperor's order. His fleet consisted of between 100 and 300 ships and carrying in total up to 27,000 men, and the largest vessels stretched to over 130 meters.[2] Zheng He's fleet was much larger than the fleets led by Christopher Columbus and Vasco da Gama that were composed of only three or four ships.

The second episode occurred in 1582, by the advice and support of European Catholic missionaries in Japan, when three Japanese Christian landlords in the Kyushu region sent four young Japanese boys as delegates to the Pope in Rome. They traveled from Japan by ship via Goa in southern India and to Portugal, and arrived at Rome where they were enthusiastically welcomed by the people and Pope Gregorio XIII. They then safely returned from Rome to Japan in 1590, supposedly being the first Japanese who traveled from Japan to Europe and back to Japan via the Indian Ocean. This delegation was supported by Portugal and Catholic missionaries. A few decades later, a famous Japanese landlord, Masamune Date in Sendai, the northeastern part of Japan, sent his diplomatic delegate, Tsunenaga Hasekura, to Spain and Rome to seek direct trade with them. In this case, Hasekura traveled by ship over the Pacific Ocean arriving at Acapulco in Mexico and then across Mexico and traveling by ship over the Atlantic Ocean to Hispania (Spain) and to Rome. He departed Sendai in 1613, and in Rome he was awarded Citizenship of Rome and safely returned by ship over the Atlantic and the Pacific Oceans to Japan in 1620. However, the purpose of his visit to Hispania

---

[1] Onuma Yasuaki, A Transcivilizational Perspective on International Law 305–313 (Pocketbooks of the Hague Academy of International Law) (2010).

[2] John Keay, China: A History 380 (2008).

and Rome, namely starting direct trade with Europe, was not successful because from the beginning of the 17th century, the Tokugawa Shogunate in Japan strictly prohibited trade with Europeans except with the Dutch only at Nagasaki port.

Regrettably, it is not clear what kind of "rules" of diplomatic law or commercial law were applied at that time on the occasions of these encounters between the peoples in East Asia and Europe. However, it could be imagined that some kind of common "rules" for both sides, in other words, some sort of *jus gentium* might have been applied between the peoples in East Asia and the peoples in Europe. It should be noted that at this stage in the 15th and 16th centuries, neither peoples in East Asia nor in Europe, which included mainly missionaries and merchants, would enforce their own rules against the other. As a result, we can find that European powers like Portugal and Spain could never make substantial colonies in the East Asian region in the 15th and 16th centuries, and it was completely different from the situation, for instance, on the South American continent at that time.

2. The Nerchinsk Treaty in 1689: The First International Treaty between the East and the West?

From a historical point of view, the first written "legal" document that might be called a treaty in the sense of Article 2(a) of the 1969 Vienna Convention on the Law of Treaties concluded between an East Asian power and an European power was the Nerchinsk Treaty which was agreed to between the Qing Dynasty in China and Russia in 1689. It should be noted that this treaty demarcated the boundary between the Qing and Russia in western Siberia and northern Manchuria along with the Stanovoi Mountains. The Nerchinsk Treaty is considered to be the first international agreement between an East Asian and European state to settle the land boundary between them. It is worth mentioning that both sides adopted a rather pragmatic approach in the negotiations concluding the treaty. Latin was adopted as the common language for the negotiations and as the authentic version of the treaty because among the members of the Qing delegation were two Jesuits who resided in Beijing.[3] Manchu, Mongol, Chinese, and Russian versions of the treaty were also produced. These historical facts remind us of the rules of contemporary international law regarding the "interpretation of treaties authenticated in two or more language" as prescribed in the 1969 Vienna Convention on the Law of Treaties.[4]

During the negotiations of this treaty, the Russian side consistently insisted that each party should have equal status, but the Qing delegates refused and insisted on their own ideas, namely that the Qing Emperor was superior in

---

[3] KEAY, *supra* note 2, at 439.

[4] Article 33 of the Vienna Convention on the Law of Treaties prescribes the detailed rules regarding this issue.

status at the top of the whole world and advocated that the traditional notion of "peace-through-kinship" and "trade-as-tribute" should be observed. As a result, the Qing preserved the vast territories along the Amur River, and Russian territory was confined to north of the Stanovoi Mountains. On the other hand, the Russian side obtained through the treaty commercial access to the Qing territories, and the Russian Orthodox Church and a Russian language school were established in Beijing.[5] Rosalyn Higgins, former President of the International Court of Justice, observed that "[t]his treaty provided for free commerce between the parties and confirmed the territorial jurisdiction of the Chinese authorities over those charged with incursions."[6] She also added that the Treaty of Kiakhta in 1727 concluded between the same parties that demarked the Russo-Mongolian border provided for certain extra-territorial jurisdiction in Russia's favor.[7] However, until the beginning of the 19th century, the relationship and the contents of treaties between East Asia and Europe were largely on equal terms in contrast to the latter half of the same century.

B. *International Law in East Asia in the 19th Century*

1. Application of International Law outside European Soil in 19th Century

James Crawford mentioned in his famous monograph, *The Creation of States in International Law*, that "Asian States such as (for example) China, Ottoman Empire, Afghanistan, Japan, Korea, Thailand (Siam), and the Maratha Empire in India were early recognized as sovereign States subject to international law."[8] He also argued, however, that "[t]his did not of course mean that identical rules were applied to such States as were by European States *inter se*, but that is to be explained not by any distinction between 'civilized' and 'barbarous' States but because many of those rules were what would now be called regional custom rather than general international law."[9]

As for the application of "European" international law to the non-European territories in the 19th century, especially to "the Orient," both Charles de Visscher and *Oppenheim's International Law* edited by Sir Robert Jennings and Sir Arthur Watts, similarly pointed out the importance of the 1856 Peace Treaty

---

[5] Keay, *supra* note 2, at 439.

[6] Rosalyn Higgins, Conflict of Interests: International Law in a Divided World, A Background Book 37 (1965).

[7] *Id.*

[8] James Crawford, The Creation Of States in International Law 176 (2nd ed. 2006).

[9] *Id.* Here, Crawford mentions the Dissenting Opinion of Judge Spender in the Temple of Preah Vihear Case in 1962, and the Judgment of the Right of Passage over Indian Territory Case in 1960. *Temple of Preah Vihear* (Cambodia v. Thai.), 1962 I.C.J. 162; *Temple of Preah Vihear* (Cambodia v. Thai.), 1960 I.C.J. 37, 91–92.

of Paris. Article 7 of the Paris Treaty, signed by five European powers at that time (Britain, France, Austria, Prussia, Sardinia, and the Ottoman Empire), expressly acknowledged Turkey's membership in the (European) international community.[10] *Akehurst's International Law* pointed out that "[i]n the case of old powers, such as Turkey, Siam (Thailand), China and Japan, Western states basically relied on the so-called capitulation system, treaties which were designed to establish lasting privileges for European trade and commerce in those states and which exempted European from local jurisdiction."[11]

In 1873, the *Institut de Droit International* was established in Gent, Belgium, and the first session of the *Institut* was held in Geneva. In 1875, the *Institut* sought to provide clarity on the issue of the possibility of applying customary (European) international law "in the Orient" by commencing a study under the chairmanship of Sir Travers Twiss. A questionnaire was sent to experts in Oriental law to find out whether the beliefs and legal institutions of Oriental and Christian states were sufficiently similar to admit the former "into the general community of international law."[12] In this questionnaire, eight questions were included, and included for instance, the second question which was drafted as follows: "Les notions des peoples orientaux concernant l'obligation d'observer les stipulations des traités different-elles quant au fond même, de celles des peoples chrétiens sur la meme matière?"[13] Two other questions focused on missionaries and another two questions dealt with consular jurisdiction.[14] From the results of this questionnaire, Twiss found that it was very difficult to answer these questions in general terms. He pointed out in his report to the *Institut* that "On ne saurait mettre sur la même ligne tous les peoples orientaux. Les habitants de l'empire ottoman, les Persans, les Chinois, les Japonais doivent être distingués des populations payennes et demi-sauvages. Les relations de l'Europe avec Chine et le Japan sont tout autres que celles avec les populations non civilisêes."[15]

---

10 Article 7 of Paris Treaty 1856 states expressly "déclarent Sublime Porte admise à participer aux avantages du droit public et du concert Européens." 1 OPPENHEIM'S INT'L L., PEACE, INTRODUCTION AND PART 1, 88 (Sir Robert Jennings & Sir Arthur Watts eds., 9th ed. 1992); CHARES DE VISSCHER, THÉORIES ET RÉALITÉS EN DROIT INTERNATIONAL PUBLIC 61 (1970).

11 PETER MALANCZUK, AKEHURST'S MODERN INTRODUCTION TO INTERNATIONAL LAW 13 (7th rev. ed. 1997). In this book, it is also pointed out that "Turkey was expressly admitted (as the first non-Christian nation) to Concert of Europe." *Id.* at 12.

12 MARTTI KOSKENNIEMI, THE GENTLE CIVILIZER OF NATIONS: THE RISE AND FALL OF INTERNATIONAL LAW 1870–1960, 132 (2004).

13 INSTITUTE OF INTERNATIONAL LAW, 1 ANNUAIRE DE L'INSTITUT DE DROIT INTERNATIONAL 141 (2010).

14 *Id.* at 141–42.

15 RAPPORT DE SIR TRAVERS TWISS, 3–4 ANNUAIRE DE L'INSTITUT DE DROIT INTERNATIONAL 301, 1879–1880 (Hans Wehberg ed., 1957).

2. International Law Applied in East Asia in the 19th Century

Even though "European" international law could be applicable, as Sir Travers pointed out in his report regarding the countries in East Asia, what was the reality of applying these rules to East Asia in the 19th century? Rosalyn Higgins argued in her book that

> [t]he era of unequal treaties was inaugurated by the Treaty of Nanking, which the British imposed upon China in 1842 after the Opium War. Under the terms of this treaty, British subjects and their families were to be allowed to live without restriction in several important towns of commerce including Canton. British consuls were to act as intermediaries with the Chinese authorities and an "equitable" customs duty was to be established in ports open to foreigners.[16]

France and the United States rapidly followed Britain and concluded with the Qing the Treaties of Wanghsia and Whampoa respectively in 1844. During the "Arrow War" from 1856, the Qing government was forced by Britain and France to conclude the punitive Treaty of Tianjin in 1858, and after the invasion of the Emperor's summer palace in Beijing by Anglo-French soldiers, the Qing government had no other choice but to conclude the humiliating Convention of Peking in 1860. At this stage, Russia managed to conclude a treaty with the Qing that demarcated a new boundary line between the two states along the Amur River and Wusuli River.

Shortly after the defeat at the hand of these European powers, the Qing government established a new government bureau, Zongli Yamen, to deal with foreign affairs. Zongli Yamen was led by Li Hongzhang, a governor of Anhui who was transferred to Tianjin as governor-general, who occupied this pivotal position until his death in 1901.[17] One of the first official tasks of Zongli Yamen was the introduction of European international law with Henry Wheaton's book, *Elements of International Law*, which was translated into Chinese and published in 1864.[18] As the result of the Treaty of Tianjin in 1858 and Convention of Peking in 1860, Britain, France, Russia, and the United States, began to send their permanent diplomatic missions to Beijing, the capital of the Qing Dynasty. However, it was after the 1870s that the Qing also sent her permanent diplomatic missions to the capitals of these Western states.[19]

---

16 HIGGINS, *supra* note 6, at 37–38.

17 KEAY, *supra* note 2, at 485; *Bankoku-Koho-no-Jidai, Youmu-Henpou Undou* [*The Era of Public Law of Nations, Movement of Westernization and Self-Strengthening*], 2 SHIN-PEN GENTEN-TSYUGOKU-KINDAI-SHISOUSHI [NEW SERIES OF ORIGINAL CHINESE MODERN HISTORY OF IDEAS] 1–2 (Yuichiro Murata ed., 2010).

18 Era of Public Law of Nations, *supra* note 17, at 2.

19 *Id.* at 6–7.

It is worth mentioning here the interesting case in 1864 when Qing officials, by referring to the rules of international law found in Wheaton's treatise, strongly protested Prussia's capture of a Danish merchant ship at Tianjin port during the Schleswig-Holstein War between Prussia and Denmark. As a result, the Prussian Minister in Beijing agreed to free the Danish ship. It was a case in which Qing government officials successfully used the rules of "European" international law to achieve their diplomatic objective.[20]

At that time, in the middle of the 19th century, Japan was also forced to conclude agreements with the United States and European powers. According to these treaties, the Japanese Shogunate opened several ports in Japan to trade with their Western counterparts. The terms of these treaties were unequal for Japan as consular jurisdiction was conferred to the Western countries along with the power to determine custom duties. As a result, for both China and Japan, the revision of these unequal treaties became one of the most important diplomatic goals to be achieved from the latter half of the 19th century to the beginning of the 20th century.

Around the same time, China, Korea, and Japan began to change their relations into European style inter-state relationships. Bilateral treaties between them were concluded one after another: between China and Japan in 1871 and between Korea and Japan in 1876. The relationship between China and Korea was unclear because the Sino-Korean Agreement concluded in 1882 still provided to some degree the traditional tributary relationship between them.[21]

In Japan, the westernization and modernization of its domestic social system was very rapid from the 1870s to the beginning of the 20th century. As for international law, the Japanese Society of International Law was established in 1897, and after the Russo-Japanese War from 1904 to 1905, Sakuyé Takahashi, a prominent international lawyer in Japan and professor of international law of the Imperial University of Tokyo, published a vast monograph written in English and French to show European countries and the United States how the rules of international law were applied and observed, especially by the Japanese navy, during the Russo-Japanese War.[22]

---

20 *Id.* at 23–25.

21 Pae-Keun Park, *Chouchu-Shoumin-Suiriku-Boueki-Shoutei ni Kansuru Sobyo: Higashi-Ajia ni okeru Kokusaihou no Jyuyou to Chosen no Kokusaihouteki-Chii no Kanten kara [A Sketch on the Agreement between Chosen and China for the Trade and Commerce in Land and Sea: From the viewpoint of the Acceptance of International Law in East Asia and the Status of Chosen under International Law]*, *in* KOKUSAI-HOUGAKUNO CHIHEI: REKISHI,RIRON, JISSHOU, HORIZON OF INTERNATIONAL LAW, HISTORY, THEORY AND EXAMINATION, FESTSHRIFT FOR PROFESSOR ONUMA YASUAKI, 216–49 (Jyunji Nakagawa & Hiroshi Teraya eds., 2008).

22 SAKUYE TAKAHASHI, INTERNATIONAL LAW APPLIED TO THE RUSSO-JAPANESE WAR: WITH THE DECISIONS OF THE JAPANESE PRIZE COURTS (1908).

II. International Law in East Asia in the 20th Century and the Future

A. *The Development of International Law in the 20th Century and East Asia*

1. League of Nations Era

Towards the beginning of the 20th century, the breakout and the catastrophe of the First World War had a great impact on international society and the international system as a whole. As a result, the League of Nations and the Permanent Court of International Justice (PCIJ) were established, and a new system of international law began with them. As for East Asian countries, Japan became a Permanent Member of the Council in the League of Nations, and among judges of the PCIJ, one Chinese judge and three Japanese judges were elected during the 1920s and the 1930s. Judge Mineichiro Adatci was elected President of the PCIJ from 1930 to 1933 and he died in The Hague in 1934. However, just before his death, the Japanese government announced at the General Assembly of the League in 1933 that it would withdraw from the League. At this point, Japan's positive attitude toward international law and the international regime under the League of Nations substantially came to an end. In East Asia, like other parts of the world, peoples in this region suffered "untold sorrow"[23] during the Second World War. In June 1945, just 50 days before the surrender of Japan, the Charter of the United Nations was signed in San Francisco, and the Charter came into force in October 1945.

2. United Nations Era

After 1945, under the newly created United Nations system, East Asian countries started in relatively low profiles during the 1950s and 1960s. China was one of the original members of the United Nations having the status of a permanent member of the Security Council, but it was only after 1971 for the Chinese government in Beijing that it began to actively participate in United Nations organs. Japan was regarded as an "enemy State" under the United Nations Charter.[24] Shortly after the restoration of her independence in 1952 through the entry into force of the San Francisco Peace Treaty, Japan had applied for the membership in the United Nations according to Article 4 of the U.N. Charter, but admission for membership was rejected until 1956 because of the objection by the Soviet Union in the

---

23 U.N. Charter, Preamble, para. 1.

24 *See* U.N. Charter arts. 53, 107. For the interpretation of these Enemy State Clauses, see Hans Kelsen, The Law of the United Nations: A Critical Analysis of Its Fundamental Problems 805–15 (1950); Leland M. Goodrich, Edward Hambro and Anne Patricia Simons, Charter of the United Nations, Commentary and Documents 367–68, 633–37 (3rd rev. ed. 1969); The Charter Of The United Nations: A Commentary, Vol. I, at 870–90, Vol. II, at 1330–40 (Bruno Simma ed., 2nd ed. 2002).

Security Council. It was on December 18, 1956, just six days after the entry into force of the Soviet-Japanese Joint Declaration signed by Japanese Prime Minister Ichiro Hatoyama and his Soviet counterpart in Moscow when the Soviet Union and Japan agreed to re-establish their diplomatic relations, that the Soviet side admitted Japan's application for United Nations membership. This was the political reality during the Cold War era. For Korea, joining the United Nations was achieved much later in September 1991 after Korea's diplomatic relationship with the former Socialist countries had been dramatically eased.

B. *East Asia's Contribution to International Law in the 21st Century*

In stark contrast, during the first decades of the 21st century, East Asian contributions to the United Nations and other related international organizations have been highly remarkable. For instance, at the moment, two of the highest international offices, namely the Secretary-General of the United Nations and the President of the International Criminal Court (ICC) are occupied by two distinguished Koreans, Secretary-General Ki-Moon Ban of the United Nations and President Sang-Hyun Song of the ICC. China has of course a permanent seat on the Security Council of the United Nations which has the unique power to make enforcement measures under Chapter VII of the U.N. Charter. In that regard, China is in a strong position and also owes a responsibility to maintain international peace and security provided for in Article 24 of the U.N. Charter through the decisions of the Security Council.

As for international judicial bodies, Judge Shigeru Oda from Japan, who had been a judge of the International Court of Justice (ICJ) in The Hague, the principal judicial organ of the United Nations,[25] from 1976 to 2003, was the only judge that served for three terms for a total of 27 years on the Court. After that, Judge Jiuyong Shi became the first President of ICJ from the East Asian region from 2003 to 2006. From 2009 to 2012, Judge Hisashi Owada was in the same position. It is remarkable that within these ten years two Presidents have been elected from East Asia. It should be also noted that Sadako Ogata from Japan served as the United Nations High Commissioner for Refugees (UNHCR) from 1990 to 2000, and she played a very important role in the recognition of the notion of "human security" as one of the co-chairpersons of the Committee on Human Security.

These facts mentioned above indicate that academics and government officials from East Asia have had a very active role and have made more positive contributions in the field of international law than any other region in the world, and it might be correctly said that East Asia will become the center of international law in the 21st century. Now, after a decade of the 21st century, the peoples of East

---

[25] U.N. CHARTER art. 92.

Asia are arriving at the position as active participants and players of international law in contemporary world society. International law is becoming a part of "our own" law, not "their (Western)" law, by which another enforces upon us to apply "their" own rules that are not familiar to us. After the encounter with European international law in the middle of the 19th century, East Asian peoples are now stepping on to a new stage upon which they themselves are actively engaged in both rule-making and theorizing on the future of "our own" international law.

CHAPTER FOUR

THE DECLARATION ON THE CONDUCT OF PARTIES AND A CODE OF CONDUCT IN THE SOUTH CHINA SEA: RECENT ACTIONS TAKEN BY ASEAN

Yann-huei Song*

I. Introduction

Recent developments in the South China Sea (SCS) has shown the ineffectiveness of the Declaration on the Conduct of Parties in the South China Sea (DOC) that was signed by the foreign ministers of the member states of the Association of Southeast Asian Nations (ASEAN) and special envoy and vice minister of the foreign ministry of the People's Republic of China (China) in Phnom Penh, Cambodia in November 2002.[1] All of the parties involved in the sovereignty and maritime disputes in the SCS signed the declaration, with the exception of the government of the Republic of China (Taiwan) due to the sensitive political issue relating to the Chinese insistence on the so-called "One China" principle.

Under the declaration, the parties concerned in the SCS agreed "to exercise self-restraint in the conduct of activities that would complicate or escalate disputes and affect peace and stability including, among others, refraining from action of inhabiting on the presently uninhabited islands, reefs, shoals, cays, and other features and to handle their differences in a constructive manner."[2] Since the signing of the DOC, however, all of the parties concerned, perhaps with the exception of Brunei and Taiwan,[3] have conducted a series of activities that not only are con-

* Research Fellow, Institute of European and American Studies, Academia Sinica.

[1] Declaration on the Conduct of Parties in the South China Sea, adopted by the Foreign Ministers of ASEAN and the Peoples Republic of China at the 8th ASEAN Summit in Phnom Penh, Cambodia, *available at* http://www.asean.org/13163.htm.

[2] *Id.* at para 5.

[3] Brunei is the only party involved with the sovereignty and maritime disputes in the Spratly Islands which has not sent military forces to occupy her claimed island. While it is clear that Taiwan is a party concerned in the SCS issues, she has been excluded from signing the 2002 DOC and therefore, politically speaking, is not bound by the DOC.

sidered breaking their political commitments made under the declaration, but also lead to increasing tensions in the SCS area.

In April 2010, the ASEAN-China Joint Working Group on the Implementation of the DOC (JWG-DOC) met in Hanoi, Vietnam to review the implementation of the DOC and discussed concrete measures for co-ordination and the effective realization of the declaration.[4] In July 2010, Hillary Clinton, the U.S. Secretary of State, stated in Hanoi that the United States supports the DOC, encourages the parties to reach agreement on a full code of conduct (COC), and is prepared to facilitate initiatives and confidence building measures consistent with the declaration.[5] Both ASEAN and China are also taking the position on the need to enhance the effectiveness of the DOC and the eventual conclusion of a regional COC in the SCS.[6]

The year 2011 was designated as the ASEAN-China Exchange and Friendship Year that marked the 20th anniversary of the ASEAN-China dialogue relations. Are there any possibilities for ASEAN and China to establish a regional COC in the SCS in the coming years?

The purpose of this chapter is to examine recent developments in the SCS by focusing on the actions taken by ASEAN over the past few years to ensure the effective implementation of the DOC and move toward the eventual conclusion of a regional COC in the SCS. After the introductory section, a summary report on recent rising tensions in the SCS will be provided. This will be followed by a discussion of the adoption of the DOC, the difficulties ASEAN encountered in dealing with the SCS issues as a group, and recent actions taken by ASEAN in relation to the implementation of the DOC and adoption of a regional COC in the SCS. This chapter will conclude with remarks on the prospect for implementation of the DOC and adoption of a regional COC, and a call for Taiwan's inclusion in the negotiating process that deals with the SCS issues and in particular the DOC and COC-related matters.

---

[4] *ASEAN-China joint working group discusses East Sea conduct*, VNA NEWS AGENCY WEBSITE (Hanoi), Apr. 17, 2010 (citing BBC MONITORING ASIA-PAC. POLITICAL, Apr. 18, 2010).

[5] *See* Hilary Clinton, U.S. Sec'y of State, Remarks at the National Convention Center in Hanoi, Vietnam (July 23, 2010), *available at* http://www.state.gov/secretary/rm/2010/07/145095.htm.

[6] *See* the Joint Communiqué, the 43rd ASEAN Foreign Ministers Meeting in Hanoi, Vietnam (July 19–20, 2010) para. 28, *available at* http://www.aseansec.org/24899.htm; Chairman, Statement for the 13th ASEAN-China Summit in Hanoi (Oct. 29, 2010) para. 17, *available at* http://www.aseansec.org/25481.htm.

II. Rising Tensions in the SCS: 2007–March 2011

Tensions in the SCS have escalated over the past few years. In April 2007, Beijing accused Hanoi of infringing on China's sovereignty by agreeing with British Petroleum (BP) on a natural gas field and pipeline project in the SCS. In response, Vietnam asserted that the islands in the SCS are historically Vietnamese. In June 2007, BP announced that it was halting seismic work in the disputed waters in the SCS after China hinted that the company's actions were infringing on China's sovereignty. In July 2007, a ship belonging to the Chinese navy fired at Vietnamese fishing vessels near the disputed Spratly Islands in the SCS, injuring five Vietnamese fishermen.[7] In December 2007, Vietnam registered her protest against China's plan to set up San Sha City to manage the three group of islands in the SCS, including the Macclesfield Bank (Zhongsha Qundao in Chinese), Paracel Islands (Xisha Qundao in Chinese and Quần đảo Hoàng Sa in Vietnamese) and Spratly Island (Nansha Qundao in Chinese and Quần đảo Trường Sa in Vietnamese). In addition, a group of students gathered in front of the Chinese Embassy in Hanoi and Consulate in Ho Chi Minh City to oppose China's establishment of San Sha City in Hainan.[8]

In June 2008, China asked ExxonMobil, a U.S. corporation, to withdraw from an exploration deal it had with Vietnam in the SCS, claiming that the blocks under contract are in Chinese waters and therefore constitute a breach of Chinese sovereignty.[9] In August 2008, Taiwan issued a statement reiterating its sovereignty over the Spratly Islands after Datuk Seri Najib Tun Razak, Deputy Prime Minister of Malaysia, led members of the media to Swallow Reef (Pulau Layang-Layang) and proclaimed Malaysia's sovereignty over the disputed island.[10] During the second half of 2008, under Chinese pressure, the Philippine government suspended its legislative process for its archipelagic baselines bill. However, in January 2009, the legislative process resumed and ended with the approval of the Archipelagic Baselines Act by the Senate in February 2009, in which the Philippines claims sovereignty over part of the disputed Spratly Islands and Scarborough

---

[7] *Chinese navy fires at Vietnamese fishing ship, injuring 5*, Japan Econ. Newswire, July 20, 2010; Written testimony, U.S.-China Economy and Security Review Comm'n, Hearing on China's Emerging Military Aerospace and Commercial Aviation Capabilities (May 20, 2010) (prepared by Jeff Hagen); 2010 Report to Cong. of the U.S. Econ. and Sec. Comm'n, at 134, 111th Cong. 2nd Sess. (Nov. 2010).

[8] *Viet Nam assets sovereignty over Truong Sa, Hoang Sa Islands*, Vietnamese News Agency, Dec. 3, 2007; *Vietnam protest against China's San Sha City Spontaneous*, Thai Press Reports, Dec. 12, 2007.

[9] *China Warns Exxon To quit Vietnam Deal*, Asia Pac. Oil and Gas Insights, July 1 2008.

[10] Ministry of Foreign Affairs, Republic of China, Media Center, Aug. 15, 2008, *available at* http://www.mofa.gov.tw/webapp/fp.asp?xItem=32920&ctNode=1014.

Shoal located in the SCS. On March 10, 2009, President Gloria Arroyo signed the Archipelagic Baselines Act, claiming that the Kalayaan Island Group in the Spratly Islands and Scarborough Shoal, classified as a "regime of islands," is part of the country's territory.[11] China, Taiwan, and Vietnam lodged protests against the legislation.[12] In March, China sent its largest fishery patrol ship *Yuzheng 311* to the SCS. We Zhuang, director-general of the Administration for Fishing Affairs and Fishing Ports on South China Sea, was quoted by *China Daily* as saying that "[t]he patrol ship will safeguard China's sovereignty in the South China Sea and protect the nation's marine rights and interests."[13]

In early March 2009, China, Taiwan, and Vietnam reiterated, respectively, their sovereignty claims over the Spratly Islands after Malaysian Prime Minister Badawi's visit to Swallow Reef.[14] On March 8, 2009, the U.S. surveillance ship USNS *Impeccable* was involved in a skirmish with five Chinese vessels 75 miles off the Hainan Islands in the SCS. The United States protested the Chinese actions

---

11 Republic Act No. 9522 of The Philippines, An Act to Amend Certain Provisions of Republic Act No. 3046, as amended by Republic Act No. 5466, To Define the Archipelagic Baselines of the Philippines, and for Other Purposes, approved Mar. 10, 2009, Republic of the Philippines, Cong. of the Philippines, 14th Cong., 2d Regular Sess., *available at* www.lawphil.net/statutes/repacts/ra2009/ra_9522_2009.html; *See also PGMA Signs Baselines Bill into Law*, THE PHILIPPINES, Mar. 11, 2009, *available at* www.gov.ph/index.php?option=com_content&task=21961&itemid=2; *Arroyo Signs into Law Bill Claiming Islands' Sovereignty*, GULF NEWS (United Arab Emirates), Mar. 12, 2009.

12 *See* Letter to Sec'y of Gen. of the U.N. by People's Republic of China, U.N. Doc. CML/12/2009, Apr. 13, 2009, *available at* www.un.org/Depts/los/LEGISLATIONANDTREATIES/Statefiles/phil.htm; Vietnam, Permanent Mission to the U.N., Vietnam's Response to Philippine President's signing of Baseline Act, Mar. 13, 2009, *available at* www.vietnam-un.org/en/news.php?id=77&act=print; *see generally* Head Bayron, *New Philippine Border Law Re-ignites Territorial Disputes in South China Sea*, VOICE OF AMERICA, Mar. 17, 2009, *available at* www.voanews.com/english/archive/2009-03-2009-03-17-voa15.cfm?renderforprint=1. *See also* Kristina Kazmi, *China Protests Philippine Bill Laying Claim to Disputed Spratly Islands*, GLOBAL INSIGHT, Feb. 19, 2009; Joyce Pangco Panares, *Vietnam Joins Protest Against Baseline Bill*, MANILA STANDARD, Feb. 21, 2009; *see* The statement made by the Ministry of Foreign Affairs, Republic of China (Taiwan) (Feb. 4, 2009), *available at* www.mofa.gov.tw/webapp/fp/asp?xItem=36869&ctnode=1548 (in Chinese). *See also Taiwan Lodges Protest Against Philippines Act*, BBC MONITORING ASIA PAC. POLITICAL, Mar. 13, 2009.

13 Bernama, *China Sends Fishery Patrol to South China Sea After Skirmish*, THE MALAYSIAN NAT'L NEWS AGENCY, Mar. 12, 2009.

14 *Vietnam reiterates sovereignty claim after Malaysian PM's island visit*, BBC MONITORING ASIA PAC.—POLITICAL, Mar. 10, 2009; The Gov't of the Republic of China (Taiwan) reiterates its sovereignty over the Nansha Islands and surrounding waters, Gov't Info. Office, Republic of China (Taiwan), Mar. 11, 2009, *available at* http://www.gio.gov.tw/ct.asp?xItem=46362&ctNode=2462; *China—Beijing reiterates sovereignty over disputed islands*, PERISCOPE DAILY DEF. NEWS CAPSULES, Mar. 10, 2009.

and said that the U.S. Navy ships will continue to operate in international waters in the SCS.[15]

In mid-March 2009, Vietnam protested against China's decision to allow a company to operate tours to Phu Lam Island in the Paracel Islands. Vietnam stressed that this seriously infringed on its territorial sovereignty and was unhelpful to bilateral negotiations.[16] The incident was followed in April 2009 by Vietnam appointing a government official to the disputed Paracel Islands and sending a high-ranking delegation of the Communist Party of Vietnam's Central Committee for Education and Propagation to visit the islands. China protested and called the acts "illegal and invalid."[17]

On May 7, 2009, China sent two notifications to the Secretary-General of the United Nations[18] in response to the joint submission made by Vietnam and Malaysia on May 6, 2009[19] and the separate submission made by Vietnam on May 7, 2009[20] delivered to the Commission on the Limits of the Continental Shelf (CLCS) in relation to two areas of outer continental shelf located beyond the two countries' respective 200-nautical-mile exclusive economic zones (EEZs) in the SCS.[21] In the two notifications, China stated that it "has indisputable sovereignty

---

15 Pauline Jelinek, *Pentagon: Chinese vessels harassed unarmed ship*, Assoc. Press Online, Mar. 9, 2009. For further on this issue, *see* Chris Rahman and Martin Tsamenyi, *A Strategic Perspective on Security and Naval Issues in the South China Sea*, 41 Ocean Dev. and Int'l L. 315–33 (2010).

16 *Vietnam Reaffirms Sovereignty over Paracel and Spratly Islands*, Thai Press Reports, Mar. 16, 2009.

17 *World—China slams Vietnam's Paracel post*, Morning Star, Apr. 29, 2009; *Vietnam Appointment of Hoang Sa District's Mayor Is Normal and Legal, Says FM Spokesman*, Thai Press Reports, May 1, 2009; *Vietnam CPV's High-ranking Delegation Visits Truong Sa Archipelago*, Thai Press Reports, May 1, 2009.

18 Note Verbale from the Permanent Mission of the Peoples Republic of China to the United Nations, U.N. Doc. CML/17/2009, N.Y., May 7, 2009 and Note Verbale from the Permanent Mission of the Peoples Republic of China to the United Nations, U.N. Doc. CML/18/2009, N.Y., May 7, 2009, Commission on the Limits of the Continental Shelf, *available at* www.un.org/Depts/los/clcs_new/clcs_hime.htm. [hereinafter Note Verbale 17 & 18]

19 Exec. Summary, Malaysia-Vietnam Joint Submission to the Comm'n on the Limits of the Continental Shelf Pursuant to art. 76, para. 8 of the U.N. Convention on the Law of the Sea 1982 in Respect of the South Part of the South China Sea (May 2009). Note Verbale 17 & 18, *supra* note 18.

20 Exec. Summary, Vietnam Submission to the Comm'n on the Limits of the Continental Shelf Pursuant to art. 76, para. 8 of the U.N. Convention on the Law of the Sea 1982, Particval Submission in Respect of Vietnam's extended Continental Shelf: North Area (VNM-N) (Apr. 2009). Note Verbale 17 & 18, *supra* note 18.

21 The Comm'n on the Limits of the Continental Shelf was established by Annex II of the 1982 U.N. Convention on the Law of the Sea, done at Montego Bay, Jamaica, (Dec. 10, 1982, entered into force Nov. 16, 1994) 166 parties (as of Oct. 5, 2010), 1833 U.N.T.S. 397. Regarding the work of the Comm'n, *see* Note Verbale 17 & 18, *supra* note 18.

over the islands in the South China Sea and the adjacent waters" and "enjoys sovereign rights and jurisdiction over the relevant waters as well as the seabed and subsoil therefore."[22] This sovereign and jurisdictional claim is manifested in a map attached to the notifications. In addition, China pointed out that the submissions by Vietnam and by Vietnam and Malaysia "has seriously infringed China's sovereignty, sovereign rights and jurisdiction in the South China Sea."[23]

In mid-June 2009, China seized three Vietnamese fishing boats and arrested 37 fishermen in the waters near the Paracel Islands for violating China's fishing law. Vietnam protested and stated that China's actions had infringed its sovereignty and jurisdiction of the SCS.[24] In early August 2009, Chinese naval patrols again seized a Vietnamese fishing boat in the disputed Paracel Islands in the SCS.[25] Also, in June 2009, General Zhang Li, former deputy chief of the General Staff of the People's Liberation Army (PLA), presented a proposal at the sixth meeting of the 11th National Committee of the Chinese People's Political Consultative Conference's Standing Committee, calling for China to build an airport and naval dock on Mischief Reef located in the Spratly Islands in the SCS. The former PLA general stated that such facilities would permit China to carry out air patrols of the area, support Chinese fishing vessels, and underline the country's claims to sovereignty of the disputed Spratly Islands in the SCS.[26]

In response to the friction in the SCS area, the *Impeccable* incident, and possible challenges to U.S. maritime strategy and interests, a hearing was held before the Committee on Foreign Relations of the U.S. Senate on July 15, 2009. During the hearing, Peter Dutton asserted:

> Since all of the islands in the South China Sea are claimed as Chinese territory and included in the baselines section of the 1992 Territorial Sea Law, the effect of the 1988 law [the People's Republic of China Law on Exclusive Economic Zone and Continental Shelf] is to claim an exclusive economic zone around each of them. In combination, therefore, the two Chinese laws effectively claim a Chinese EEZ covering nearly the entire South China Sea.[27]

---

22 Note Verbale 17 & 18, *supra* note 18, at para. 2.

23 *Id.*

24 *Politics & Law: China Asked to Release Vietnamese Fishermen*, VIETNAM NEWS BRIEF, June 29, 2009; Kristina Kazmi, *Tensions Rise Between China and Vietnam over Disputed Islands*, GLOBAL INSIGHT, June 29, 2009.

25 *China detain Vietnamese fishermen fleeing storms*, EARTH TIMES, Aug. 2009, *available at* http://ww.earthtimes.org/articles/printstory.php?news=280123.

26 Russell Hsiao, *PLA General Advises Building Bases in the South China Sea*, CHINA BRIEF, Vol. 9, Issue 13, June 24, 2009, *available at* http://www.jamestown.org/programs/chinabrief/single/?tx_ttnews%5Btt_news%5D=35169&tx_ttnews%5BbackPid%5D=414&no_cache=1.

27 Written Testimony, U.S. S. Comm. on Foreign Relations Hearing on Maritime Disputes and Sovereignty Issues in E. Asia (July 15, 2009), at 1–2 (*prepared by Peter Dutton*), *available at* http://vietnam.usembassy.gov/uploads/images/5vXRK-sXHTxpgAzsVHcEqw/DuttonTestimony090715p.pdf.

On July 31, 2009, it was reported that China increased midair refueling training for its J-10 fighters that are stationed in Guangzhou. The main purpose of stepping up the training is to extend the projection power of the Chinese Air Force beyond China's border and to enforce its claims to territories in the SCS.[28]

In November 2009, Vietnam protested the Chinese sending two fishery patrol ships to the Paracel Islands and one medical ship to the Spratly Islands. Vietnam considered the move a violation of its sovereignty over the two archipelagos.[29] In the same month, Vietnam for the first time held an international conference on SCS issues in Hanoi where 150 scholars and officials participated. It was speculated that because Vietnam would be taking over the chair of ASEAN in 2010, it would try to persuade the member states of ASEAN to come together in a territorial negotiation with China.[30] On December 16, 2009, it was reported that Vietnam had purchased six diesel-electric Kilo class submarines and was considering ordering 12 Sukhoi Su-30MK2 fighter jets from Russia, all aimed at bolstering its claims against China over the disputed Paracel and Spratly Islands.[31]

In January 2010, Vietnam again protested against China's plan to develop tourism in the Paracel Islands,[32] and China warned the Philippine government against conducting seismic tests in the Reed Bank Basin off the Kalayaan Island Group in the Spratly archipelago.[33] In April and July respectively, China conducted naval exercises in the South China Sea. In June 2010, U.S. defense secretary Robert Gates stated in Singapore that the SCS is an area of growing concern for Washington "because the sea is not only vital to countries bordering it but to all nations with economic and security interests in Asia."[34] The Secretary also pointed out that the United States "objects to any effort to intimidate U.S. corporations or those of any nations engaged in legitimate economic activity"[35] in the SCS.

In July 2010, U.S. officials leaked to the Japanese media an exchange they had with Chinese officials in March 2010, in which the Chinese reportedly said the

---

28 *Jet-10 Midair Refueling, Monitoring and Controlling the South China Sea*, UNITED DAILY NEWS, July 31, 2009, *available at* http://www.haixiainfo.com.tw/64305.html.

29 *Vietnam Decries Chinese Ship Incursion*, VIETNAMESE NEWS AGENCY, Nov. 27, 2009.

30 Edward Wong, *Vietnam, Taking on China, Seeks Allies in Island Clash*, INT'L HERALD TRIBUNE, Feb. 5, 2010, at 3.

31 Nga Pham, *Vietnam Buy Russian submarines*, BBC NEWS, Dec. 16, 2009, *available at* http://news/bbc.co.uk/go/pr/f/-/2/hi/asia-pacific/8415380.stm.

32 *Vietnam Demands China End Tourism on Hoang Sa Islands*, THAI PRESS REPORTS, Jan. 2010, LexisNexis.

33 *China Warns Philippines Against Conducting Seismic Tests in Kalayaan Islands*, BBC MONITORING ASIA PAC. POLITICAL, Jan. 25, 2010.

34 *See* Robert Gates' Speech delivered during the 9th International Institute for Strategic Studies Asia Security Summit held in Singapore (June 5, 2010); Llanesca t. Panti, *South China Sea disputes spook US*, MANILA TIMES PHILIPPINES, June 8, 2010.

35 Gates, *supra* note 34.

SCS was their "core interest," putting it on a par with Taiwan and Tibet.[36] The remark caused great concern in Southeast Asia over China's seeming assertiveness in the SCS. Then, on July 23, 2010, at the 17th ARF, U.S. Secretary of State Hillary Clinton declared that the U.S. had a "national interest" in the freedom of navigation in the SCS, and urged China and ASEAN to formulate a regional COC to resolve their territorial disputes.[37] China reacted angrily and conducted a large-scale naval exercise in the SCS that same month.[38] This was followed by a joint U.S.-Vietnam naval training exercise in the SCS in August 2010, which involved the super-carrier USS *George Washington* and the USS *John S. McCain*.[39]

In early November 2010, China conducted a "live action drill" with over 100 warships and submarines in the SCS.[40] On November 8, 2010, Vietnam accused China's National Bureau of Surveying and Mapping (NBSM) of encroaching upon its sovereignty over the Paracel and Spratly archipelagos and the surrounding territorial waters by launching an online mapping service, Map World (Tianditu),[41] which depicts the Chinese claimed 9 dotted lines in the SCS that overlapped with Vietnam's claimed islands and waters in the sea. Vietnam claimed that NBSM's act violated Vietnam's sovereignty, sovereign rights, and territorial jurisdiction over the continental shelf and 200-nautical-mile EEZ, and broken the 1982 United Nations Convention on the Law of the Sea (UNCLOS) and the DOC.[42]

In January 2011, the Vietnamese controlled media reported, citing the Japanese newspaper *Asahi Shinbum*, that China drew up a military plan to seize control of the islands in the SCS that are under the effective control of other nations.[43] Also

---

36 In March 2010, U.S. Deputy Secretary of State James Steinberg and Senior Director for Asian Affairs of the National Security Council Jeffrey Bader visited China and had talks with Chinese state councilor Dai Bingguo where the remark was made and then leaked to the media. *See China tells U.S. that S. China Sea is 'core interest' in new policy*, JAPAN ECON. NEWS WIRE, July 3, 2010.

37 The text of the Secretary's speech is available at the website of the U.S. Department of State at http://www.state.gov/secretary/rm/2010/07/145095.htm.

38 Wendell Minnick, *China Is Checkmated at ASEAN*, DEF. NEWS, Aug. 2, 2010; Daniel Schearf, *China Conducts Military Exercise in South China Sea*, VOICE OF AMERICA NEWS, July 30, 2010.

39 *US, Vietnam to Launch Unprecedented Naval Exercises*, VOICE OF AMERICA NEWS, Aug. 10, 2010; Donald Kirk, *US-Vietnam ties strengthen with military exercises, to China's chagrin*, THE CHRISTIAN SCIENCE MONITOR, Aug. 12, 2010.

40 K. J. M. Varma, *China begins 'live action drill' in South China Sea, The Press Trust of India*, Nov. 3, 2010.

41 The service is available at http://www.sianditu.cn and http://www.chinaonmap.cn.

42 *Vietnam Protests China's Sovereignty—Violating Acts*, THAI PRESS REPORTS, Nov. 8, 2010.

43 *Politics & Law China Builds Military Plan to Seize Isles in East Sea*, VIETNAM NEWS BRIEFS, Jan. 5, 2011; Adm. James A. Lyons, Special to the Washington Times, *China's imperialism on full display; PLA weapons upgrades signal goal of Pacific hegemony*, THE WASH. TIMES, Jan. 12, 2011, at. 1.

in January, Vietnam protested against information provided by China to the Map World service, in which the nine-segment claim line in the SCS continued to be present, and asked China to remove the data immediately.[44] In February 2011, the Energy Department of the Philippines gave the go-signal to Forum Energy Plc of the United Kingdom to proceed with the exploration of the Reed Bank basin near the disputed Kalayaan off the SCS.[45] China protested against this act and sent patrol vessels in early March 2011 to order the Singapore-registered and French-owned research vessel to leave the site.[46] In response, the Philippines dispatched an OV 10-bomber plane and a Navy Islander to the Reed Bank area to protect its survey activities. In addition, Philippine President Aquino sent the Commission on Maritime and Ocean Affairs Secretary-General Henry Bensurto to discuss the incident.[47] On March 25, 2011 at a news conference in Beijing, China's foreign ministry spokesman Jiang Yu warned that, "Oil and gas exploration activities by any country or company in the waters under China's jurisdiction without permission of the Chinese government constitute a violation of China's sovereignty, rights, and interests."[48] Also in March 2011 officials of the Armed Forces of the Philippines-Western Command recommended that the Latag (Lawak) and Patag Islands (Flat Island) in the Philippine-occupied Kalayaan Island Group be turned into a tourist spot to strengthen the country's territorial claim. Top Philippine military officials also urged Senate President Pro Tempore Jinggoy Estrada to help pass legislation that would support the proposed revision of Presidential Proclamation 72 to expand the security coverage to all service contracts.[49] The Philippines bought a large Hamilton-class patrol craft from the United States to help it guard its waters amid tensions over territorial claims in the SCS.[50] The Philippines plans to acquire patrol ships, aircraft, and an air defense radar system in order to help secure its territorial claim in and near the disputed Spratly

---

[44] *Vietnam Calls on Map World to Rectify East Sea Line Error*, THAI PRESS REPORTS, Jan. 28, 2011.

[45] *Forum Energy Obtains Nod to Explore Reed Bank Gas Project*, MANILA STANDARD, Feb. 8, 2011.

[46] Tom Grieder, *Sino-Philippine Tensions Rise in South China Sea As Chinese Patrol Boats Threaten Seismic Vessel*, GLOBAL INSIGHT, Mar. 8, 2011.

[47] Press Release, Department of Foreign Affairs, Continuing dialogue essential on the South China Sea, THE PHILIPPINES (Mar. 18, 2011), *available at* http://www.gov.ph/2011/03/18/continuing-dialogue-essential-on-the-south-china-sea/.

[48] Alastair McIndoe, *Philippines stirs waters off Spratlys*, THE STRAITS TIMES (Singapore), Mar. 31, 2011, *available at* http://www.viet-studies.info/kinhte/Phillipin_stirs_Spratlys.htm.

[49] *Philippine president rules out unilateral action Chinese harassment in Spratlys*, BBC MONITORING ASIA PAC. POLITICAL, Mar. 9, 2011.

[50] *Philippine Navy acquire US patrol ship*, AGENCE FRANCE-PRESSE, Mar. 7, 2011, *available at* http://www.abs-cbnnews.com/nation/03/07/11/philippine-navy-acquires-us-patrol-ship.

Islands in the SCS. The Philippines also plans to repair the worn-out airstrip on Pag-asa (Thitu Island) in the Spratly archipelago.[51]

In early March 2011, the Vietnamese Foreign Ministry raised a protest against an anti-piracy exercise conducted by China's eighty naval escort flotilla in the waters near the Spratly Islands, claiming that the exercise "seriously violated Vietnam's sovereignty over the archipelago" and was in violation of the 2002 ASEAN-China DOC.[52] On March 10, 2011, Vietnamese Foreign Ministry spokesperson Nguyen Phuong Nga issued a statement, opposing Taiwan's training on artillery shelling around Taipin Island (Itu Aba) of the Spratly archipelago. Vietnam considered that the act "seriously violated the country's sea and island sovereignty, causing tensions, complicating the regional situation and directly threatening maritime security, especially travel of boats and fishing."[53] In addition, the Vietnamese Foreign Ministry registered its protest against China's 12th five-year Socio-Economic Development Plan Summary, which mentions creating plans for exploitation of resources in the Paracel Islands and Spratly Islands and surrounding territorial waters in the SCS, and the plan to strengthen tourism development in the Paracel Islands.[54]

Rising tensions in the SCS over the past few years highlights not only the ineffectiveness of the DOC but also the necessity of concluding a regional COC in the area. In addition, it demonstrates the importance of the role played by existing regional organizations, in particular, ASEAN, and dialogue mechanisms in the region, such as the ASEAN Ministerial Meeting (AMM), ASEAN Summit, ASEAN Regional Forum (ARF), ASEAN Defense Ministers Meeting Plus (ADMM+), ASEAN + 3 (China, S. Korea and Japan), ASEAN-China Summit, ASEAN-US National Leaders Meeting, East Asia Summit (EAS), Council for Security Cooperation in the Asia-Pacific (CSCAP), the Informal Workshop on Managing Potential Conflicts in the South China Sea (SCS Workshop), the Shangri-La Dialogue in Singapore, and others to help manage potential conflicts in the SCS. As commented, if the potential conflicts in the SCS cannot be properly managed, "it may not be long before it [(the SCS)] is seen once again as a major potential regional flashpoint."[55]

---

51 Jim Gomez, *Philippines seeks patrol ships, aircraft, radar to bolster watch in and near the Spratlys*, The Associated Press, Mar. 28, 2011, http://www.carstairscourier.ca/article/GB/20110328/CP01/303289935/-1/car0806/philippines-seeks-patrol-ships-aircraft-radar-to-bolster-watch-in&template=cpArt.

52 *Vietnam Opposes China's Truong Sa Military Exercise*, Thai Press Reports, Mar. 7, 2011.

53 *VN Opposes China's Violations on Sovereignty*, The Vietnam News Agency, Mar. 10, 2011.

54 *Id.*

55 Ian Storey, *Impeccable Affair and Renewed Rivalry in the South China Sea*, China Brief, Vol. 9, Issue 9, *available at* http://www.jamestown.org/programs/chinabrief/single/?tx_ttnews%5Btt_news%5D=34922&tx_ttnews%5BbackPid%5D=414&no_cache=1.

III. The Origin and Development of a Regional COC and the Signing of the DOC in the SCS

The idea for concluding a regional COC in the SCS came from a proposal made by the government of the Philippines in 1992[56] mainly in response to the enactment of the Chinese territorial sea law in February the same year, which claims that the land territory of China includes "the mainland of the People's Republic of China and its coastal islands; Taiwan and all islands appertaining there to including the Diaoyu Islands; the Penghu Islands; the Dongsha Islands [Pratas Islands]; the Xisha Islands [Paracel Islands]; the Zhongsha Islands [Macclesfield Bank] and the Nansha Islands [Spratly Islands]; as well as all the other islands belonging to the People's Republic of China."[57] It was also a response to the contract signed between China's National Offshore Oil Company and Crestone Energy Corporation of the United States in the area near Wan'an Tan (Vanguard Bank) in the Spratly Islands in May 1992 for oil exploration work.[58] The Philippines successfully obtained the support from the participating foreign ministers to adopt a declaration on the SCS (Manila Declaration), in which they "COMMEND all parties concerned to apply the principles contained in the Treaty of Amity and Cooperation in Southeast Asia as the basis for establishing a code of international conduct over the South China Sea."[59] The ASEAN foreign ministers also invited "all parties concerned" to subscribe to the declaration of principles.[60] In March 1995, in response to the Mischief Reef incident,[61] the ASEAN foreign ministers issued a statement on recent developments in the SCS in which they urged all the parties concerned to remain faithful to the letter and spirit of the Manila Declaration and to resolve differences by peaceful means and to refrain from taking actions that would destabilize the situation in the SCS.[62]

---

56 *See* Nguyen Hong Thao, *The 2002 Declaration on the Conduct of Parties in the South China Sea*, 34 Ocean Dev. & Int'l L. 279 (2003).

57 Law on the Territorial Sea and the Contiguous Zone, adopted at the 24th Meeting of the Standing Committee of the Seventh National People's Congress (Peoples Republic of China) (Feb. 25, 1992), promulgated by Order No. 55 of the President of the Peoples Republic of China on Feb. 25, 1992, and effective as of the date of promulgation. The Chinese and English text of the law is available at http://www.lawinfochina.com/law/display.asp?id=670.

58 Barry Wain, *Beijing and Hanoi Play with Fire in SCS*, The Asian Wall St. J., July 20, 1994, at 5.

59 *See* the ASEAN Declaration on the South China Sea, Manila, Philippines (July 22, 1992), para. 5, *available at* http://www.asean.org/5370.htm.

60 *Id.*

61 In February 1995, the Philippines detected that structures had been built by China on Meiji Jiao (Mischief Reef), which was also claimed by Manila and was located in the Philippines' claimed EEZ in the South China Sea.

62 *See* Recent Developments in the South China Sea (1995), Mar. 18, 1995, *available at* http://www.asean.org/5364.htm.

At the 2nd ARF, held in Brunei in August 1995, the Philippines again proposed the adoption of a multilateral COC for the SCS to help reduce uncertainty and suspicion between and among the claimants in the Spratlys/SCS area. Domingo L. Siazon, Secretary of Foreign Affairs of the Philippines, proposed that:

> Pending a final resolution of the fundamental question of sovereignty in the South China Sea, all concerned countries should strive to arrive at an informal arrangement, a modus vivendi, a code of conduct, which would give all of us a clearer idea of what to expect from one another in terms of our behavior in the area.[63]

The idea of formulating a regional COC for the SCS was endorsed by the foreign ministers who attended the 29th AMM in July 1996.[64]

The issue of developing a regional COC in the SCS was also discussed at the Second Meeting of the Technical Working Group on Legal Matters in the SCS held in Chiang Mai, Thailand, May 13–17, 1997. The participants noted that the issue of developing the code had been discussed in other fora, formal and informal. They agreed that the conclusion of the COC would be an important confidence building measure in the SCS, and therefore supported the effort to establish such a code.[65] On December 16, 1998, at the 6th ASEAN Summit held in Hanoi, Vietnam, the ASEAN leaders picked up the proposal again and agreed to promote efforts to establish the COC in the SCS among the parties directly concerned.[66]

Accordingly, the idea was then discussed at the 5th ASEAN-China Senior Officials Consultation Meeting (SOM) which was held in Kunming in early April 1999. Initially China said that there was no need to sign the proposed code, mainly because the Joint Statement signed between the ASEAN and Chinese leaders were sufficient and presented a confidence building measure.[67] However, its position changed in 2000. At the 6th China-ASEAN SOM held in Kunching, Malaysia, April 25–26, 2000, the two sides agreed to establish a joint working group to formulate a regional COC in the SCS. In 2001, in his speech delivered at the meeting of the 8th ARF, Chinese Foreign Minister Tang Jiaxuan stated that positive progress had been made in consultations between China and ASEAN concerning the COC in

---

63 DFA News Release, Department of Foreign Affairs, Philippines Raises Regional Security Concerns in ARF, THE PHILIPPINES, No. BSB 23 (Aug. 1, 1995).

64 *See* the Joint Communique of the Twenty-Ninth ASEAN Ministerial Meeting, Jakarta (July 20–21, 1996) para. 11, *available at* http://www.aseansec.org/politics/pramm29.htm.

65 *See* the Statement of the Second Meeting of the Technical Working Group on Legal Matters (May 13–17, 1997), para. 12 (*prepared by Chiang Mai*) (Copy of the statement on file with author).

66 *See* the Joint Communiqué of the 32nd AMM held in Singapore (July 23–24, 1999), para. 39, *available at* http://www.aseansec.org/politics/pramm32.htm.

67 In particular this was referred to the Joint Statement of the Meeting of the President of the People's Republic of China and the Heads of State/Gov't of the Member States of ASEAN, Dec. 16, 1997, *available at* http://www.aseansec.org/5476.htm.

the SCS.[68] On November 6, 2001, Chinese Premier Zhu Rongji pointed out at the 5th China-ASEAN Summit that "[i]n order to achieve a more stable situation in the South China Sea, China is ready to complete the consultations with ASEAN on the code of conduct for the South China Sea region at an early date."[69]

In April 2002, after attending the Malaysia-China delegation meeting, Malaysia's Deputy Prime Minister Datuk Seri Abdullah Ahmad Badawi stated at a media conference that Malaysia and China agreed on the need to implement a COC in the disputed areas in the SCS including the Spratly Islands. However, he stressed that certain aspects of the code must be studied to enable countries to deal with sensitive issues such as overlapping claims or multiple claims made against territories in the SCS. Within ASEAN, particularly among the member states that are directly involved in the territorial disputes in the SCS, there were four differences over the text of the ASEAN-drafted COC: the geographical scope of the COC; the issues relating to new occupation and construction; joint military exercises; and humane treatment of fishermen in the disputed areas. Among these differences, the geographical scope of the SCS was the most difficult one to be dealt with.

In order to break the deadlock, in July 2002, Malaysia decided to push for signing a non-binding document called "the Declaration on the Conduct of Parties in the South China Sea" instead of adopting a regional COC for the sea. The proposal was included in the agenda of the 35th AMM that was held in Bandar Seri Begawan on July 29–30, 2002. In the Joint Communiqué of the 35th AMM, the ASEAN foreign ministers reaffirmed the adoption of a COC in the SCS that would further promote peace and stability in the region and agreed to work towards a Declaration on the Conduct of Parties in the South China Sea. The ministers agreed to work closely with China with a view to adopting the DOC.[70] On October 11, 2002, the ASEAN SOM was held in Phnom Penh, Cambodia, in which differences among the member states of ASEAN over the scope, wording, and application of the political declaration proposed by Malaysia were ironed out. On October 31, 2002, senior officials of the member states of ASEAN and China discussed the text of the declaration in Phnom Penh and reached agreement to sign the document.

After three years of negotiations, the member states of ASEAN and China finally signed the DOC at the end of the sixth ASEAN-China summit that was held

68 *See* Tang Jiaxuan, Chinese Foreign Minister, Address at the 8th Foreign Ministers' Meeting of ASEAN Regional Forum (July 25, 2001), *available at* http://www.fmprc.gov.cn/eng/wjb/wjbz/2461/t14066.htm.

69 Zhu Rongji, Premier of the Peoples Republic of China, Address at 5th China-ASEAN Summit, Working Together to Create a New Phase of China-ASEAN Cooperation, *available at* http://www.fmprc.gov.cn/eng/wjdt/zyjh/t25046.htm.

70 *See* the Joint Communiqué of the 35th ASEAN Ministerial Meeting, Bandar Seri Begawan (July 29–30, 2002), para. 40, *available at* http://www.aseansec.org/10189.htm.

in Phnom Penh, Cambodia on November 4, 2002.[71] The signing of the declaration was described as "a major leap for peace and would lead to an eventual adoption of a regional code of conduct in the SCS."[72]

IV. The ASEAN-China Declaration on Conduct of Parties in the SCS

In the declaration, ASEAN and China recognized the need to promote a peaceful, friendly, and harmonious environment in the SCS for the enhancement of peace, stability, economic growth, and prosperity in the region. The two sides reaffirmed their commitment to the purposes and principles provided in the international agreements such as UNCLOS and other universally recognized principles of international law.[73] The declaration added that the member states of ASEAN and China would avoid undertaking activities that had the potential to complicate or escalate disputes and affect peace and stability in the SCS. An example was given in the Declaration, stating that the parties concerned would refrain from the action of inhabiting the presently uninhabited islands, reefs, shoals, cays, and other features.[74]

Under the Declaration, freedom of navigation in and over-flight in the SCS would be respected; territorial and jurisdictional disputes would be resolved by peaceful means; efforts would be undertaken to build trust and confidence; cooperative activities would be explored or conducted; and consultations/dialogues would be continued. ASEAN and China also reaffirmed that the adoption of a regional COC in the SCS would further promote peace and stability in the region and therefore agreed to work towards the eventual attainment of that goal.[75]

The Declaration contains several important confidence building measures which include: holding dialogues and exchange of views between defense and military officials; ensuring just and humane treatment of all persons who are either in danger or in distress; and notifying on a voluntary basis other parties concerned of any impending joint/combined military exercises conducted in the Spratly/SCS region.[76] Under the Declaration, the parties concerned may explore or undertake cooperative activities such as the following: (a) marine environmental protection; (b) marine scientific research; (c) safety of navigation and communication at sea; (d) search and rescue operation; and (e) combating transnational

---

[71] *See* News Release, ASEAN and China Sign Declaration on the Code of Conduct in the South China Sea, ASEAN Secretariat, Jakarta, Indonesia (Nov. 4, 2002), *available at* http://www.aseansec.org/13166.htm.

[72] *ASEAN-China Accord Is A Major Leap for Peace: Philippine FM*, Asia Pulse, Nov. 6, 2002.

[73] Declaration on the Conduct of Parties in the South China Sea, *supra* note 1, at para. 1.

[74] *Id.* at para. 5.

[75] *Id.* at para. 10.

[76] *Id.* at para. 5.

crime, including but not limited to trafficking in illicit drugs, piracy and armed robbery at sea, and illegal traffic in arms. However, the modalities, scope and locations, in respect of bilateral and multilateral cooperation, should be agreed upon by the parties concerned prior to their actual implementation.[77]

The DOC is not a legal instrument and therefore does not have legal binding force. By signing the political declaration, the member states of ASEAN and China express their commitment or intent as to future conduct in the SCS. While noting the non-legal character of the signed declaration, attention should also be drawn to the inclusion of provisions that recognize existing rules or principles of international law, namely, the Charter of the United Nations, UNCLOS, the Treaty of Amity and Cooperation in Southeast Asia, the Five Principles of Peaceful Coexistence, and other universally recognized principles of international law.[78]

V. The Implementation of the DOC

In 1997, the Joint Statement of the Meeting of the Heads of State/Government of the Member Countries of ASEAN and the President of the People's Republic at Kuala Lumpur, Malaysia, was issued that laid a good political foundation for the two sides to enhance cooperation at bilateral and multilateral levels.[79] In November 2002, China and ASEAN signed the DOC and the Framework Agreement on Comprehensive Economic Cooperation. The framework agreement set the target for establishing an ASEAN-China Free Trade Area by 2010 for the six core member countries of ASEAN.[80] Certainly Beijing's non-devaluation of the *ren min bi* (RMB) at the time of the 1997/98 Asian financial crisis also helped in fostering closer relations between ASEAN and China. In October 2003, the heads of state/government of member countries of ASEAN and China issued the Joint Declaration of the PRC and ASEAN State Leaders: A Strategic Partnership for Peace and Prosperity.[81] In the Joint Declaration, China and ASEAN agreed to implement the DOC, and discuss and plan the concrete modes, areas, and projects of follow-up actions.[82] In the same month, China acceded to the Treaty of

---

[77] *Id.* at para. 6.

[78] *Id.* at para. 1.

[79] The Joint Statement of the Meeting of the Heads of State/Gov't of the Member Countries of ASEAN and the President of the People's Republic of China at Kuala Lumpur, Malaysia (Dec. 16, 1997)—ASEAN-China Cooperation Toward the 21st Century, *available at* http://www.aseansec.org/5476.htm.

[80] For the Framework Agreement on Comprehensive Economic Cooperation Between ASEAN and the People's Republic of China, Phnom Penh (Nov. 4, 2002), *available at* http://www.aseansec.org/13196.htm.

[81] The text of the Joint Declaration is *available at* http://aseansec.org/15265.htm.

[82] *Id.* at sec. (4)—Security Cooperation.

Amity and Cooperation in Southeast Asia.[83] The Joint Declaration was followed by agreement on a detailed "Plan of Action to Implement the Joint Declaration on ASEAN-China Strategic Partnership for Peace and Prosperity" on November 29, 2004,[84] which "serve as the 'master plan' to deepen and broader ASEAN-China relations and cooperation in a comprehensive and mutually beneficial manner for the next five years (2005–2010) with the view to strengthening the strategic partnership for regional peace, development and prosperity and playing a proactive role to tap the opportunities and meet the challenges of the new millennium." With regard to the DOC, ASEAN and China planed to pursue the following joints actions and measures:

- Implement in an effective way the Declaration on the Conduct of Parties (DOC) in the South China Sea to maintain regional stability and promote cooperation in the South China Sea;
- Convene regular ASEAN-China Senior Officials Meeting (SOM) on the realization of the DOC to provide guidance for and review the implementation of the DOC;
- Establish a working group to draw up the guidelines for the implementation of the DOC and to provide recommendations to the ASEAN-China SOM on policy and implementation issues;
- Promote joint cooperation and dialogue in areas such as marine scientific research, protection of the marine environment, safety of navigation and communication at sea, search and rescue operation, humane treatment of all persons in danger or distress, fight against transnational crimes as well as cooperation among military officials;
- Promote trust and confidence building through cooperative activities, in accordance with the principles of the DOC, in particular, those of consultations and consensus among the concerned parties in the South China Sea, pending the peaceful settlement of the territorial and jurisdictional issues as stated in the DOC;
- Affirm the vision of the DOC state parties to work, on the basis of consensus, on the eventual adoption of a code of conduct in the South China Sea; and
- Adhere to the terminologies used in the UN Convention on the Law of the Sea and other instruments of the International Maritime Organization.[85]

---

83 Instrument of Accession to the Treaty of Amity and Cooperation in Southeast Asia, done at Bali, Indonesia on Oct. 8, 2003, and signed by Li Zhaoxing, Minister of Foreign Affairs, the People's Republic of China, *available at* http://www.aseansec.org/15271.htm.

84 Plan of Action to Implement the Joint Declaration on ASEAN-China Strategic Partnership for Peace and Prosperity, *available at* http://www.aseansec.org/16805.htm.

85 *Id.* at 1.5—Declaration on the Conduct of Parties in the South China Sea.

In accordance with the 2004 Plan of Action, the 1st ASEAN-China SOM on the implementation of the DOC was held on December 7, 2004, which decided to establish the JWG-DOC. The main task of the joint working group is "to study and recommend measures to translate the provision of the DOC into concrete cooperative activities that will enhance mutual understanding and trust."[86] The ASEAN-China JWG-DOC is tasked to formulate recommendations on:

1. guidelines and the action plan for the implementation of the DOC;
2. specific cooperative activities in the South China Sea, particularly in the following areas:
   - marine environmental protection;
   - marine scientific research;
   - safety of navigation and communication at sea;
   - search and rescue operation; and
   - combating transnational crime;
3. a register of experts and eminent persons who may provide technical inputs, non-binding and professional views or policy recommendations to the ASEAN-China JWG; and
4. the convening of workshops as the need arises.[87]

The ASEAN-China JWG-DOC is asked to meet regularly at least twice a year and submit a report and recommendation to the ASEAN-China SOM at the end of each meeting.[88]

The 1st JWG-DOC was held on August 4–5, 2005 in Manila, the Philippines, where the ASEAN side presented a draft of guidelines for the implementation of the DOC. The proposed guidelines consist of the following seven points:

1. The implementation of the DOC should be carried out in a step-by-step approach in line with the provisions of the DOC.
2. ASEAN will continue its current practice of consulting each other before meeting China.
3. The implementation of the DOC should be based on activities or projects clearly defined.
4. The participation in the activities or projects should be carried out on a voluntary basis.
5. Initial activities to undertaken under the ambit of the DOC should be confidence-building measures.

---

86 *See* Terms of Reference of the ASEAN-China Joint Working Group on the Implementation of the Declaration on the Conduct of Parties in the South China Sea, *available at* http://www.aseansec.org/16886.htm.

87 *Id.* at para. 7.

88 *Id.* at para. 10.

6. The decision to implement concrete measures or activities of the DOC should be based on consensus among parties concerned, and lead to the eventual realization of the Code of Conduct.
7. In the implementation of the agreed projects under the DOC, the services of the Expert and Eminent Persons, if deemed necessary, will be sought to provide specific inputs on the projects concerned.[89]

The 2nd ASEAN-China JWG was held in Sanya, Hainan, China, February 8–9, 2006, where the representatives of all parties to the DOC agreed upon the following six projects to be implemented from 2006:

1. Joint ASEAN-China Table Top Maritime Search and Rescue Exercise. The Philippines are in charge of preparing a paper on the project.
2. Workshop on Marine Ecosystems and Biodiversity. This Workshop will be funded by the ASEAN-China Cooperation Fund (ACCP).
3. Workshop on Regional Oceanographic and Climate Exchange in the South China Sea. Vietnam is responsible for preparing and circulating a paper on the project.
4. Workshop on Disaster Prevention and Reduction, Establishing Disaster Monitoring and Warning System in the South China Sea.
5. Training Program on Ecosystem Monitoring and Monitoring Technology.
6. Regional Oceanographic Exchange around the South China Sea. China will take charge of providing further details on the last three projects for consideration at later meetings.[90]

The agreed projects were reported at the 2nd ASEAN-China SOM held in Siem Reap, Cambodia on May 30, 2006. The meeting also discussed and exchanged views on the guidelines proposed by ASEAN and approved the aforementioned six projects. However, the agreed projects will not be implemented before a consensus was reached on the guidelines for the implementation of the DOC.[91] The 3rd ASEAN-China SOM was held in Bandar Seri Begawan on March 26, 2008, but no consensus was reached on the ASEAN-proposed guidelines. The main reason for the stalemate of negotiations between China and ASEAN for the adoption of the proposed guidelines to implement the DOC was the difference over the modality of their consultation. ASEAN member countries insisted that they

---

89 Nguyen Hong Thao, *The Declaration on the Conduct of Parties in the South China Sea: A Vietnamese perspective, 2002–2007*, in SECURITY AND INTERNATIONAL POLITICS IN THE SOUTH CHINA SEA: TOWARDS A COOPERATIVE MANAGEMENT REGIME 218 (Sam Bateman and Ralf Emmers eds., 2009).

90 *Id.* at 215.

91 *Id.* at 218.

should consult among themselves first before they consult with China.[92] However, China argued that the approach is not in line with the understanding of the DOC, where modalities, scope and location of bilateral and multilateral cooperation are left flexible to the parties concerned in the SCS. China insisted that the whole issue of the SCS was not a matter between ASEAN as an organization and China, but among the relevant countries. In addition, China was concerned about the actions taken recently by some claimant states in the SCS, which were in violation of the principles contained in the DOC, namely the parties concerned were asked to genuinely observe the DOC to exercise self-restraint not to complicate the situation and escalate the disputes in the SCS.[93]

VI. ASEAN's Dealing the SCS Issues

While the member states of ASEAN were able to take a common position in dealing with China on SCS issues first in 1992 by adopting the Manila Declaration and then in 1995 by issuing a statement on the SCS as a group, they have been divided on SCS issues and the call for a united ASEAN position to check China since 1995. As it can be recalled, when China and member states of ASEAN were negotiating for the adoption of a regional COC, differences had been seen not only between China and member states of ASEAN, but also within the organization. Vietnam, Malaysia, and China took different positions on the area of application of the document. Vietnam and Malaysia also had different views on the binding nature of the agreement. In the end, the DOC signed between ASEAN and China in November 2002 left the Vietnamese feeling abandoned by the rest of the organization. In response, Vietnam insisted with the support of other member countries in ASEAN that the ultimate aim is a regional COC in the SCS.[94]

Customarily, the governments of Cambodia, Laos, Myanmar, and Thailand have close political and economic relations with China and therefore have been taking a lukewarm attitude on the SCS issues. When Thailand served as the rotating chair of ASEAN, SCS issues were not on the top of ASEAN's agenda. It is clear that Singapore's concern about the SCS issues, and in particular, the need to foster a common position of ASEAN to check China's assertive moves in the SCS is not as strong as those of Vietnam and the Philippines. These two countries

---

92 *See* point 2 of the guidelines proposed by ASEAN; Declaration on the Conduct of Parties in the South China Sea, *supra* note 1, at para. 5.

93 *See* Madam Xue Hanquin, Chinese Ambassador to ASEAN, Speech entitled China-ASEAN Cooperation: A Model of Good-Neighbourliness and Friendly Cooperation at ASEAN Studies Centre, Institute of Southeast Asian Studies (ISEAS), Singapore (Nov. 19, 2009), *available at* http://www.iseas.edu.sg/aseanstudiescentre/Speech-Xue-Hanqin-updated.pdf.

94 *See* Rodolfo C. Severino, *ASEAN and the South China Sea*, Security Challenges 45, Vol. 6, Issue 2 (Winter 2010).

have long-standing conflicting claims with China over the Paracel and Spratly Islands in the SCS. As a result of the Chinese submission of an official map to the UN Secretary-General in May 2009 and the expansion of the Chinese patrolling activities to the southern part of the SCS, Malaysia's and Indonesia's concerns have increased since then.

Despite the existing differences, however, member states of ASEAN have continuously sought to "internationalize" the SCS issues "not only in ASEAN and ARF meetings but in other international gatherings as well."[95] At the 36th AMM held in Phnom Penh on June 16–17, 2003, the ASEAN foreign ministers exchanged views on a number of important issues including the situation in the SCS. The foreign ministers reaffirmed the DOC as an important step towards a COC in the SCS and as a valuable contribution to peace and stability in the region. They stressed the need for observance of the provisions of the Declaration and urged all concerned parties to undertake the confidence-building and cooperative measures called for in accordance with the DOC. In addition, they reiterated the call for continued self-restraint and the avoidance of any action that would complicate the situation in the SCS. Moreover, they emphasized the need for all concerned to seek to deal with the disputes in the SCS by peaceful means in conformity with international law, including UNCLOS. Finally, they encouraged the continuation of the informal SCS Workshops.[96] The same statements can be found in the Joint Communiqué of the AMM that were held between 2004 and 2009.[97] The need to intensify efforts to move forward the implementation of the DOC, including the early finalization of the Guidelines on the Implementation of the Declaration, was emphasized in the Joint Communiqué of the 42nd AMM. The foreign ministers also looked forward to the eventual conclusion of a regional COC in the SCS.[98]

---

[95] For example, the member states of ASEAN have raised the SCS issues at the meeting of the Non-aligned Movement in which China is an observer. [hereinafter SCS issues] *See id.* at 44.

[96] *See* Joint Communiqué of the 36th ASEAN Ministerial Meeting, Phnom Penh (June 16–17, 2003), para. 26, *available at* http://www.aseansec.org/14880.htm.

[97] Joint Communiqué of the 37th ASEAN Ministerial Meeting, Jakarta (June 29–30, 2004), paras. 22–24, *available at* http://www.aseansec.org/16192.htm; Joint Communiqué of the 38th ASEAN Ministerial Meeting, Vientiane (July 26, 2005), para. 13–15, *available at* http://www.aseansec.org/18781.htm; Joint Communiqué of the 39th ASEAN Ministerial Meeting, Kuala Lumpur (July 25, 2006), paras. 27–28, *available at* http://www.aseansec.org/18782.htm; Joint Communiqué of the 40th ASEAN Ministerial Meeting, Manila (July 29–30, 2007), paras. 30–31, *available at* http://www.aseansec.org/21785.htm; Joint Communiqué of the 41st ASEAN Ministerial Meeting, Singapore (July 21, 2008), paras. 20–21, *available at* http://www.aseansec.org/21784.htm; and Joint Communiqué of the 42nd ASEAN Ministerial Meeting, Phuket, Thailand (July 20, 2009), paras. 20–21, *available at* http://www.aseansec.org/21784.htm.

[98] Joint Communiqué of the 42nd ASEAN Ministerial Meeting, *supra* note 97, at para. 21.

At the ASEAN Summit, the SCS issues have also been discussed. The ASEAN leaders at the 10th ASEAN Summit held in Vientiane on November 29, 2004 welcomed the steps being taken by ASEAN and China to implement the DOC in the SCS.[99] Relevant statements are also included in the Chairman's Statement of the 11th and 12th ASEAN Summits held in 2005 and 2006 respectively.[100]

The SCS issues have also been included in the agenda of ARF since its 2nd meeting held in Brunei Darussalam on 1 August 1995[101] and the discussion of the DOC/COC since its 10th meeting held in Phnom Penh on June 18, 2003.[102] In addition to the ten member countries of ASEAN, foreign ministers or their representatives from Australia, Canada, China, the EU, India, Japan, New Zealand, South Korea, Russia, the United States, PNG, North Korea, Mongolia, Pakistan, East Timor, Bangladesh, and Sri Lanka participated in the ARF meetings annually. At the 10th ARF, for example, the participating foreign ministers welcomed the DOC and expressed their confidence that efforts made by ASEAN and China in compliance with the Declaration's provisions and commitments would contribute valuably to the security and stability of the Asia-Pacific and would help create the conditions for the peaceful settlement of the disputes in the SCS.[103] At the 15th meeting of the ARF:

---

99 Chairman, Statement at the 10th ASEAN Summit, Vientiane (Nov. 29, 2004), para. 13, *available at* http://www.aseansec.org/16631.htm.

100 Chairman, Statement at the 11th ASEAN Summit, Kuala Lumpur (Dec. 12, 2005), para. 6, *available at* http://www.aseansec.org/18039.htm; Chairperson, Statement at the 12th ASEAN Summit, Cebu, Philippines (Jan. 13, 2007), para. 14, *available at* http://www.aseansec.org/19280.htm.

101 Chairman, Statement at the 2nd Meeting of the ASEAN Regional Forum, Brunei, Darussalam (Aug. 1, 1995), *available at* http://www.aseanregionalforum.org/PublicLibrary/ARFChairmansStatementsandReports/ChairmansStatementofthe2ndMeetingoftheASE/tabid/199/Default.aspx.

102 Chairman, Statement at the 11th Meeting of the ASEAN Regional Forum, Jakarta (July 2, 2004), para. 14; Chairman, Statement at the 12th Meeting of the ASEAN Regional Forum, Vientiane (July 29, 2005), para. 18; Chairman, Statement at the 13th Meeting of the ASEAN Regional Forum, Kuala Lumpur, Malaysia (July 28, 2006), para. 18; Chairman, Statement at the 14th Meeting of the ASEAN Regional Forum, Manila, Philippines (Aug. 2. 2007), para. 17; Chairman, Statement at the 15th Meeting of the ASEAN Regional Forum, Singapore (July 24, 2008), para. 12; and Chairman, Statement at the 16th Meeting of the ASEAN Regional Forum, Phuket, Thailand, (July 23, 2009), para. 12, *available at* http://www.aseanregionalforum.org/PublicLibrary/ARFChairmansStatementsandReports/tabid/66/Default.aspx.

103 *See* Chairman, Statement at the 10th Meeting of ASEAN Regional Forum, Phnom Penh (18 June 2003), para. 19, *available at* http://www.aseanregionalforum.org/PublicLibrary/ARFChairmansStatementsandReports/ChairmansStatementofthe10thMeetingoftheAS/tabid/76/Default.aspx.

> The Ministers reaffirmed the continuing importance of the Declaration on the Conduct of Parties in the South China Sea of 2002 (DOC) as a milestone document between ASEAN and China, embodying their collective commitment to ensure the peaceful resolution of disputes in the area. They believed that the Declaration has been effective in building mutual trust and confidence among the claimants in the area and in maintaining peace and stability in the region. They reiterated the hope that ASEAN and China would expeditiously conclude the Guidelines on the Implementation of the DOC, and looked forward to the eventual conclusion of a Regional Code of Conduct in the South China Sea. They encouraged the continued exercise of self-restraint by all the parties concerned and the promotion of confidence-building measures in this area and welcomed their commitment to resolving disputes in the South China Sea by peaceful means in conformity with the spirit of the DOC and recognised principles of international law including the United Nations Convention on the Law of the Sea.[104]

There is another ASEAN-related dialogue process that is also dealing with SCS issues and DOC/COC matters, namely, the ASEAN-China Summit that is referred to as the ASEAN+1 meeting. The ASEAN and Chinese leaders witnessed the signing of the DOC at the 6th ASEAN-China Summit in November 2002. In addition, the two sides adopted the Joint Declaration of ASEAN and China on Cooperation in the Field of Non-Traditional Security Issues and tasked their ministers to expeditiously specify mechanisms for such cooperation. Moreover, China acceded to the Treaty of Amity and Cooperation in Southeast Asia and stated its willingness to work with ASEAN to push for early accession to the Southeast Asia Nuclear Weapons-Free Zone (SEANFWZ).[105] China and ASEAN also discussed SCS issues and the DOC/COC at the 9th Summit (December 12, 2005), the Commemorative Summit (October 30, 2006), and the 11th Summit (November 20, 2007).[106]

VII. Recent Actions Taken by ASEAN in Relation to the DOC and COC

ASEAN has become more active in dealing with the SCS issues since 2010. Three reasons can be given to help explain this new gesture: (1) the rising tensions in

---

104 *See* Chairman, Statement at the 15th Meeting of ASEAN Regional Forum, Singapore (July 24, 2008), para. 12, *available at* http://www.mofa.go.jp/region/asia-paci/asean/conference/arf/pdfs/ARF_15_CS.pdf; Thao, *supra* note 89.

105 *See* Chairman, Press Statement at the 8th ASEAN Summit, the 6th ASEAN+3 Summit and the ASEAN-China Summit, Phnom Penh, Cambodia (Nov. 4, 2002), para. 28, *available at* http://www.aseansec.org/13188.htm.

106 *See* Chairman, Statement at the 9th ASEAN-China Summit, Kuala Lumpur (Dec. 12, 2005), para. 10, *available at* http://www.aseansec.org/18048.htm; Joint Statement of ASEAN-China Commemorative Summit, Nanning, China (Oct. 30, 2006), paras. 3 and 14, *available at* http://www.aseansec.org/18894.htm; Chairman, Statement at the 11th ASEAN-China Summit, Singapore (Nov. 20, 2007), para. 8, *available at* http://www.aseansec.org/21106.htm.

the SCS and the perceived increasing Chinese assertive moves in the region; (2) Vietnam's taking over the rotating chair of ASEAN; and (3) the intention of the United States to re-involve itself in Southeast Asia via the SCS issue. Section II of this chapter has already cited a number of unilateral actions taken by the claimants that are considered in violation of the DOC and lead to rising tensions in the SCS. The second reason relates to Vietnam's interests in limiting perceived Chinese assertive moves in the SCS over the past few years.

Vietnam joined ASEAN in 1995 and its role in the organization has been growing rapidly over the past 15 years. Since Vietnam has long-standing conflicting claims with China over the Paracel Islands and the Spratly Islands, it has been very active in bringing up its interests in the SCS over the past few years. Vietnam is keen to see ASEAN member countries taking a firmer stance on the issue of determining the sovereignty of disputed islands in the SCS. Efforts have also been made by Hanoi to encourage member countries of ASEAN to act as a bloc in dealing with Beijing on the SCS issues. Vietnam's taking over the rotating chair of ASEAN[107] in 2010 provided Hanoi a good opportunity to achieve the stated goal. It is therefore not surprising that the SCS issues have been put on top of the ASEAN agenda during the Vietnamese chairmanship.

As far as the U.S. intention to re-involve itself in Southeast Asia via SCS issues are concerned, a number of statements made by top U.S. officials who are in charge of diplomatic and security affairs over the past two years can be summarized to support this observation. On May 31, 2008, in his speech delivered at the 7th IISS Asia Security Summit (Shangri-La Dialogue), Robert Gates, the U.S. Secretary of Defense, stated that:

> We welcomed back in the mid-1990s moves toward a "code of conduct" among states with competing territorial and resource claims in South China Sea. We stressed then, as we do today, that we do not favor one claim, or one claimant country, over another. We urged then, as we do today, the maintenance of a calm and non-assertive environment in which contending claims may be discussed and, if possible, resolved. All of us in Asia must ensure that our actions are not seen as pressure tactics, even when they coexist beside outward displays of cooperation.[108]

---

107 According to the ASEAN Charter, the Chairmanship of ASEAN shall rotate annually, based on the alphabetical order of the English names of Member States. Thailand was the chair in 2009 and therefore Vietnam took over the chairmanship from Thailand in January 2010. For more information, *see* Press Report, Indonesia Replaces Brunei as Chair of ASEAN 2011, ASEAN SECRETARIAT (Apr. 12, 2010), *available at* http://www.aseansec.org/24547.htm.

108 Robert Gates, Challenges to Stability in the Asia-Pacific, *available at* http://www.iiss.org/conferences/the-shangri-la-dialogue/shangri-la-dialogue-2008/plenary-session-speeches-2008/first-plenary-session-challenges-to-stability-in-the-asia-pacific/first-plenary-session-the-hon-robert-gates/.

In July 2009, in his testimony given at a hearing before the Subcommittee on East Asian and Pacific Affairs, Committee on Foreign Relations, U.S. Senate, Deputy Assistant Secretary of State Scot Marciel stated that "the United States has a vital interest in maintaining stability, freedom of navigation, and the right to lawful commercial activity in East Asia's waterways"[109] and that "the United States object to any efforts to intimidate U.S. companies."[110]

In November 2009, President Obama met with ASEAN leaders in Singapore where he said that the United States is committed to engaging ASEAN at the highest levels and proposed that he meet with ASEAN leaders again in 2010. In January 2010, in her speech made at the East-West Center, Hawaii, Secretary Clinton stated that "America's future is linked to the future of the Asia Pacific region, and the future of this region depends on America" and that "to promote regional security, we must address nuclear proliferation, territorial disputes and military competition—persistent threats of the 21st century."[111] On July 23, 2010, in her remarks made at National Convention Center in Hanoi, Vietnam when attending the 17th ARF meeting, Secretary Clinton stated that:

> The United States, like every nation, has a national interest in freedom of navigation, open access to Asia's maritime commons, and respect for international law in the South China Sea. We share these interests not only with ASEAN members or ASEAN Regional Forum participants, but with other maritime nations and the broader international community.
>
> The United States supports a collaborative diplomatic process by all claimants for resolving the various territorial disputes without coercion. We oppose the use or threat of force by any claimant. While the United States does not take sides on the competing territorial disputes over land features in the South China Sea, we believe claimants should pursue their territorial claims and accompanying rights to maritime space in accordance with the UN Convention on the Law of the Sea. Consistent with customary international law, legitimate claims to maritime space in the South China Sea should be derived solely from legitimate claims to land features.
>
> The U.S. supports the 2002 ASEAN-China declaration on the conduct of parties in the South China Sea. We encourage the parties to reach agreement on a full code of conduct. The U.S. is prepared to facilitate initiatives and confidence building measures consistent with the declaration. Because it is in the interest of all claimants and the broader international community for unimpeded commerce to proceed under lawful conditions. Respect for the interests of the international community and responsible efforts to address these unresolved claims and help create the conditions for resolution of the disputes and a lowering of regional tensions.[112]

---

109 Testimony of Deputy Assistant Secretary Scot Marciel, Bureau of East Asian & Pacific Affairs, U.S. Department of State, *available at* http://foreign.senate.gov/imo/media/doc/MarcielTestimony090715p1.pdf.

110 *Id.* at 4.

111 Hillary Clinton, Remarks on Regional Architecture in Asia: Principles and Priorities, *available at* http://www.state.gov/secretary/rm/2010/01/135090.htm.

112 For the remarks, *see* Hillary Clinton, Remarks on Press Availability, *available at* http://www.state.gov/secretary/rm/2010/07/145095.htm.

In response to Secretary Clinton's remarks, in particular relating to the DOC and COC, Chinese foreign minister Yang Jiechi highlighted the consensus reached between ASEAN and China that the sovereignty and maritime disputes in the SCS should be solved peacefully through friendly consultations in the interest of peace and stability in the region and good-neighborly relations and that the parties concerned, in accordance with the DOC, should exercise restraint, and not to make it an international issue or multilateral issue. He also stressed that the disputes should not be viewed as ones between China and ASEAN as a whole just because the countries involved are ASEAN members. The foreign minister insisted that the SCS issues should not be internationalized and warned that if the SCS disputes are turned into international or multilateral issues, it will only make matters worse and the resolution more difficult. He urged that the best way to resolve the SCS disputes is for countries concerned to have direct bilateral negotiations.[113]

However, at the 5th EAS, the U.S. policy on the SCS issues was reiterated by Secretary Clinton, stating that, "the United States has a national interest in the freedom of navigation and unimpeded lawful commerce. And when disputes arise over maritime territory, we are committed to resolving them peacefully based on customary international law." She added, "With regard to the South China Sea, we are encouraged by China's recent steps to enter discussions with ASEAN about a more formal binding code of conduct."[114] It is observed that the Obama administration is trying to boost the confidence of Southeast Asian nations to stand up to China. U.S. intervention in the SCS disputes is considered part of its broad plan to reassert itself in Southeast Asia. In addition, in particular from the perspective of China, a U.S.-led evolution of a pan-Asian NATO is forming.

It is against this background that a number of actions have been taken by ASEAN in 2010 that are related to SCS issues in general and DOC/COC matters in particular. As the rotating chair of ASEAN, Vietnam hosted a number of ASEAN-related meetings in which SCS issues and DOC and COC matters had been discussed. In addition, the second ASEAN-US leaders meeting was held in New York in September 2010 where the leaders also discussed SCS issues.

In April 2010, the 4th JWG-DOC was convened in Hanoi, where the representatives of the member countries of ASEAN and China underlined the significance of the DOC, reviewed the implementation of the declaration, and discussed concrete measures for coordination and effective realization of the declaration.[115] However, there was no progress reported on the adoption of the guidelines

---

113 For "Foreign Minister Yang Jiechi Refutes Fallacies on the South China Sea Issue," *see* the Ministry of Foreign Affairs of the Peoples Republic of China *available at* http://www.fmprc.gov.cn/eng/zxxx/t719460.htm.

114 *See* the Secretary's "Intervention at the East Asia Summit," the U.S. Dep't of State, *available at* http://www.state.gov/secretary/rm/2010/10/150196.htm.

115 *See ASEAN-China joint working group meets in Hanoi, available at* http://asean2010.vn/asean_en/news/36/2DA87B/ASEAN-China-joint-working-group-meets-in-Hanoi.

to implement the DOC that was drafted at the 1st JWG-DOC in 2005. In early October 2010, both the Chinese ambassador and U.S. ambassador to the Philippines talked about the willingness to establish or to help craft a regional COC in the SCS. Chinese ambassador Liu Jianchao said that a draft code of conduct was being discussed by the member countries of ASEAN and China at the working level. The inclusion of sanctions in the draft against claimant states that will violate the code "is under the process of consultations."[116] U.S. ambassador Harry Thomas said that the United States was willing to help craft a legally binding "code of conduct" to end the sovereignty and maritime disputes between ASEAN member countries and China that threaten stability in the SCS region.[117]

In December 2010, the 5th JWG-DOC was held in Kunming, Yunnan Province, China, which reviewed the progress of the implementation of the DOC.[118] All parties at the meeting reaffirmed the importance of the DOC and agreed to make the SCS a place of peace, cooperation, and friendship. China made a 4-point proposal for ASEAN member states to take back for their consideration. One of the most controversial points in the Chinese proposal was to delete paragraph 2 of the Implementation Guidelines.[119] ASEAN member states agreed that they would respond to China's proposal. The 5th JWG-DOC recommended that ASEAN-China SOM on the DOC would be held at an appropriate time. In addition, the meeting agreed to convene the 6th JWG-DOC in Indonesia in the second half of March 2011. While it was possible to see the adoption of the guidelines to implement the DOC and progress made in the drafting a regional COC at the upcoming JWG-DOC and ASEAN-China SOM meetings, it is believed that the goals would not be achieved soon.

According to the ASEAN Charter, the chairmanship of ASEAN shall rotate annually, based on the alphabetical order of the English names of member states. In principle, 2011 would have seen Brunei succeeding the chairmanship from Vietnam, and Indonesia would have taken over from Cambodia in 2013. Due to Indonesian concerns about the heavy burden for hosting the APEC and other summit meetings including the G-20, Indonesia assumed the chairmanship in 2011 with Brunei chairing ASEAN in 2013. A member state assuming the

---

116 Michaela P. del Callar, *Asean, China start dialogue on code of conduct*, The Daily Tribune, *available at* http://www.tribuneonline.org/nation/20101001nat5.html.

117 *US willing to help craft a South China Sea code of conduct*, Taipei Times, Oct. 5, 2010, *available at* http://www.taipeitimes.com/News/front/archives/2010/10/05/2003484579.

118 *ASEAN, China to meet on S. China Sea code of conduct in December*, The Mainichi Daily News, Oct. 28, 2010, *available at* http://mdn.mainichi.jp/mdnnews/news/20101028p2g00m0in006000c.html and Mustaqim Adamrah, *China 'softens' South China Sea stance*, The Jakarta Post, Nov. 24, 2010, *available at* http://www.thejakartapost.com/news/2010/11/24/china-%E2%80%98softens%E2%80%99-s-china-sea-stance.html.

119 The paragraph is read as "ASEAN will continue its current practice of consulting among each other before meeting China."

chairmanship shall chair the ASEAN Summit and related summits, the ASEAN Coordinating Council, the three ASEAN Community Councils, relevant ASEAN Sectoral Ministerial Bodies and senior officials, and the Committee of Permanent Representatives. Cambodia assumed the chairmanship of ASEAN in 2012 and is followed by Brunei in 2013, and Myanmar in 2014.

Over the past twenty years, Indonesia has been playing a very important role in managing potential conflicts in the SCS by establishing the SCS workshop process and hosting SCS workshop relevant meetings since 1990. Jakarta's concern about Chinese assertive moves in the SCS has also increased over the past years. Indonesia has played a more active role in getting member countries of ASEAN to act as a bloc against China when it took over the chairmanship of ASEAN in January 2011 by putting SCS issues and the DOC/COC matters on top of the ASEAN agenda in 2011. The recent rapidly improved US-Indonesia relations and the visit of President Obama to Indonesia and attending the 6th EAS have led to this development. If no progress were made on the discussion of the COC and the deadlock continues in relation to the adoption of the guidelines that is aimed to ensure effective implementation of the DOC, there could be seen a risk of losing ASEAN's momentum in pressuring China to accept a much more stronger document that govern the acts of the claimant countries in the SCS. It is further observed that Cambodia, which took the chair of ASEAN in 2012 and has maintained close political and economic relations with China, and Brunei, to be the chair in 2013, have been passive in the past in dealing with SCS issues.

Under the Vietnamese chairmanship of ASEAN, the 43rd AMM was held in Hanoi in July 2010, where the foreign ministers discussed SCS issues and DOC/COC matters. The ASEAN discussion on and concerns about SCS issues are reflected in paragraphs 28 and 29 of the Joint Communiqué of the 43rd ASEAN Foreign Ministers Meeting. The ASEAN foreign ministers reaffirmed the significance of the DOC as a "milestone document" between ASEAN and China, "embodying the collective commitment to promoting peace, stability and mutual trust and to ensuring the peaceful resolution of disputes in the area."[120] The ministers underscored the need to intensify efforts to ensure the effective implementation of the Declaration and looked forward to the eventual conclusion of a regional COC in the SCS. In this connection, they welcomed the reconvening of the JWG-DOC in April 2010 in Hanoi and tasked ASEAN senior officials to work closely with their Chinese counterparts to reconvene the ASEAN-China SOM at the earliest opportunity. In addition, the ASEAN foreign ministers stressed the importance of maintaining peace and stability in the SCS and encouraged the continued exercise of self-restraint by all the parties concerned and the promotion of confidence-building measures in the area. They emphasized the importance of all parties to respect the freedom of

---

120 For the joint communiqué, *see* ASEAN Secretariat, para. 28, *available at* http://www.aseansec.org/24899.htm.

navigation in and over-flight above the SCS as provided for by universally recognized principles of international law. Finally they welcomed the commitment of all the parties concerned to resolving the SCS disputes through peaceful means in conformity with the spirit of the DOC and recognized principles of international law, including UNCLOS.[121] The same is observed in the Chairman's Statement of the 17th meeting of the ARF that include the same wording that appears in the joint communiqué of the 43rd AMM.[122]

Possibly due to the efforts made by Chinese senior officials secretly to prevent a broad discussion on the SCS disputes by member countries of ASEAN at the meetings, the unwillingness of some of the ASEAN members to openly confront China over the SCS issues, and the close political relations between the ASEAN chair and China, the SCS issues and the DOC/COC matters were not put on the agenda of the 13th (hosted by Singapore), 14th (hosted by Thailand), 15th (hosted by Thailand), and the 16th ASEAN Summit (hosted by Vietnam). As a result, SCS issues were not included in the chairman's statement of these four summits. However, mainly because of the U.S. strategy to contain China and get involved in the SCS issues by fostering a close strategic relations with ASEAN at the 17th ASEAN Summit hosted by Vietnam on October 28, 2010, not only were SCS issues widely discussed but also the results of the discussion were included in the chairman's statement of the meeting that stated:

> We reaffirmed the importance of the Declaration on the Conduct of Parties in the South China Sea (DOC) signed between ASEAN and China, which embodies the collective commitment to promoting peace and stability in this area through dialogue and cooperation and peaceful resolution of disputes in accordance with universally agreed principles of international law including the United Nations Convention on the Law of the Sea (UNCLOS 1982) and other relevant international maritime laws. We stressed the need to intensify efforts to ensure the effective implementation of the DOC and move toward the eventual conclusion of a regional Code of Conduct in the South China Sea (COC). In this connection, we encouraged continued consultations between ASEAN and China, including the early convening of the ASEAN-China SOM on the DOC.[123]

At the 13th ASEAN-China Summit, chaired by Nguyen Tan Dung, Prime Minister of the Socialist Republic of Vietnam and held in Hanoi in October 2010, the leaders of ASEAN member states and Wen Jiabao, Premier of the State Council of the People's Republic of China, discussed a number critical issues concerning the two sides, including SCS issues and DOC/COC matters. Paragraph 17 of the

---

121 *Id.* para. 29.

122 *See* Chairman, Statement at the 17th ASEAN Regional forum, the 43rd AMM/PMC/17th ARF VIETNAM 2010, Ha Noi (July 23, 2010), para. 12, *available at* http://www.aseansec.org/24929.htm.

123 Chairman, Statement at the 17th ASEAN Summit, Hanoi (Oct. 28, 2010), para. 12, *available at* http://www.aseansec.org/25452.htm.

Chairman's Statement of the 13th ASEAN-China summit states that the leaders of ASEAN member states and China reaffirmed their commitment to fully and effectively implement the DOC and work towards the eventual adoption, on the basis of consensus, of a COC in the SCS, to further contribute to peace, stability and cooperation in the region. They welcomed the progress made in this regard, including the convening of the 4th Meeting of JWG-DOC, and stressed the importance of close consultation and coordination between the ASEAN member states and China in the implementation of the DOC, including the re-convening of the ASEAN-China SOM on the DOC.[124] More importantly, ASEAN and China adopted the Plan of Action to Implement the Joint Declaration on ASEAN-China Strategic Partnership for Peace and Prosperity on October 31, 2010, that extended the framework of the implementation of the Plan of Action for another five years between 2011 to 2015.[125] This plan of action is very important for the implementation of the DOC and possible adoption of a regional COC mainly because it includes the following joint actions and measures:

1. Push forward the full and effective implementation of the DOC in the South China Sea to maintain regional stability and promote cooperation in South China Sea including through the regular convening of the ASEAN-China SOM on the DOC and the ASEAN-China Joint Working Group on the Implementation of the DOC and continued joint efforts in drafting the Guidelines for the implementation of the DOC while working toward the eventual conclusion, on the basis of consultations and consensus, of a code of conduct in the South China Sea;
2. Promote trust and confidence building through cooperative activities, in accordance with the principles of the DOC, in particular, those of consultations and consensus among the concerned parties in the South China Sea, pending the peaceful settlement of the territorial and jurisdictional issues as stated in the DOC.
3. Adhere to the terminologies used in the UN Convention on the Law of the Sea and other instruments of the International Maritime Organization;
4. Promote joint cooperation and dialogue in areas such as marine scientific research, protection of the marine environment, safety of navigation and communication at sea, search and rescue operation, humane treatment of all persons in danger or distress, fight against transnational crimes as well as cooperation, among military officials.[126]

---

124 *See* ASEAN Secretariat *available at* http://www.aseansec.org/25481.htm.

125 *See* http://asean2010.vn/asean_en/news/48/2DAA16/Plan-of-Action-to-Implement-the-Joint-Declaration-on-ASEAN-China-Strategic-Partnership-for-Peace-and-Prosperity.

126 *Id.*

Vietnam has also been successful in inserting SCS issues into the meeting agenda of ASEAN-US Summit, ADMM+, and EAS, and bringing the United States to participate in the dialogue processes. Before the second ASEAN-US Summit that was held in New York in September 2010, it was believed that the meeting would result in a joint statement addressing the SCS issues by reiterating the intent and direction of Secretary Clinton's remark at the 17th meeting of ARF in Hanoi with a focus on China. However, partially due to the efforts made by Chinese senior officials in New York and the unwillingness of the ASEAN member countries to thumb their nose at China so openly over the SCS issue in the territory of the United States, the participating leaders did not accept the U.S. proposal to specifically include the wording, such as the SCS or the name of certain claimant countries in the dispute, that would be considered provocative by China. As a result, the softened paragraph in the Joint Statement of the 2nd ASEAN-U.S. Leader Meeting reads as follows:

> We reaffirmed the importance of regional peace and stability, maritime security, unimpeded commerce, and freedom of navigation, in accordance with relevant universally agreed principles of international law, including the United Nations Convention on the Law of the Sea (UNCLOS) and other international maritime law, and the peaceful settlement of disputes.[127]

This concern also appears in the Chairman's Statement of the 1st ASEAN Defense Ministers' Meeting Plus (ADMM+) that was held in Hanoi on October 12, 2010.[128] While the remarks made by Secretary Robert Gates at the meeting reiterated the U.S. commitment to fundamental principles that are essential to regional peace, prosperity, and stability, which include: (1) U.S. commitment to free and open commerce; (2) a just international order that emphasizes the rights and responsibilities of nations, and fidelity to the rule of law; (3) open access by all to the global commons of sea, air, space, and now, the cyberspace domain; and (4) the principle of resolving conflict without the use of force.[129] The participating defense ministers only noted that "the member states are interested in maritime security cooperation and agreed that the collective efforts are required to address the challenges of piracy, human trafficking and disasters at sea."[130] It was included in the statement that "[s]ome delegates touched upon traditional security challenges, such as disputes in the East Sea [South China Sea]" and that

---

127 Joint Statement of the 2nd U.S.-ASEAN Leaders Meeting, para. 18, *available at* http://www.whitehouse.gov/the-press-office/2010/09/24/joint-statement-2nd-us-asean-leaders-meeting.

128 *See* Chairman's Statement, *available at* http://english.vovnews.vn/Home/First-ADMM-Chairmans-Statement/201010/120438.vov.

129 For the Secretary's remarks, *see* Robert Gates, Remarks at ASEAN Defense Ministers Meeting Plus, *available at* http://sharing.govdelivery.com/bulletins/GD/USDOD-FC8AC.

130 Del Callar, *supra* note 116, at para. 12.

the meeting welcomed efforts by concerned parties to address the issue by peaceful means in conformity with the spirit of the DOC and recognized principles of international law, including UNCLOS.[131]

When it was expected that the United States would soon join the 16-nations EAS, it was worried that America would try to put the SCS issue on the agenda of the summit. This development has the potential to aggravate US-China tensions. It would also jeopardize the future of the expanded EAS. In October 2010, Secretary Clinton attended the 5th EAS as invited special guest. In her remarks at the summit, she reiterated the U.S. position on SCS issues and the intention to be involved in the discussion of the COC. She said:

> The United States has a national interest in the freedom of navigation and unimpeded lawful commerce. And when disputes arise over maritime territory, we are committed to resolving them peacefully based on customary international law. With regard to the South China Sea, we are encouraged by China's recent steps to enter discussions with ASEAN about a more formal binding code of conduct.[132]

As an invited guest, the Secretary's remarks were not included in the Chairman's Statement of the 5th EAS. Paragraph 5 of the statement only states that the participating leaders of the ASEAN member countries, Australia, China, India, Japan, South Korea, and New Zealand "noted with pleasure its important contributions toward maintaining regional peace and stability, maritime security and safety, and peaceful settlement of disputes in accordance with universally agreed principles of international law."[133]

In January 2011, the ASEAN Foreign Ministers' Retreat was convened in Lombok, Indonesia and attended by eight foreign ministers of ASEAN and the Secretary-General of ASEAN, which marked the first of a string of meetings hosted by Indonesia during its chairmanship of ASEAN in 2011. At the meeting, the foreign ministers discussed a number of important regional and international issues of common concern, including SCS issues. The ministers underlined the 9 years of negotiation at the JWG-DOC level, which failed to make progress on the adoption of the Implementation Guidelines for the DOC. They called for cooperation between ASEAN and China to create stability in the SCS by implementing the DOC. In addition, they hoped that discussions on the Guidelines would not slow down the immediate implementation of the DOC and eventually lead to the possible adoption of a regional COC for the SCS.[134] After the meeting, Indonesian Foreign Minister Marty Natalegawa said that of maritime disputes

---

131 *Id.*

132 For the Secretary's remarks, *see* Hillary Clinton, Intervention at the East Asia Summit, *available at* http://www.state.gov/secretary/rm/2010/10/150196.htm.

133 For the statement, *see* Japanese Ministry of Foreign Affairs, para. 5, at http://www.mofa.go.jp/region/asia-paci/eas/pdfs/state101030.pdf.

134 Press Release, ASEAN Foreign Ministers' Retreat (AMM Retreat), Lombok (Jan. 16–17th, 2011), *available at* http://www.deplu.go.id/Pages/PressRelease.aspx?IDP=1070&l=en.

in the SCS: "these can spiral out of control" and that "there must be a greater sense of urgency in finalising guidelines."[135] The AMM retreat was followed by a meeting held in Kunming, China on January 24, 2011 to celebrate the 20th anniversary of establishing dialogue relationship between ASEAN and China. At the meeting, the ministers stressed the importance of effectively implementing the DOC, which contributes to peace and stability in the region.[136] In March 2011, Indonesian Minister of Foreign Affairs Marty Natalegawa said that Indonesia, as the ASEAN chair, stood ready to help create a conductive situation for the solution of territorial disputes in the SCS, including bringing them up at the next ASEAN summit for deliberation. In addition, he asked for the stoppage of polemics and the need to settle the SCS conflict at the bilateral, regional, and global levels as well as all those approaches that are of a mutually complimentary and supportive nature.[137]

VIII. Conclusion

ASEAN member states have been divided on SCS issues, in particular with regard to whether or not and how to act as a group to deal with an increasingly assertive China in the SCS. Over the past few years, ASEAN has indeed become more active in dealing with SCS disputes and calling for the need to adopt guidelines between itself and China to ensure effective implementation of the DOC as well as the eventual conclusion of a regional COC. There are a number of reasons that account for the shift of ASEAN's posture in dealing with SCS issues, which include: recent developments in the SCS that involve long-standing conflicting sovereignty and maritime claims over the Paracel and Spratly Islands and the accompanied unilateral actions taken by the claimants to support their respective claims; rising tensions in the SCS; China's assertive posture; and the increasing U.S. interest and intervention in Southeast Asia via SCS issues; the inclusion of the SCS issues to the top of the agenda of a number important ASEAN-related meetings such as AMM, ASEAN Summit, ARF, ASEAN+1, ADMM+, ASEAN-US Summit, and EAS; and Vietnam's taking over the ASEAN chairmanship. In 2010, ASEAN responded to the rising tensions in the SCS, the changing strategic and security environment as a whole in the region, and the increasingly perceived competition for influence in Southeast Asia between the United States and China by reiterating its previous

---

135 *Southeast Asia seeks common ground on sea disputes with China*, Reuters, Jan. 16, 2011, http://af.reuters.com/article/idAFTRE70F1G320110116.

136 *ASEAN, Chinese foreign ministers gather in Kunming*, VietNamNet, http://english.vietnamnet.vn/en/politics/4272/asean--chinese-foreign-ministers-gather-in-kunming.html.

137 *South China Sea Disputes May be Taken to ASEAN Summit: Indonesian FM*, Asia Pulse, Mar. 9, 2011.

position on the SCS issues that emphasized the importance of the DOC and the need to conclude a regional COC, and asking the parties concerned to promote peace and stability in the SCS through dialogue and cooperation and resolve disputes in accordance with universally agreed principles of international law.

ASEAN's concerns and position on the recent developments can be observed by reading the chairman's statements or joint communiqués of the relevant ASEAN meetings held in 2010 as examined in this chapter. It can be expected to see that the SCS remains an issue for the agenda of ASEAN-related meetings in the years to come. Indonesia played an important role in dealing with SCS issues and DOC/COC matters given that the country took over the chairmanship of ASEAN in 2011, and Jakarta has undertaken great efforts to help manage the potential conflicts in the SCS over the past two decades via the SCS workshop process that was established by Indonesia in 1990.

In addition, it is likely that the United States, just like the approach it took with Vietnam, will work closely with Indonesia to bring up the SCS issues at ASEAN-related meetings to check China's assertive moves in the SCS and its growing military power that is considered to be a potential threat to U.S. interests in East Asia.

For China, in order to counter U.S. involvement in SCS issues and in particular Washington's intention to internationalize the issues and adopt a multilateral approach to manage the potential conflicts in the area, it is likely that Beijing will take a softened position in dealing with the claimant countries either bilaterally or multilaterally. As indicated in the ASEAN-China 2011–2015 action plan, the two sides will push forward the full and effective implementation of the DOC and work toward the eventual conclusion of a regional COC in the SCS. It is possible to see some progress made in the years to come by China and member states of ASEAN. It can also be expected to see China increasing its efforts to cooperate with the member states of ASEAN in a comprehensive way, given that the 2002 ASEAN-China Free Trade Agreement came into effect on 1 January 2010 which establishes a free trade area that is the largest in the world in terms of population and third largest in terms of nominal GDP, and that the member countries of ASEAN are keen to maintain their close economic and political relations with China.

Finally, as far as Taiwan is concerned, while it has been excluded from participation in the ASEAN-China negotiating process since the late 1990s for the consideration of a regional COC and the adoption as well as implementation of the DOC until today, recent developments in the SCS and the rapidly improving cross-strait relations since 2008, the possibilities for Taiwan to be involved in the discussion of the guidelines to implement the DOC and the eventual conclusion of a regional COC in the SCS are indeed increasing. If Beijing is willing to discuss with Taipei on the issue of Taiwan's participation in the ASEAN-China negotiating process, a number of flexible arrangements could be made. These include: an extension of an invitation to Taiwan's scholars, or even better, governmental officials in their personal capacity to participate in the JWG-DOC or the ASEAN-China SOM meetings as resource persons, observers, or special guests; or the invitation extended to Taiwan to accede to the DOC 2002 and then participation in the six agreed cooperative projects that have been proposed in 2006 by China and ASEAN; or other agreed projects to be implemented in the future. In that regard, the best approach is to sign an agreement or memorandum of understanding between Beijing and Taipei on the modality of Taiwan's participation in the DOC/COC-related negotiation process and implementing activities. The China-Taiwan agreement or MOU would then be endorsed by the member states of ASEAN based on a new ASEAN+1+1 formula and understanding of adherence to the "One China" principle.

In July 2011, China and ASEAN eventually agreed to the text of the guidelines to implement the DOC. At the 18th ASEAN Regional Forum, held on the 23rd of the same month in Bali, Indonesia, the participating foreign ministers welcomed the finalization and adoption of the guidelines and considered it "a milestone document" between ASEAN member countries and China. In December 2011, a Workshop on the Regional Oceanography of the South China Sea was held in Qingdao, China, which was the first cooperation project of all parties under the framework of the DOC. In the same month, a workshop on "Implementing DOC: Maintaining Freedom and Safety of Navigation in the South China Sea" was held in Hainan's Haikou City, China, which was one of the cooperative initiatives proposed by China in July 2011 at the 3rd China-ASEAN SOM to implement the DOC. In January 2012, at the 4th ASEAN-China SOM to implement the DOC, the two sides agreed to organize workshops and seminars on issues related to the South China Sea which include maritime disaster prevention and mitigation, marine ecological environment and surveillance technology, maritime search and rescue, and marine ecology and biological diversity. The participating senior officials from ASEAN member states and China stated that they were committed to promoting the comprehensive implementation of the DOC and advance pragmatic cooperation in the South China Sea. In July 2012, at the 45th ASEAN Ministerial Meeting held in Phnom Penh, Cambodia, the foreign ministers were divided over the SCS issue and ended the meeting without a joint communiqué for the first time in the Association's forty-five year history. To help maintain the Association's common position on the SCS issue, Indonesian foreign minister Marty Natalegawa made a special diplomatic effort which resulted in the Statement of ASEAN Foreign Ministers on ASEAN's Six-Point Principles on the South China Sea released on July 20, 2012.

CHAPTER FIVE

RESOLUTION TO HIGH SEAS FISHERIES ISSUE: A VIEW FROM THE SOUTH CHINA SEA AND AN EXPECTATION ON NATIONAL OCEAN POLICY

Kuan-Hsiung Wang*

I. Introduction

Globalization has already become an important phenomenon in modern international society. This phenomenon has been demonstrated in the economic elements of production that have flowed with unprecedented speed and scale on a global scale. Although the process of globalization has been witnessed for several decades, there is still debate over whether globalization will cause the collapse of national boundaries. Furthermore, will states collapse in the future because their functions have been restricted?

In previous discussions or debates on "globalization," there has been a focus on international financial transactions, technology flows, transnational cooperation, capital flows, the cross border movements of people, and so forth. In other words, states, as members of the international community, are becoming closer and sharing common interests. Therefore, more functional fields, such as the interaction between the fish products trade and marine environmental protection, and even disputes are emerging.

It is clear that national sovereignty has been challenged by the developments mentioned above. Not only has such a phenomenon appeared in daily economic life, but it has also appeared in the development of the international legal system, especially in the areas of high seas fisheries and international environmental protection. This chapter will deal with the high seas fisheries issue from the approach of regional cooperation.

There are a great number of management tools, institutions, and international instruments, such as conventions, treaties, and arrangements that have been developed to protect fish stocks. These policy means should be practiced in an integrated mechanism at the national, regional, and international levels so that these policy objectives can be accomplished.

* Professor and Director, Graduate Institute of Political Science, National Taiwan Normal University.

II. Crisis: High Seas Fish Stocks Depletion

Human society is faced with three interrelated problems: a rising population; the need to provide adequate food; and increasing levels of carbon dioxide in the atmosphere. According to the United Nations,[1] by the year 2100, it is predicted that the world's population will have more than doubled its 1990 level of 5.2 billion people and will approach 11.5 billion. In such circumstances, providing sufficient food will become an urgent task for the present generation. It is apparent that the ocean plays an important role at present by providing animal protein to the human population.[2]

Statistics from the Food and Agriculture Organization of the United Nations shows that global production from fisheries and aquaculture supplied about 101 million tonnes of food in 2004, providing for a per capita supply of 16.6 kg (live weight equivalent) which is the highest on record. Of this total, aquaculture accounted for 43 percent. Outside China, per capita supply has shown a modest growth rate of about 0.4 percent per year since 1992 (following a decline from 1987), as growth in the supply from aquaculture more than offset the effects of the static capture of fishery production and a rising population. In 2004, the per capita fish supply was estimated at 13.5 kg if data from China is excluded. Overall, fish provided more than 2.6 billion people with at least 20 percent of their average per capita animal protein intake. The share of fish protein among the total animal protein supply grew from 14.9 percent in 1992 to a peak of 16.0 percent in 1996, declining to about 15.5 percent in 2003. Notwithstanding the relatively low fish consumption by weight in low-income food-deficit countries of 14.1 kg per capita in 2003, the contribution of fish to the total animal protein intake was significant—at about 20 percent—and is probably higher than indicated by official statistics in view of the unrecorded contribution of subsistence fisheries. Preliminary estimates for 2005 based on reporting by major fishing countries indicate that total world fishery production reached almost 142 million tonnes, representing an increase of over 1 million tonnes compared with 2004, a record high production. Although the total amount of fish available for human consumption is estimated to have increased to 107 million tonnes, the global per capita supply remained at about the same level as in 2004 because of population growth.[3]

---

1 United Nations, Long Range World Population Projections, Dep't of Int'l Econ. and Social Affairs, U.N. Doc. ST/ESA/SER.A/125 (1992), no. 125.

2 Ian S. F. Jones & Helen E. Young, *Engineering A Large Sustainable World Fisheries*, 24 Env't Conservation 99, n. 2 (1996).

3 Food and Agriculture Organization of the United Nations, FAO Fisheries and Aquaculture Dept., The State of World Fisheries and Aquaculture 2006 (Rome: FAO, 2007), at 3–4, *available at* http://www.fao.org/docrep/009/A0699e/A0699e00.htm.

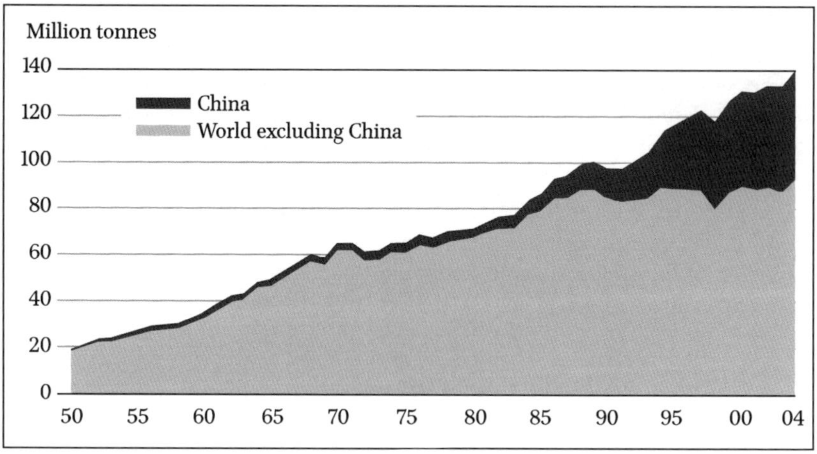

Source: Food and Agriculture Organization of the United Nations, FAO Fisheries and Aquaculture Dept., *The State of World Fisheries and Aquaculture 2006* (Rome: FAO, 2007), p. 4.

Figure 1. World capture and aquaculture production.

Figure 1 demonstrates that fish captured from the ocean and harvested from aquaculture has increased six times in the past five decades. Furthermore, fish capture from the ocean had doubled in the last 20 years of the 20th century. This fact leads to one result and one question. The result is that fishery resources are under increasing pressure and the question is what impact will it have on the environment?

Taking the Atlantic bluefin tuna (*Thunnus thynnus*) as an example, such a species spends most of its life in the cool waters of temperate zones. They are pelagic during all stages of their life, and they are extremely fecund, releasing millions of eggs each time a female bluefin spawns. However, "only a fraction of the eggs spawned and fertilized survive to become adults..."[4] Notwithstanding the low survival rate of juvenile bluefin tuna, commercial demand for the bluefin has been steadily increasing since the 1960s. Consequently, the population of Atlantic bluefin tuna has declined nearly 90 percent since 1970.[5] Furthermore, other species are confronted with a similar crisis. The haddock population has fallen

---

[4] Atlantic Bluefin Tuna Status Review Team, *Status Review Report of Atlantic Bluefin Tuna* (*Thunnus thynnus*), May 20, 2011. http://www.nero.noaa.gov/nero/regs/frdoc/11/11ABTESANoticeSR.pdf.

[5] Jon Van Steenis, *Pirates as Poachers: International Fisheries Law and the Bluefin Tuna*, 29 CAP. U. L. REV. 661 (2001–2002). Another research shows that "compared to its abundance before longlines were introduced (i.e., 1960), the population is now just 3% of its former level—a 97% decline. And, ominously, it is still slowly declining toward extinction." *See* Atlantic Bluefin Tuna, Severity of Decline and its Causes, *available at* http://www.bigmarinefish.com/bluefin.html.

94 percent since 1960, Atlantic swordfish by over 50 percent, and Pacific red snapper by over 90 percent.[6]

One of the serious consequences of overfishing has been the collapse of the biosphere. Food chains, for example, have become worn down one predator species at a time, leaving the ecosystem with "junk" species and a drop in biodiversity and bio-integrity. Biodiversity relates to the number of different species within an area. Bio-integrity involves the strength of an ecosystem in terms of resisting disease, species extinction, and other ecological infirmities.[7] Therefore, depletion of fish stocks or removal of other food chain components could cause dramatic changes in whole marine ecosystems.[8]

III. Solution: Cooperation as an Obligation

It is not the purpose of this chapter to define the term "global governance" as there are a variety of definitions on this subject. Instead, the author would like to use the concept of cooperation to describe the on-going processes of managing and conserving fishery resources. Such processes include international instruments, international organizations, and the behavior of states.

A. *International Instruments: Legal Obligations*

The 1982 United Nations Convention on the Law of the Sea[9] ("UNCLOS") and the 1995 Agreement for the Implementation of the Provisions of the United Nations Convention on the Law of the Sea of 10 December 1982 Relating to the Conservation and Management of Straddling Fish Stocks and Highly Migratory Fish Stocks[10] ("UNFSA") provide certain provisions on the regulation of cooperation among states in dealing with the issues of high seas fisheries. One of the basic issues to be considered is the nature of the duty to cooperate of which the performance of such duty varies state to state. Such a concept can be traced back to certain documents

---

6 Zachary Tyler, *Saving Fisheries on the High Seas: The Use of Trade Sanctions to Force Compliance with Multilateral Fisheries Agreements*, 20 Tul. Envtl. L.J. 47–48 (2006–2007).

7 Peter Jacques and Zachary A. Smith, Ocean Politics and Policy: A Reference Handbook 26 (Oxford: ABC-CLIO, 2003).

8 James M. Broadus & Raphael V. Vartanov, The Oceans and Environmental Security: Shared US and Russian Perspectives 58 (1994).

9 UNCLOS entered into force on Nov. 16, 1994 and there are 160 states that have ratified this Convention. *See* Status of the United Nations Convention on the Law of the Sea of the Agreement relating to the implementation of Part XI of the Convention and of the Agreement for the implementation of the provisions of the Convention relating to the conservation and management of straddling fish stocks and highly migratory fish stocks, *available at* http://www.un.org/Depts/los/reference_files/status2010.pdf.

10 The UNFAS entered into force on Dec. 11, 2001 and there are 67 states that have ratified this Agreement. *Id.*

made more than three decades ago such as in a United Nations General Assembly declaration in 1970[11] that provided "States have the duty to co-operate with one another, irrespective of the differences in their political, economic and social systems, in the various spheres of international relations..."

This duty can be characterized into one of two forms: a duty to enter into negotiations; and a duty to negotiate and to reach an agreement. Obviously, both duties of cooperation will require negotiations entered into good faith. Moreover, the parties concerned shall be obliged to work together in a good faith effort to reach an agreement and to carry that agreement through to a successful conclusion.[12] Under such considerations, certain provisions in UNCLOS and UNFSA embrace the spirit of cooperation.

According to Article 118 of UNCLOS, countries that fish in the same living marine resources area or in the same area of the high seas shall cooperate in the conservation of these resources. With respect to straddling fish stocks and highly migratory species in the high seas, such an obligation is supplemented with the special obligations of the relevant coastal states and states fishing for these stocks in adjacent areas of the high seas to cooperate for the conservation of these stocks.[13] Taking into consideration of the practices in recent years from states and international organizations, these obligations have become a part of customary international law.[14]

Part 3 of UNFSA includes several provisions for mechanisms for cooperation in the conservation of straddling fish stocks and highly migratory species. Although the introductory paragraph of Article 8 seems to leave states a choice as to whether to cooperate directly or through regional or sub-regional fisheries management organizations or arrangements, the ensuing paragraphs place radical limits on this freedom. Where there exists a fisheries management organization or an arrangement competent to regulate the fishery for a specific straddling fish stock or highly migratory fish stocks, those states fishing for these stocks on the high seas and the relevant coastal states shall become members of the organization or participants of that arrangement.[15]

---

11 1970 Declaration on Principles of International Law concerning Friendly Relations and Cooperation among States in accordance with the Charter of the United Nations. GA Res. 2625(XXV), U.N. Doc. A/8082 (Oct. 24, 1970).

12 L. Guruswamy, *The Promise of the United Nations Convention on the Law of the Sea: Justice and Environmental Disputes*, 25 Ecology L.Q. 189 (1998) (quoting from Stuart M. Kaye, *International Fisheries Management*, The Hague: Kluwer L. Int'l 111 (2001)).

13 United Nations Convention on the Law of the Sea, arts. 63(2)–64(1), Dec. 10, 1982, U.N. Doc. A/CONF. 62/122, 21 I.L.M. 1245 (1982).

14 *See also* Tore Henriksen, Geir Honneland & Are Sydnes, Law and Politics in Ocean Governance: The UN Fish Stocks Agreement and Regional Fisheries Management Regimes 15 (2006).

15 Agreement for the Implementation of the Provisions of the United Nations Convention on the Law of the Sea of Dec. 10, 1982 relating to the Conservation and Management

States fishing for these stocks on the high seas may choose not to join or participate but are then obligated to apply the management measures adopted by the organization or arrangement in order to be entitled to fish on these stock.[16] If the straddling fish stocks or highly migratory fish stocks are not subjected to the regulatory competence of any organization or arrangement, the states that fish for these stocks on the high seas and the relevant coastal states are obligated to establish either an organization or other appropriate arrangements.[17]

B. *International Organizations: Regional Fisheries Management Organizations*

In the absence of an effective centralized authority in dealing with fishing matters, a regional fisheries organization is an alternative to secure sustainable conservation and management of transboundary marine resources. Such regional fisheries cooperation involves efforts by states to overcome collective action problems related to the use of shared and common fisheries. This cooperation arises when two or more states concerned identify a shared problem or goal which requires a common and cooperative solution. Such cooperation is often formalized through bilateral or multilateral agreements establishing principles, rules, procedures, and institutional organizations for the implementation of cooperation between the parties. In many cases these agreements are institutionalized by the formation of Regional Fishery Management Organizations (RFMOs).[18]

Most of the RFMOs operative in developing regions during the period of the 1950s and 1960s were established at the initiative of the Food and Agriculture Organization of the United Nations (FAO). They were initiated with broad mandates to promote research, development and management, but were without regulatory powers. Moreover, these organizations were established as development mechanisms; their operations dependent on funding from FAO and other donors. Thus, for their functions to be fulfilled, they relied heavily on the political will of members of the RFMOs to enforce regulations.[19]

---

of Straddling Fish Stocks and Highly Migratory Fish Stocks, U.N. Doc. A/CONF.164/37 (Sept. 8, 1995); United Nations Conference on Straddling Fish Stocks and Highly Migratory Fish Stocks, art. 8(3), 6th Sess., N.Y. (July 24–Aug. 4, 1995), *available at* http://daccess-dds-ny.un.org/doc/UNDOC/GEN/N95/274/67/PDF/N9527467.pdf?OpenElement.

16 United Nations Conference on Straddling Fish Stocks and Highly Migratory Fish Stocks, *supra* note 15, art. 8(4).

17 *Id.* at art. 8(5).

18 Are K. Sydnes, *Regional Fishery Organizations: How and Why Organizational Diversity Matters*, 32 Ocean Dev't and Int'l L. 350–51 (2001). *See also* Are K. Sydnes, *Regional Fisheries Organizations and International Fisheries Governance, in* A Sea Change: The Exclusive Economic Zone and Governance Institutions for Living Marine Resources 117–33 (Syma Ebbin, Alf Hoel & Are K. Sydnes eds., 2005).

19 Are K. Sydnes, *Regional Fishery Organizaitons in Developing Regions: Adapting to Changes in International Fisheries Law*, 26 Marine Policy 374 (2002).

Table 1. List of selected RFMOs.

APFIC	Asia-Pacific Fisheries Commission
ATLAFCO	African Atlantic Fisheries Conference
CCAMLR	Commission for the Conservation of Antarctic Marine Living Resources
CCSBT	Commission for the Conservation of Southern Bluefin Tuna
CECAF	Committee for the Eastern Central Atlantic Fisheries
COREP	Regional Fisheries Committee for the Gulf of Guinea
CPPS	Permanent Commission for the South Pacific
CRFM	Caribbean Regional Fisheries Mechanism
FFA	South Pacific Forum Fisheries Agency
GFCM	General Fisheries Commission for the Mediterranean
IATTC	Inter-American Tropical Tuna Commission
IBSFC	International Baltic Sea Fishery Commission
ICCAT	International Commission for the Conservation of Atlantic Tunas
IOTC	Indian Ocean Tuna Commission
IPHC	International Pacific Halibut Commission
NAFO	Northwest Atlantic Fisheries Organization
NASCO	North Atlantic Salmon Conservation Organization
NEAFC	North East Atlantic Fisheries Commission
NPAFC	North Pacific Anadromous Fish Commission
PSC	Pacific Salmon Commission
RECOFI	Regional Commission for Fisheries
SEAFO	South East Atlantic Fisheries Organization
SRCF	Sub-Regional Commission on Fisheries
SWIOFC	South West Indian Ocean Fisheries Commission
WCPFC	Western and Central Pacific Fisheries Commission
WECAFC	Western Central Atlantic Fisheries Commission
WIOTO	Western Indian Ocean Tuna Organization

Source: Organized by the author. Further detailed information can be obtained from Directorate-General for Maritime Affairs and Fisheries, European Commission, *see* http://ec.europa.eu/fisheries/cfp/international/rfmo/index_en.htm.

Scholars have pointed out that the cooperative governance problem in marine resources management is to provide the adequate means for achieving three major tasks: (1) generation of adequate and reasonably consensual scientific knowledge to permit informed judgments about whether and how exploitation of resources shall be conducted; (2) adoption of legitimate and appropriate regulatory measures to govern economic activities while taking heed of existing knowledge; and (3) a system to promote compliance with such measures among those engaged in resource use in the area.[20] Therefore, the latter two goals, i.e., regulatory measures and compliance of the members, rely heavily upon the members' positive practices.

[20] Olav Schram Stokke, *Governance of High Seas Fisheries: The Role of Regime Linkages*, *in* ORDER FOR THE OCEANS AT THE TURN OF THE CENTURY 159, 162–70 (Davor Vidas & Willy Ostreng, eds., 1999).

Even so, some of the RFMOs have taken steps to improve their performance in managing and conserving marine living resources. For example, the Inter-American Tropical Tuna Commission (IATTC) has demonstrated these efforts. IATTC was established in 1950 in accordance with the entry into force of the 1949 Convention for the Establishment of an Inter-American Tropical Tuna Commission.[21] After almost fifty years of operation, it was decided that the IATTC (Commission) and the 1949 IATTC (Convention) should be strengthened and modernized to take into account recently adopted international instruments such as the 1982 UNCLOS, the 1992 Agenda 21 and Rio Declaration, the 1993 FAO Agreement to Promote Compliance with International Conservation and Management Measures by Fishing Vessels on the High Seas, the 1995 FAO Code of Conduct for Responsible Fisheries, and the 1995 UNFSA.[22] An ad hoc Working Group was formed to review the 1949 Convention.[23]

The revising work was done in June 2003 with the adoption of an amended convention.[24] According to Article 10 of the Antigua Convention, a Committee for the Review of Implementation of Measures Adopted by the Commission was established to: (a) review and monitor compliance with conservation and management measures adopted by the Commission, as well as other cooperative measures; (b) analyze information and any other information necessary to carry out its functions; (c) provide the Commission with information, technical advice and recommendations relating to the implementation of, and compliance with, conservation and management measures; (d) recommend to the Commission means of promoting compatibility; (e) recommend to the Commission the means to promote the effective implementation of the Antigua Convention; (f) in consultation with the Scientific Advisory Committee, recommend to the Commission the priorities and objectives of the program for data collection and monitoring of this Convention and assess and evaluate the results of that program; and (g) perform other functions.[25]

---

21 For 1949 Convention, *see* http://www.iattc.org/PDFFiles/IATTC_convention_1949.pdf.

22 Resolution on the Establishment of a Working Group to Review the IATTC Convention, Inter-American Tropical Tuna Commission (IATTC) (June 1998), *available at* http://www.iattc.org/PDFFiles/C-98-02%20Convention%20WG%20resolution%20Jun%2098.pdf.

23 *Id.*

24 Convention for the Strengthening of the Inter-American Tropical Tuna Commission Established by the 1949 Convention between the United States of America and the Republic of Costa Rica (also known as "Antigua Convention"). For the full text, *see* http://www.iattc.org/PDFFiles2/Antigua_Convention_Jun_2003.pdf.

25 Committee for the Review of Implementation of Measures Adopted by the Commission, Antigua Convention, Annex 3, *available at* http://www.iattc.org/pdffiles2/antigua_convention_jun_2003.pdf.

Furthermore, Article 18 provides that the parties shall take measures necessary to ensure the implementation of and compliance with the Antigua Convention and any conservation and management measures adopted pursuant thereto, including the adoption of necessary laws and regulations. Also, the parties shall provide to the Commission all the information that may be required for the fulfillment of the objectives of the Antigua Convention, including statistical and biological information and information concerning its fishing activities in the Convention Area, and shall provide to the Commission information regarding actions taken to implement the measures adopted in accordance with the Antigua Convention. Except for the actions made by the IATTC, other RFMOs take similar actions either by adopting resolutions or taking related measures so that the conservation and management measures can be achieved.[26]

From the aforementioned discussion, it is safe to conclude that RFMOs and arrangements are given exclusive competence to regulate the high seas fisheries of straddling and highly migratory fish stocks.[27]

C. *Regional Cooperation in a Semi-Enclosed Sea: Case of the South China Sea*[28]

In terms of geographical features, the South China Sea can be categorized as a "semi-enclosed sea," that is provided for in Article 122 of UNCLOS as an "enclosed or semi-enclosed sea" which is "a gulf, basin, or sea surrounded by two or more States and connected to another sea or the ocean by a narrow outlet or consisting entirely or primarily of the territorial seas and exclusive economic zones of two or more coastal States."

Because the South China Sea is semi-enclosed, any change in its ecosystem will have a significant impact on the whole area. It is generally recognized that the living resources in the South China Sea area migrate from one EEZ to another,

---

26 For example, on Dec. 27, 2000, the International Commission for the Conservation of Atlantic Tunas (ICCAT) adopted a resolution under the title of "Supplemental Resolution by ICCAT to Enhance the Effectiveness of the ICCAT Measures to Eliminate Illegal, Unregulated and Unreported Fishing Activities by Large-Scale Tuna Longline Vessels in the Convention Area and Other Areas." Under this resolution, the ICCAT Commission urged Japan and Taiwan to take the necessary measures to complete the scrapping of IUU vessels built in Japan and Taiwan.

27 Tore Henriksen, Geir Honneland, & Are Sydnes, Law and Politics in Ocean Governance: The UN Fish Stocks Agreement and Regional Fisheries Management Regimes 16 (Martinus Nijhoff Publishers 2006); Robin Churchill & A. V. Lowe, The Law of the Sea 309 (1999); F. O. Vicuna, *The International Law to High Seas Fisheries: From Unrestricted Freedom of Fishing to Sustainable Use*, *in* Governing High Seas Fisheries 40–42 (O. S. Stokke, ed., 2001).

28 Unless specifically mentioned, this sub-section is basically quoted from Kuan-Hsiung Wang, *Bridge over Troubled Waters: Fisheries Cooperation as a Resolution to the South China Sea Conflicts*, 14 The Pac. Rev. 541–43, n. 4 (2001).

particularly highly migratory species such as tuna and other shared stocks. Each country may already have its own assessment of its living resources in its EEZ, assuming that the definition and delineation of each EEZ is clear. The problem is that many of those EEZ boundaries are not well-defined nor mutually agreed upon by the relevant parties. Likewise, there are various conflicting claims to islands that complicate and defer the determination of EEZ boundaries. For this reason, many experts and scholars are convinced of the need to cooperate on the assessment of the living resources in the South China Sea area without regard to jurisdictional boundaries. The basis for this endeavor is Article 123 of UNCLOS regarding enclosed and semi-enclosed seas.[29] UNCLOS has foreseen this problem as Article 123 provides:

> States bordering an enclosed or semi-enclosed sea should co-operate with each other in the exercise of their rights and in the performance of their duties under this Convention. To this end they shall endeavour, directly or through an appropriate regional organisation:
> (a) to co-ordinate the management, conservation, exploration and exploitation of the living resources of the sea;
> (b) to co-ordinate the implementation of their rights and duties with respect to the protection and preservation of the marine environment;
> (c) to co-ordinate their scientific research policies and undertake where appropriate joint programmes of scientific research in the area;
> (d) to invite, as appropriate, other interested states or international organisations to co-operate with them in furtherance of the provisions of this article.

Therefore, all parties concerned should be aware that fish are migratory and that fishery resources are exhaustible such that the rational use of the South China Sea and the preservation of its marine environment are important to all parties. Thus, cooperation among littoral states in the region is essential. In order to avoid overfishing or depletion of resources, conservation and management measures have to be conducted under a collective manner. Such measures are not possible without regional cooperation and require close coordination among the parties concerned, especially in a semi-enclosed sea.

Indeed, a semi-enclosed sea concept could conceivably provide the catalyst to promote cooperation and coordination of the management of resources in the South China Sea.[30] Under such circumstances, for all the littoral states to make the boundary delimitation issue as a first priority seems unwise. Rather, concentrating upon common interests will be an essential element to resolve these conflicts rationally.

---

29 Hasjim Djalal, *Issue Paper for Technical Working Group on the Resources Assessment of the South China Sea Informal Workshop, in* the Second Working Group Meeting on Resources Assessment and Ways of Development in the South China Sea, Jakarta, Indonesia, July 5–6, 1993, at 1–2.

30 Lee G. Cordner, *The Spratly Islands Dispute and the Law of the Sea*, 25 OCEAN DEV'T AND INT'L L. 71 (1994).

Fishery cooperation can be the most feasible course of action for these littoral states because through cooperation, fishery resources can be properly conserved and managed such that economic waste and over-exploitation can be avoided. Cooperation in the utilization of fishery resources is a feasible and practical way to start a regional cooperation regime. It sidesteps the issue of sovereignty and focuses upon a common interest, namely the utilization of living resources. It also defers long-term negotiations with respect to the delimitation of the continental shelf relating to the hydrocarbon resource issue. Thus, as cooperative relationships are forged with regard to fishery resources, mutual confidence can build among the various parties that may eventually contribute to successful cooperation with respect to hydrocarbon resources. Fishery resources management is crucial in preventing over-exploitation and overfishing and may be a touchstone the efforts of littoral states to resolve these important issues.

Without affecting the jurisdictional boundaries as laid down in UNCLOS, it is certainly possible to have regional joint fishery management in the South China Sea as the starting point for further cooperation. If all states in this region treat cooperation as a key step toward achieving mutual benefits, then the future for such a regional cooperation mechanism is assured.

IV. Conclusion

Fishing is a vital element of the world's diet, economy, and biodiversity. However, overwhelming evidence shows that these crucial uses of the marine world are in danger. Under such circumstances, the depletion of fishery resources is not just a crisis for food, but also a crisis for the environment.

The history of high-seas fisheries management over the last 150 years can be classified into three phases. The first phase, up until the early 1970s, saw a rapid increase in both the number of fishing vessels operating in the individual oceans and advances in technology which allowed greater catches. This phase was characterized by generally narrow coastal state maritime zones and large areas identified as high seas. By the mid-1970s, a considerable proportion of fisheries in the high seas fell under the jurisdiction of international or regional fishery commissions. The second phase, the period from the mid-1970s up until the early 1990s, reflected the developments and negotiations of the Third United Nations Conference on the Law of the Sea. Owing to the practices of claiming exclusive economic zone, coastal states extended their jurisdiction out to 200 nautical miles so that many areas (and fisheries) that were previously classified as high seas came under a national jurisdiction. The area defined as high seas was thus considerably reduced, and consequently, so was the area under the jurisdiction of regional and international fisheries commissions. Since the mid-1990s, high seas fisheries management has entered its third phase. This phase reflects the international community's concerns about overfishing in the high seas. Even greater emphasis has been placed on the international duties and responsibilities of all nations in the conservation of ocean resources, as well as the importance of cooperation between states both adjacent to the fisheries and those exploiting them.[31]

For the purpose of conserving and managing marine living resources, traditional concepts of "utilization" should be transformed to "sustainability." In that regard, "sustainable development" is one of the main policy foundations whereby "the needs of the present generation [can be met] without compromising the ability of future generations to meet their own needs."[32] Governments should take this position in making their fishery policies rather than concentrate on increasing fishing capacity or the amount of fishing especially when the FAO has reiterated the serious situation in its 1999 International Plan of Action for the Management of Fishing Capacity.[33]

Following the concept of the sustainable development of fisheries, another consideration that should be taken when making policy regarding fisheries is the "precautionary approach." This approach was developed since the mid-1980s when regional legal instruments called for the protection of the terrestrial, and subsequently, marine environment, and was finally enshrined in Principle 15 of the 1992 Rio Declaration.[34] It provides that:

> In order to protect the environment, the precautionary approach shall be widely applied by States according to their capabilities. Where there are threats of serious or irreversible damage, lack of full scientific certainty shall not be used as a reason for postponing cost-effective measures to prevent environmental degradation.

Based on the precautionary approach, UNFSA not only includes this approach as a type of duty to cooperate,[35] but also demands the application of the precautionary approach. This can be seen from Article 6 of UNFSA that provides:

> 1. States shall apply the precautionary approach widely to conservation, management and exploitation of straddling fish stocks and highly migratory fish stocks in order to protect the living marine resources and preserve the marine environment.
> 2. States shall be more cautious when information is uncertain, unreliable or inadequate. The absence of adequate scientific information shall not be used as a reason for postponing or failing to take conservation and management measures.
> 3. In implementing the precautionary approach, States shall:

---

31 Sevaly Sen, *The Evolution of High-Seas Fisheries Management in the North-East Atlantic*, 35 Ocean & Coastal Mgmt. 85–86, n. 2–3 (1997).

32 World Commission on Environment and Development, Our Common Future 43 (1987).

33 Rosemary Rayfuse, The Challenge of Sustainable High Seas Fisheries, in International Law and Sustainable Development: Principles and Practice 469–77 (Nico Schrijver & Friedl Weiss, eds., 2004).

34 United Nations Conference on Environment and Development, Rio de Janeiro, June 3–14, 1992, U.N. Doc. A/CONF.151/26, Vol. I (Aug. 12, 1996), *available at* http://www.un.org/documents/ga/confl51/aconf15126-1.

35 United Nations Conference on Straddling Fish Stocks and Highly Migratory Fish Stocks, *supra* note 14, art. 5(c).

(a) improve decision-making for fishery resource conservation and management by obtaining and sharing the best scientific information available and implementing improved techniques for dealing with risk and uncertainty;...

Such a consideration even has to be taken when a natural occurrence has a significant adverse impact on the status of straddling fishing stocks or highly migratory fish stocks. In such a case, states shall adopt conservation and management measures on an emergency basis to ensure that their fishing activity does not exacerbate such adverse impacts. States shall also adopt such measures on an emergency basis where fishing activity presents a serious threat to the sustainability of such stocks.[36]

Policy assessment is one of the most important elements in policy-making. During the period of focusing on economic development and trade, exploring marine living resources and increasing its production might be the right choice. However, in a globalized world, as it is difficult to distinguish between the complicated web of influences between trade and the environment; so it is with fisheries. Nonetheless, since the phase of conserving and managing fishery resources is at hand, and international instruments and RFMOs have already embedded the concepts of sustainability and precaution into fishing, it appears to be the right time and prudent course to adjust fishing policies in line with environmental deliberations. Moreover, states that border semi-enclosed seas should give priority to regional cooperation in its national ocean policies.

[36] *Id.* art. 6(7).

CHAPTER SIX

THE ISSUE OF *NON LIQUET* IN RECENT ADVISORY PROCEEDINGS OF THE ICJ

Bing Bing Jia*

I. Introduction

The presumption of a legal system as a complete body of rules may be tested in the face of the reality where the law of the system has no answer to issues that demand one. It is suitable that such a test has just taken place before the International Court of Justice (ICJ or the Court) with regard to an issue fundamental to the system of contemporary international law. The issue has had to do with the unilateral declaration of independence by the Provisional Institutions of Self-Government in Kosovo in early 2008. It became subject to a United Nations General Assembly (UNGA) resolution in late 2008 requesting the ICJ to provide an advisory opinion on the conformity or otherwise of this declaration.[1] Over 30 states provided written and oral comments on the issue in the course of the advisory proceedings, including China and Japan.[2] The Court delivered its opinion in July 22, 2010.[3]

The case provides a fascinating account of many aspects of the creation of a state in international law. But the conclusion of the Court may just raise again the issue of *non liquet* that occasionally piques international lawyers. The interest in the issue lies on two sides of a well-known debate, that international law, despite its many shortcomings, is a legal system nevertheless, admitting of no gaps that

* Professor of International Law, Tsinghua University Law School.

[1] Request for an advisory opinion of the International Court of Justice on whether the unilateral declaration of independence of Kosovo is in accordance with international law, G.A. Res.10764, 63d Sess. plen. mtg. at 71, U.N. Doc. A/63/PV.22 (Oct. 8, 2008).

[2] The written pleadings and oral Statements made in this case are published by the I.C.J. website, http//www.icj-cij/.

[3] Accordance with International Law of the Unilateral Declaration for Independence in Respect of Kosovo, Advisory Opinion, 2010 I.C.J. 403 (July 22).

may exist where they are least desired, and that the system is not complete as the domestic model, with the result that the gaps in it are duly representative of the system's odd parings with morality and the alike. It is felt that this body of rules is better cast somewhere in between those two descriptions, but probably closer to the second position, except that the nature of the system is totally one of law, rather than ethics or morality. Gaps become revealed only when a legal solution is called for but there is none derivable from existing sources of law. This is a feature of all legal systems in their growth towards ascending levels of maturity. The system of international law is no exception. But is this the case?

That is the basic question to be explored briefly in this chapter. It is in this context that China's and Japan's response in the Kosovo advisory proceedings will be compared. It seems that at least in some cases, a *non liquet* might have to do with the way parties to a case formulate their submissions. In a way, the responses from the two countries in East Asia, both with residual territorial disputes with other countries, can support or disprove the existence of a *non liquet* in this case. What can be surmised at the beginning is that China's response is one way to avoid a finding of *non liquet.* But the more interesting feature of the advisory opinion is that the Court did not avoid a definitive answer to the question posed by the UNGA after finding a *non liquet.* It may therefore be suggested that the lack of law or the existence of gaps in law do not necessarily impact on the resolution of a case. If so, there seems to be a practical innocuousness to the doctrine, in the sense that its role is much more limited than the interesting debate over it has suggested.

However, it may be useful first to consider whether a case of *non liquet* is something that must be avoided at all costs by a legal system like the one of international law. In addition, it may also be interesting to look at a precedent to the 2010 advisory opinion: the advisory opinion given by the ICJ in 1996 on the legality of threat or use of nuclear weapons. This earlier case is to be mentioned as a clear instance of *non liquet,* somewhat bucking the trend of past jurisprudence shown in a consistent silence towards this doctrine by international tribunals and the ICJ.

II. Completeness of a Legal System

The question is whether any legal system must be an all-embracing one that admits of no gap in its reach, in order to maintain that status as a system. It is proposed first to examine the understanding of the notion of *non liquet* as generally accepted in practice and literature. Then the question of the completeness of a legal system will be reflected upon.

A. *The Notion of* Non Liquet

The notion, according to *Black's Law Dictionary,* signifies that the law is not clear, with "the law" understood to include not only international law but domestic law.[4] In both Lauterpacht's and Stone's view, it signifies the lack of suitable rules in respect of a certain case pending before a judicial body.[5] What has become the dispute in this regard is not so much with this notion's content as with its consequences. For Lauterpacht, the notion persists in practice to form the root of the doctrine, recognised by both writers and practitioners, that seeks to limit the judicial function of international tribunals through the treatment of the issue as to the justiciability of disputes.[6] For Stone, while the notion has enjoyed "much distinguished juristic interest," the actuality of state practice has not attached similar attention to it. Indeed, he sees the debate over the notion as proceeding at the level of *de lege ferenda*, i.e. on the issue as to whether a *non liquet* "should" be admissible.[7]

It seems that the two writers differ immediately after they are agreed on the content of the notion and the fact that there have never been cases in which international tribunals actually pronounced a *non liquet*. The difference may lie in part in the differing views of the function and nature of international law as a system. In Stone's view, it is a debate bordering on the meta-legal.[8] In Lauterpacht's view, three approaches may exist with the positivist, the naturalist, and the adherent to the PCIJ/ICJ Statute.[9] The positivist will consider nothing to be binding except a positive rule, and where there is no such a rule, the judicial way to resolve a dispute is precluded. The naturalist prepares to rely on "the law of nature and the principle of natural justice,"[10] which may well put in question what is allowed to states pursuant to existing international law.[11] The Statutes for both Courts envisage a role for general principles of law, beside the sources of treaty and custom. While the helpfulness of the general principles is readily conceded, it is not certain that gaps in current law will never appear, as when a matter, unregulated by any rule of law, requires a Court seized of it to take the lead in developing the law through its decision.[12] He then proclaimed that his view was based on a study of positive international law, especially judicial decisions of international tribunals.

---

4 BLACK'S LAW DICTIONARY (7th ed. 1999).

5 HERSCH LAUTERPACHT, THE FUNCTION OF LAW IN THE INTERNATIONAL COMMUNITY 51–52 (1933); JULIUS STONE, LEGAL CONTROLS OF INTERNATIONAL CONFLICT: A TREATISE ON THE DYNAMICS OF DISPUTES AND WAR-LAW 153 (1954).

6 *See* LAUTERPACHT, *supra* note 5, at 54.

7 *See* STONE, *supra* note 5, at 154.

8 *Id.* at 153.

9 *See* LAUTERPACHT, *supra* note 5, at 57.

10 *Id.*

11 LUCIEN SIORAT, LE PROBLÈM DES LACUNES DANS LE DROIT INTERNATIONAL 241 (1958) (citing Julius Stone, *Non Liquet and the Function of Law in the International Community*, 35 BRIT. Y. INT'L L. 124, 126–27, n. 1 (1960)).

12 Bing Bing Jia, *The Doctrine of Command Responsibility Revisited*, 3 CHINESE J. INT'L. L. 1, 7–12 (2004).

It is felt that the notion, as presented here, is sometimes entangled with the question of how the notion manifests itself in reality. It is logical that the appearance of the notion can be varying from one situation to another, and that it may be true that the factual existence of cases of *non liquet* is not equivalent to their admissibility in judicial proceedings. As will be shown below, the forms of appearance of the notion in reality are many.

B. *The Manifestations of* Non Liquet

The traditional form in which the notion appears is where the judicial body finds a gap in the law with regard to a dispute before it. In *Haya de la Torre,* the ICJ found a gap in the 1928 Havana Convention as to the manner in which asylum should be terminated.[13] The gap would cover "cases in which the asylum has not been regularly granted or maintained," in respect of which no provision was made in the Havana Convention as to the method of termination; nor was "any provision made in this matter in cases where the territorial state has not requested the departure of the refugee."[14] The Court inferred from the silence of the convention in this regard the intention of the signatory states to leave the consequences of those cases to decisions inspired by "considerations of convenience or of simply political expediency."[15] The Court then refrained from filling the gap.[16] The final result was deemed to be a *non liquet,* and the view has been expressed that the Court could of course display a preference when faced with conflicting legal rights.[17] It may be wondered whether this conclusion could be seen as evidence that the Court, even in a case where the applicable law is not available to the issue falling for decision, would give an answer within its judicial powers. The refrainer itself, therefore, constituted the answer demanded by law in that case. Otherwise, the Court could have faced the difficulty that it moved into a non-legal province where it was simply not authorised by law to operate. In this light, the Court did not rely on a *non liquet,* even in the sense of the term as upheld by Lauterpacht.[18]

---

[13] Haya de la Torre Case (Colombia v. Peru), 1951 I.C.J. 71, at 83 (June 13).

[14] *Id.* at 80.

[15] *Id.* at 81.

[16] *Id.* at 83 where the Court felt unable to provide "any practical advice" in the context of the case, without running the risk of going beyond its judicial function.

[17] HERSCH LAUTERPACHT, THE DEVELOPMENT OF INTERNATIONAL LAW BY THE INTERNATIONAL COURT 145–46 (1958).

[18] He considered that the term *non liquet* reveals itself in a refusal by a court to "give a decision," which seems to suggest that, as long as the court gives a decision, even if it is in the form of an indecision of the issue before it, there is no question of *non liquet.* Hersch Lauterpacht, *Some Observations on the Prohibition of Non Liquet and the Completeness of International Law,* SYMBOLAE VERZIJL 196, 198–99 (1958).

The notion may, alternatively, take the form that the judicial body finds itself in lack of jurisdiction or the case in point is inadmissible.[19] This instance of *non liquet* often results from the defective formulation of the dispute by the parties submitting it for judicial settlement.[20] It could also result from a defective expression of the will of the parties.[21] Where there is an improper or insufficient formulation of a dispute or question for judicial advice, due to errors on the part of the proponents, it is doubtful whether that constitutes a case of *non liquet*. For in that scenario, the law is not found to contain a gap. Instead, it is the parties' own fault not to follow proper procedural requirements, by formulating a question that reaches beyond existing law, that renders the judicial body incapable of proceeding with the case on its merits. It should be borne in mind that, where the wording of the question contained in a request for judicial decision appears to be vague or less accurately stated, the ICJ can broaden, interpret, and even reformulate the question put.[22] It is a question that falls for the Court to decide how to deal with such a situation: to decide that the dispute so formulated to be inadmissible, or after reaching a satisfactory understanding of the dispute so formulated by the Court's own interpretation, to proceed to deal with it in its newly conferred meaning.

Yet another possible form of expression of the notion may exist where the issue in contention is deemed non-justiciable by the protagonist concerned with the issue. Reference is made to a well-known instance in which international law was not deemed suitable to interfere in the event that involved the threat or use of force by a sovereign state. A deep impression has been formed of Mr. Acheson's remarks during the Cuban missile crisis, that the establishment of the quarantine in the circumstances in which "the power, position and prestige of the United States has been challenged by another state" was not a legal issue, and that "the survival of states is not a matter of law."[23] The influence of international law in that episode was seen as being procedural, and in the view of the speaker, "the law through its long history has been respectful of power."[24] That instance was not, of course, submitted for judicial determination. Where a dispute is not thus submitted, it is plainly non-justiciable. It is recognised, however, that this instance of non-justiciability is not equivalent to a *non liquet*. Without a

---

[19] Judgements of the Administrative Tribunal of the ILO upon Complaints Made against UNESCO, Advisory Opinion, 1956 I.C.J. 77, 98 (Oct. 23).

[20] Shabtai Rosenne, The International Court of Justice: An Essay in Political and Legal Theory 65 (1957).

[21] *Id.*

[22] Certain Expenses of the United Nations, art. 17, para. 2, of the Charter, Advisory Opinion, 1962 I.C.J. 157–62 (July 20).

[23] Louis Henkin, *Force, Intervention, and Neutrality in Contemporary International Law*, 57 Am. Soc'y Int'l L. Proc. 147 (1963).

[24] *Id.*

judicial treatment, as it is the case here, it is not possible to know if the question is not amenable to a legal finding at all. A consideration of the *non liquet* issue in the context of the present chapter therefore requires that it is confined to those cases which are submitted by the parties thereto to a judicial organ for determination, when the organ finds the need to pass on the cases in terms of lack of law. This it can do by implication, without ever expressing in terms of *non liquet*. The attitude of the parties in those cases assumes prominence in deciding whether the judicial organ will be faced by a necessary pronouncement of *non liquet*.[25]

In a general sense, if judicial solution depends on prior consent of the parties to a situation, as is the case with the current international system, *non liquet* may well be what the parties want, in order to preserve their freedom of action. Judicial intervention does not happen at all when that will of the parties is expressed. Whether force should be used in such a situation is, from the protagonist's point of view, a matter within its sole power, a political matter. However, where use of force may affect the national interests of other states implicated by that situation, it is difficult to maintain that the matter, looked at from a systemic angle, can remain as isolated as the protagonist wishes. Law may not be called for to provide an answer, but it certainly remains a solution that is relevant to the situation.

It may be noted that, when the issue of *non liquet* arises, it seems certain to be entangled with the issue of the extent of the judicial function of international tribunals.[26] That in turn gives rise to the question as to whether the existence of gaps in a legal order contradicts the doctrine of the completeness of the order.

C. *The Extent of the Completeness of Legal Systems*

The completeness of legal systems may be understood in the following sense: in a community of states subject to the rule of law, the judicial organ of the community is not permitted not to resolve a dispute submitted to it on the pretext that the law of the community does not provide it with a ready rule.[27] The prerequisite for all that, namely the rule of law in the community, is not doubted any more, even though the state in which the ideal of the rule of law finds itself is not entirely satisfactory for the purpose of identifying the community as one enjoying the full protection of law.[28] It has been reasoned that the completeness of the rule of law within a given society is an *a priori* assumption of the corresponding

---

25 *Cf.* James Brierly, The Law of Nations 367–68 (Sir Humphrey Waldock ed., 6th rev. ed. 1963).

26 *See* Lauterpacht, *supra* note 17, at 146.

27 It is cautioned that completeness is not the only description of a legal system, as scholars of jurisprudence focus on such features as the efficacy of the rules contained in the system, in order to show the existence of a legal system. Josef Raz, The Concept of a Legal System 94, 212 (2d rev. ed. 2003).

28 The Secretary-General, *Report of the Secretary-General on the Rule of Law and Transitional Justice in Conflict and Post-conflict Societies*, at 3, 6, U.N. Doc. S/2004/616 (Aug. 23, 2004);

legal system.[29] However, it is not certain that the normative completeness cannot entertain gaps in substantive law. Even when a judge in this system is under a legal duty always to decide a dispute brought before him, it is not possible to do so if the same system also qualifies the duty by reference to, primarily, positive law. This is a fact that is inherent in the international legal system based on a consensual mode of law-making, in spite of its recognition that the ICJ, for one, may resort to general principles of law in adjudication.

It may be promptly added that there is no objection to judicial law-making in international law; on the contrary, it is suggested that such action does exist in this field, despite the terms of the ICJ Statute and the alike.[30] No attempt is to be made to discredit that creative force in the development of international law.[31] But that stand does not necessarily negate the view that international law contains gaps that can force the judge to pronounce a *non liquet*.

Having dealt with that particular criticism of *non liquet* in international law, it may be noted that the completeness of this legal system has been described in terms of a "perfect" legal system in a formal sense.[32] The label is not understood to carry a different meaning from the completeness as has been construed by Lauterpacht.

It is recalled that Lauterpacht once observed of Article 38(1)(c) of the PCIJ Statute as something that "has definitely removed the last vestige of the possibility of gaps conceived as a deadlock in the way of the settlement of a dispute."[33] He regarded the terms of that provision to be broad enough to cover "every dispute,"[34] thus helping to complete the international legal system. This approach explains the inadmissibility of *non liquet* in terms of the sources of international law.[35] Where the sources are readily identifiable, the international judge cannot avoid making a decision by ignoring them. However, it may be one thing to say that the completeness of the international legal system, if any, has been facilitated by the provision of Article 38(1)(c) of the ICJ Statute, but quite another to say that there will be, from now on, no gaps in the system, the potential for which is thus stunted.

In addition to the support drawn from a study of the sources of international law, the doctrine of the completeness of the international legal system may be

---

The Secretary-General, *Report of the Secretary-General on Strengthening and Coordinating United Nations rule of law activities*, at 3, U.N. Doc. A/63/226 (Aug. 6, 2008).

29 *See* Lauterpacht, *supra* note 5, at 64.

30 *See* Jia, *supra* note 12.

31 *See* Lauterpacht, *supra* note 5, at 68.

32 *See* Brierly, *supra* note 25, at 68.

33 *See* Lauterpacht, *supra* note 5, at 67.

34 *Id.*

35 Bin Cheng, General Principles of Law as Applied by International Courts and Tribunals 18 (1987).

partly supported by the fact that this system often takes on a life of its own, sustaining ineffective political entities that may appear plainly unable to pull themselves up by imaginary bootstraps. The entity of this type exists by law (and probably dies by it too). Even a semblance of governance by this entity seems to be sufficient to persuade a supervisory body to trust in its viability and effectiveness, as the Committee Against Torture, established under the Convention against Torture 1984, so believed in its consideration of a complaint from a Somali asylum seeker, which was raised on the ground that the return of the person to Somalia would lead to his torture.[36]

Given that the law extends the life of an entity, formerly recognised as a state, which, however, can no longer maintain effective governance over its territory or relations with other states, the gaps in this instance are factual. But the doctrine of the completeness of the law is slow to take that into account. This may well signify the negative effect of the completeness doctrine.

On a more general level, there is no inherent logical dilemma for a legal system to contain gaps; on the contrary, it is only normal to have them, whether it is viewed as *de lege ferenda* or *lex lata*. In the former sense, there seems to be an agreement between the two sides of the debate over the issue of *non liquet*. Lauterpacht saw such gaps as to exist in law in general only in terms of the existing law being unsatisfactory in deciding a particular case, which would give rise to a search for a different (but legal) solution.[37] This search would be for something not necessarily recognized by existing law, thus including the possibility for a new rule to be created. Stone also considered that the main issue with this topic "is thus remitted to the level of the desired future law."[38] This is to say that gaps in law may arise in the future. The mission of a standing legislature is just that: to fill the gaps in the light of ever evolving circumstances of daily life. The completeness of a legal system, if ever a viable topic of discourse, must allow for the view that the system is evolving constantly, with today's gaps filled by tomorrow's legislative actions. The system is, as such, dynamic and self-improving. The legislative function known to international lawyers is by no means confined to diplomatic conferences called to adopt treaties, or consistently growing state practice pointing to a certain pattern of behaviour. As Brierly once observed acutely, "a power to decide *ex aequo et bono* is a power to abrogate or modify existing legal rights,

---

36 Andrea Gattini, *Somalia: Purposes and Limits of State Fiction in International Law*, *in* 150 Krisenherde im Fokus des Völkerrechts-Trouble Spots in the Focus of International Law 160–61, n. 20 (Thomas Giegerich & Alexander Proelss eds., 2010). The author cited Y.H.A. v. Australia (Communication No. 162/2000), Convention against Torture and Other Cruel, Inhuman or Degrading Treatment or Punishment, *Report of the Committee Against Torture*, 27th & 28th Sess., ¶ 7.4, U.N. GAOR, 57th Sess., Suppl. No. 44, at 137, U.N. Doc. CAT/C.27/D/162/2000 (Nov. 23, 2001).

37 *See* Lauterpacht, *supra* note 5, at 68.

38 *See* Stone, *supra* note 5, at 163.

and essentially that is a power to *legislate*."[39] That power, it may be remembered, accrues to, among others, the ICJ by virtue of Article 38(2) of its Statute. The topic of *non liquet* is fundamentally related to the power of international tribunals to create and adapt existing law in view of new instances of disputes.[40] Furthermore, is it not open to the lawyer to argue that a future gap may exist regardless of the way in which Article 38 of the ICJ Statute is interpreted? Even assuming that international judges may be allowed to create law, which is very controversial a topic in itself, is it not possible that they find themselves in a situation in which there are no treaties, custom, general principles, or judicial precedent, and they are not permitted to proceed *ex aequo et bono*? To look prospectively at the topic of *non liquet* is faced by the pitfall that future events cannot be known until they occur, and that they may or may not support the solution envisaged now. The chances of *non liquet* must therefore be 50/50. Neither possibility can be satisfactorily answered by appealing to the completeness of a legal system, as a matter of precept. Law is defined and confined by fact.

However, the difference of opinion between the two eminent writers over the topic of *non liquet* remains in cases involving the application of existing law. It is felt that Stone's view, that the absence of any international case theretofore could not lead to the conclusion that a judicial pronouncement of *non liquet* is "as a matter of law" forbidden,[41] is supported by two cases of the ICJ in recent years, dealt with below in chronological order. The first shows a paradigm case of *non liquet* from the Court's point of view. The second shows divided state practice that may result in a *non liquet* in one perspective, but not in the other.

III. Two Cases of *Non Liquet* before the ICJ

A. *Self-Defence by Way of Nuclear Weapon in a Situation of National Survival*

In the advisory opinion of the ICJ in *Legality of the Use or Threat of Nuclear Weapons*,[42] the Court, in answer to a specific question raised by the UN General Assembly (UNGA), stated, by a vote of seven to seven, with the President's casting vote, that

> in view of the current state of international law, and of the elements of fact at its disposal, the Court cannot conclude definitively whether the threat or use of nuclear weapons would be lawful or unlawful in an extreme circumstance of self-defence, in which the very survival of a State would be at stake;. . . .[43]

---

39 *See* Brierly, *supra* note 25, at 372–73.

40 *See* Stone, *supra* note 11, 125.

41 *Id.* at 125. *See also* Stone, *supra* note 5, at 162–63.

42 Legality of the Threat or Use of Nuclear Weapons, Advisory Opinion, 1996 I.C.J. 226 (July 8).

43 *Id.* at 266.

It seems clear from the conclusion of the Court that, where national survival is in question, the government of a nuclear-weapon state may consider a resort to nuclear weapons stacked in its arsenal, as international law, as it stood at the time, did not provide for a definitive rule. Moreover, not even international humanitarian law could be violated necessarily by the use of nuclear weapons, despite the Court's view that that use "in fact seems scarcely reconcilable with respect for such requirements" as the principle of distinction and the avoidance of unnecessary suffering.[44] The question posed by the UNGA for the advisory proceedings was whether the threat or use of nuclear weapons was "in any circumstance permitted under international law."[45]

The Opinion of the Court thus ended with a *non liquet*.[46] There is no intention to look at this in greater detail than the following two comments.[47] First, a hierarchy was implied in the conclusion of the Court between the right to self-defence and the rules of humanitarian law. Secondly, the Court, by leaving open the possibility of the use of nuclear weapons *in extremis*, could be deemed to have given an answer to the UNGA question, as it were, by the insertion of the phrase "lawful or unlawful" in the *dispositif* quoted above.

With regard to the first comment, where humanitarian law is found to be clear, as was in this advisory opinion, with regard to the use of nuclear weapons, the Court still found itself unable to pronounce on the legality of the use in self-defence.[48] It must pose the question as to whether the right of self-defence ranks higher than the body of humanitarian law in this context or in general.

On the other hand, the preceding issue of the possible hierarchy of rules resultant from the Court's indecision may not give rise to disputes if it is applied to

---

44 *Id.* at 262–63. It is noteworthy that three nuclear-weapon states participating in the proceedings recognised during the proceedings that international humanitarian law (IHL) applies to nuclear weapons, *id.* ¶ 86. But France, while participating in the case, considered that the question placed before the Court was one that had been excluded from the most recent efforts in codifying and developing IHL, http://www.icj-cij.org/docket/files/95/8701.pdf.

45 *Id.* at 228. *See also* Request for an advisory opinion from the International Court of Justice on the legality of the threat or use of nuclear weapons, G.A. Res. 49/75[K], U.N. GAOR, 49th Sess., 90th plen. mtg. U.N. Doc. A/49/PV.90 (Dec. 15, 1994).

46 *Id.* at 322 (Dissenting Opinion of Judge Schwebel) and at 590 (Dissenting Opinion of Judge Higgins). *See also* Martti Koskenniemi, *The Limits of International Law: Are There Such? in* 28 Might and Right in International Relations 29 (Kalliopi Koufa ed., 1999).

47 For more details, *see* Daniel Bodansky, *Non Liquet and the Incompleteness of International Law*, in International Law, the International Court of Justice and Nuclear Weapons, ch. 10 (Laurence Boisson de Chazournes & Philippe Sands eds., 1999). *See also* Prosper Weil, *The Court Cannot Conclude Definitively… Non Liquet Revisited*, 36 Colum. J. Transnat'l L. 109 (1998).

48 *See* Legality of the Threat or Use of Nuclear Weapons, *supra* note 42, at 571 (Dissenting Opinion by Judge Koroma).

the *threat* of nuclear weapons. The threat of such weapons does not constitute a situation in which humanitarian law comes immediately into play.

With regard to the second comment, the qualification of "lawful or unlawful" in fact signifies that it may not be presumed by any state that threat or use of nuclear weapons in self-defence is a matter within the discretion of the state possessive of the weapons.[49] That state, in complying with the Court's opinion, would find it impossible to say either that it is allowed by the opinion to use or threaten or it is forbidden to do so. That would constitute a non-solution should it be faced with a decision on the issue. So, in a subtle way, the Court did not open a gate to the threat or use of such weapons. For the lack of legality or illegality is a factor that cautions any rash resort to the weapons. The state intending to threaten or use them may well consider to sound off the opinions among, say, its allies or in the UNSC. If the effect of the Court's conclusion is indeed such, it is an answer that can be applied by nuclear weapon states. It does not follow that the conclusion, as it stands, will signal to states that the threat or use of nuclear weapons is a freedom of choice to them (which would be a permission to threaten or use). On the contrary, they may be even more circumspect. Having said thus, the substance of that conclusion would still be a clear *non liquet*.[50]

Another notable fact is that the Court's indecision was voted in by the judges in a divided fashion, showing that the majority answer was not deemed by at least some members of the Court such that it must be avoided at all costs.[51]

Is international law silent at some moments of history? The answer may therefore be a tentative "yes." This is also the inference drawn from a look at a more recent advisory opinion delivered by the Court.

B. *Unilateral Declaration of Independence*

The issue in the advisory proceedings surrounding the legality of Kosovo's declaration of independence has been decided by the ICJ in favour of one answer in terms of international law.[52] Two countries' comments, out of many from others, which were made during the pleadings, are considered here.

---

49 But *see id.* at 389–90 (Dissenting Opinion by Judge Shahabuddeen). The learned judge had a different reading of this.

50 It is interesting to note the exact likeness between the Court's answer at issue and the vision of Stone in his important article on this topic, the latter of which, though directed at contentious cases before the ICJ, applies equally to advisory opinions: "it should be left open to a tribunal, in the absence of contrary requests by both parties, to decide that the authoritative legal materials and other resources available for judgment do not in the particular case enable it to make a binding judgment:" *See* Stone, *supra* note 11, at 160.

51 *See* Legality of the Threat or Use of Nuclear Weapons, *supra* note 42, at 281 (Declaration by Judge Vereshchetin).

52 *See id.* note 3, ¶ 84.

In Japan's written statement,[53] dated April 17, 2009, the two main points were that, as the issue of the declaration of independence in question was a fact,[54] international law did not speak to it,[55] and that international law "neither approves nor prohibits secession or independence by an entity which meets the requirements of statehood."[56]

In China's oral statement, on December 7, 2009,[57] one point was stressed that general international law was not "neutral" as far as unilateral secession from a sovereign state was concerned.[58] In this case, it was held by China that international law upheld the principle of "State sovereignty and territorial integrity" and that there was also the UNSC's decision as expressed in resolution 1244 (1999). Session, in the light of those two sources of obligation, could not be a solution open to the situation at issue.

The Court's finding, by a vote of 10 to four, was that "the declaration of independence by Kosovo adopted on February 17, 2008 did not violate international law."[59] One of the two main reasons for that conclusion was that "general international law contains no applicable prohibition of declarations of independence."[60]

It is not intended to debate whether the finding actually answered the question posed by the UNGA, which seems to be in some doubt after an adjustment of the question by the majority.[61] It is only intended here to consider whether this conclusion was based on a *non liquet*, and whether the submissions as represented by China and Japan, if followed to their logical conclusion, could achieve a different result. It may be said at once that there is no objection to a *non liquet*

---

53 *See* Written Statement of the Gov't of Japan, Embassy of Japan The Netherlands to Mr. Philippe Couvreur Registrar, International Court of Justice, The Hague (Apr. 17, 2009), http://www.icj-cij.org/docket/files/141/15658.pdf.

54 *Id.* at 2–3.

55 *Id.* at 3.

56 *Id.*

57 Accordance with International Law of the Unilateral Declaration of Independence by the Provisional Institutions of Self-Government of Kosovo (Req. for Advisory Op. submitted by U.N.GA) (CR 2009/29), http://www.icj-cij.org/docket/files/141/15724.pdf.

58 *Id.* at 34.

59 *See* Accordance with International Law of the Unilateral Declaration for Independence in Respect of Kosovo, *supra* note 3, ¶ 123.

60 *Id.* ¶ 84. The other reason was that the declaration did not violate Security Council Resolution 1244 (1999), adopted at its 4011th meeting on June 10, 1999 (or the Constitutional Framework) ¶ 122.

61 This occurred when the majority modified the question's reference to the Provisional Institutions of Self-Government of Kosovo as the authors of the declaration in question by questioning who were the real authors of the document, *Id.* ¶ 52. This was criticised by Judge Tomka in his Declaration, ¶¶ 10–21, http://www.icj-cij.org/docket/files/141/15989.pdf and by Judge Bennouna in his Dissenting Opinion, ¶¶ 27–35, http://www.icj-cij.org/docket/files/141/15999.pdf.

as was indeed pronounced by the Court in this case. In fact, it appears that this advisory opinion, in addition to the 1996 advisory opinion discussed above, has only confirmed Stone's view expressed 50 years ago, that international law does and will contain gaps.[62]

It is recalled that the majority construed the question posed by the UNGA in a particular way. It considered the accordance with international law part as signalling a search for an answer to the question whether international law contained a prohibitory rule with regard to a declaration of independence (by an entity like the Kosovo institutions).[63] That would mean, as the majority further elaborated, that the question to be addressed by the Court became one as to whether the declaration in question had violated international law. To compare this understanding with the conclusion of the majority quoted above, it may give rise to a question. If the UNGA question requested a finding on the accordance with international law of the Kosovo declaration, should the answer be such that it results from a choice between two versions? The first version of the answer is that as adopted by the majority in this instance. The second is that, if international law contains no prohibitory rule in this connection, as found by the majority in the instant case, the Kosovo declaration still could not be "in accordance with international law." Where the applicable rule is missing, how can a conduct be measured against it to test its own legality or else? What is not prohibited by international law is not equivalent to what is consistent with that law.[64] The absence of the prohibitory rule is not equal to the existence of a permissive rule.[65] It may be that legal neutrality, as a *non liquet* normally results, is not necessarily equivalent to legal permission. The declaration in question, for instance, may be embraced by a *non liquet*. However, it does not necessarily follow that its issuance becomes, therefore, permitted in the circumstances of the case.

It seems to the present writer that the second version of the answer set forth above may be a preferable one in respect of this case—inasmuch as general international law is concerned. Without, however, dwelling on it, it seems that the majority's finding was premised on a *non liquet* that the rules regarding secession outside a colonial context were lacking.

But the present discussion digresses at this juncture. Two countries—China and Japan—held different positions in the advisory proceedings, which will be looked at. The positions were set out above at the beginning of this section. With Japan's position, it would be certain that the declaration was in accordance with

---

62 *See* STONE, *supra* note 5, at 162.

63 *See* Accordance with International Law of the Unilateral Declaration for Independence in Respect of Kosovo, *supra* note 3, ¶ 56.

64 *Cf.* Dissenting Opinion of Judge Koroma, ¶ 23, http://www.icj-cij.org/docket/files/141/15991.pdf.

65 *Cf.* Declaration of Judge Simma, ¶ 3, http://www.icj-cij.org/docket/files/141/15993.pdf.

international law.[66] But the problem with that position would also be obvious. If the declaration was regarded already as a factual event, thus being irrelevant to international law,[67] how could it be in accordance with international law, as the position was later stated? It would have been better if the position was rounded off by the point, as intended by the draftspersons of the written statement, that the declaration did not contravene international law.

China's position, on the contrary, could both give a clear answer to the question posed by the UNGA, and avoid a *non liquet*. China held, among others, that international law was not neutral in respect of the Kosovo declaration.[68] It is recalled that, with regard to the Kosovo declaration, the Chinese view was that it would run counter to "the principle of State sovereignty and territorial integrity," besides UNSC Resolution 1244 (1999).[69] The resolution was accepted by the Court as part of international law regulating the Kosovo situation.[70] The necessary upshot of this view is therefore that the existing international law appertaining to the Kosovo declaration indicated the latter's discord with the former. Any further consequences which can be drawn from this position would be a matter to be decided by the UNGA and the member states concerned with the situation. It suffices to say that, in the light of the Chinese submissions, there would be no question of *non liquet*.

IV. Conclusion

While the doctrine of *non liquet* had been little practised by the 1950s, the recent cases before the ICJ seem to suggest that it has a reason to exist almost inevitably when important questions of national interest are involved in adjudication. The ICJ has not refused to give an answer to questions posed to it for advisory opinions in the two advisory cases mentioned above, in spite of a *non liquet* in each case, but the answers given in the cases differ markedly in content. In the 1996 opinion, a *non liquet* was conceded; so was in the 2010 opinion, but only after adjusting the question posed by the UNGA. The 1996 answer, without more, left open the question posed for the advisory opinion; whereas the 2010 answer essentially spelled out the consequences of the *non liquet* in that case, by conceding legality to the Kosovo declaration at issue. A judicial finding of *non liquet*,

---

66 *See* Statement of Japan, *supra* note 53, at 8.

67 *Id.*

68 *See* Accordance with International Law of the Unilateral Declaration of Independence by the Provisional Institutions of Self-Government of Kosovo, *supra* note 57, ¶ 17.

69 *Id.*

70 *See* Accordance with International Law of the Unilateral Declaration for Independence in Respect of Kosovo, *supra* note 3, ¶ 85.

therefore, does not necessarily mean no answer to a legal question or dispute.[71] Suppose the 2010 answer was given in a contentious case, one party would work away from it with a winning verdict, as the other party's claim was effectively rejected by the Court. This further shows the *neutral* nature of the existence of judicial findings of *non liquet*, in that the system in which the court operates contains gaps, which may just be the answers to cases whose solution turns only upon the gaps. The judges facing those gaps, under the authority vested in them by the Statute of the ICJ, have little choice but to state the law or the lack of it.[72] For their power to legislate is not commonly recognized by states, although frequently advocated by authors. As shown by this chapter, furthermore, sometimes *non liquet* arises from different understandings of existing law by states involved in cases pending before international judicial bodies. In that case, the judicial choice between the understandings determines the final result of the cases.[73] In short, there is nothing against the existence or else of *non liquet* in international law, and its occurrence, which is a matter of fact, does not necessarily end in an indecision from which parties subject to it cannot draw proper inferences to guide their subsequent practice.

---

71 This possibility has already been broached before. *See* ALF ROSS, A TEXTBOOK OF INTERNATIONAL LAW 279 (1947).

72 Where possible, they would of course try and find a rule. Barcelona Traction, Light & Power Co. (Belgium v. Spain), 1970 I.C.J. 4, 33–34 (Feb. 5).

73 *See* Weil, *supra* note 47, at 119.

CHAPTER SEVEN

THE INTRODUCTION OF WESTERN INTERNATIONAL LAW INTO JAPAN

Jon M. Van Dyke†*

I. Introduction

Japanese officials and scholars were first exposed to and started to master principles of Western international law in the years that followed Commodore Perry's visit to Japan with his "black ships" in 1853. The United States and the European powers imposed "unequal treaties" upon Japan, and Japan was determined to renegotiate those treaties and become a member of the "family of nations." To accomplish this goal, Japan needed to establish a stable legal system that would protect foreign investment and allow Japan to join the world economy, and also to master the principles of international law that would enable it to function in the world community. Prior to this era, Japan did not utilize the concepts of "law" and the "rule of law" (in the Western sense) and operated primarily through hierarchy and relationships. Japan's understanding of "law" thus came in part through its mastery of international law.

II. What Is [Western] International Law?

International law has been evolving in the West for centuries to provide a framework for international and transnational activities. Like other areas of the law, its purpose is to allow participants to deal with each other with some level of predictability and thus to reduce misunderstandings and avoid conflicts and confrontations.[1]

---

* Late Professor of Law, The William S. Richardson School of Law at the University of Hawai'i at Manoa.

1 "Law is an instrument for creating, maintaining, and changing a society. Law prescribes the behavior of the society's members so that social order—that is, regularity and predictability of social behavior—prevails, the survival of the society becomes possible, and

But international law is still a more primitive system of law than the domestic legal systems found in advanced nations. It does not have a legislative body with the capacity to enact laws binding on all nations, an executive branch or military or police force that can enforce the laws that do exist, or judicial tribunals that have broad jurisdiction or the power to issue binding and enforceable decrees. Although early versions of such bodies can be found in the United Nations and in emerging regional organizations, the process of constructing institutions that enjoy widespread support and can meet the challenges presented by a deeply divided world is just beginning.

Some have argued that because international law cannot be enforced by a superior body it is not law at all.[2] But most commentators contend that because most nations follow international law most of the time, and because those that violate its norms do frequently suffer consequences, it should be viewed as a system of law.[3]

International law is less developed than other systems of law because the larger and more powerful nations do not always accept that it is in their interest to subordinate their self-interest to an international or multinational goal.[4] Although smaller nations will see the benefit of an international structure that protects the weak against the powerful, the stronger nations do not always agree that such a

---

the members can live in peaceful coexistence." WERNER LEVI, CONTEMPORARY INTERNATIONAL LAW: A CONCISE INTRODUCTION 1 (2d ed. 1991).

2 John Austin defined a "law" as "a rule laid down for the guidance of an intelligent being by an intelligent being having power over him," and wrote that a "command" and a "sanction" are essential elements of a law. He put international law into the different category of "positive morality"—along with "the laws of honor" and "the laws of fashion"—because it consisted of "rules set and enforced merely by the opinion of an intermediate body of men." *See* JOHN BASSETT MOORE, INTERNATIONAL LAW AND OTHER CURRENT ILLUSIONS AND OTHER ESSAYS 292 (1924) (discussing John Austin's *Jurisprudence*).

3 The American scholar John Bassett Moore explained that:

> In respect of actual observance, I venture to say that international law is on the whole as well observed as municipal law. Perhaps one would not go too far in saying that it is better observed, at any rate in time of peace. In time of war, when a contest by force exists, it is needless to repeat that the application of law, whether municipal or international, becomes more or less uncertain, and that, as turmoil and excitement grow, the uncertainty increases. In time of peace, however, the regard which nations are accustomed to feel for their reputation and dignity strongly influences them, perhaps quite as much as does the dread of retaliation to respect the rules by which their intercourse is confessedly regulated.

MOORE, *supra* note 2, at 300. For a more recent study examining this question, *see* LOUIS HENKIN, HOW NATIONS BEHAVE (2d ed. 1979).

4 "There is little incentive for states to sacrifice their national interests to an international interest. Therefore, they have no incentive to create an effective international law, except insofar as this may serve their purposes." LEVI, *supra* note 1, at 4.

structure is beneficial.[5] The foundations of international law have always been, therefore, reciprocity and enlightened self-interest. "For example, the increasing cost of war, or perhaps the infeasibility of a major war, makes a legal settlement of conflicting interests more attractive. At any rate, war costs diminish the types of interests over which states are willing to fight a war."[6]

The primary sources of international law are treaties—bilateral and multilateral—and "customary international law," which emerges from the actual practices of states undertaken with an understanding that the practice is required by law (*opinio juris sive necessitatis*). The "practices" of states are usually found in actions taken by a country, but sometimes can be discovered in the statements their diplomats or leaders issue or in their votes at international organizations or diplomatic conferences. To become "custom," a practice must have the widespread (but not necessarily universal) support of countries concerned with the issue and must usually have continued for a period of time long enough to signify understanding and acquiescence. Occasionally a regional custom can emerge, if the countries of a certain part of the world order their affairs in a certain manner.

Most scholars[7] explain that "modern" international law emerged in Europe at the time of the Renaissance and Enlightenment through the Peace of Westphalia, which ended the Thirty Years War (1618–48) and gave formal recognition to the sovereign state system. This treaty-based system was designed, in part, to allow Catholic and Protestant states to coexist in Europe. International law became necessary to confirm the boundaries among these states and to bring some order to their dealings with each other. "These agreements also proclaimed the doctrine of *pacta sunt servanda* (treaties are to be observed)—a fundamental principle of international law—and established a machinery for the settlement of disputes arising between the signatories."[8]

---

[5] When the United States was a small and weak country, for instance, its leaders enthusiastically embraced international law. The First U.S. Congress enacted in 1790 a statute giving aliens the right to bring claims in U.S. courts for violations of torts committed "in violation of the law of nations." Judiciary Act of 1789, ch. 20, §. 9(b), 1 Stat. 73, 77 (codified at 28 U.S.C. §. 1350 (1789)). In 1792, Attorney General Edmund Randolph issued in opinion explaining that "The law of nations, although not specially adopted by the constitution or any municipal act, is essentially a part of the law of the land. Its obligation commences and runs with the existence of a nation, subject to modifications on some points of indifference." 1 OP. ATT'Y GEN. 26 (June 26, 1792). But now that the United States is the world's only superpower, it appears to have much less interest in multinational institutions as solutions to problems.

[6] LEVI, *supra* note 1, at 4.

[7] A leading treatise on the history of international law is ARTHUR NUSSBAUM, A CONCISE HISTORY OF THE LAW OF NATIONS (rev. ed. 1954).

[8] THOMAS BUERGENTHAL & SEAN D. MURPHY, PUBLIC INTERNATIONAL LAW 15 (4th ed. 2002).

The Final Act of the Congress of Vienna (1815), signed by Austria, France, Great Britain, Portugal, Prussia, Russia, and Sweden, which formally ended the Napoleonic Wars was another significant event, because it created a system of political and economic cooperation in Europe as well as delimiting norms of international law. Among the norms that emerged from this Congress were a set of rules governing diplomatic protocol, a condemnation of the slave trade, the principle of free navigation (not only for the riparian states but for all states) on the major rivers of Europe (the Rhine, the Neckar, the Mayne, the Moselle, the Meuse, and the Scheldt), and the neutrality of Switzerland.[9] Treaties, both bilateral and multilateral, began to cover a wide range of topics, supplementing and sometimes replacing custom as a source of law. This agreement reinforced the notion that "states" are all equal to each other, with horizontal relationships among them and complete sovereignty over their own territory. Today, 193 "states" make up the world community.

In recent years, it has become accepted that some principles of customary international law are so important that they are called "peremptory norms" or "*jus cogens*" (commanding law) of international law, and that no nation is permitted to depart from these principles.[10] Among these norms are the right to self-determination and the prohibitions on aggression, genocide, crimes against humanity, slavery, extrajudicial murder, prolonged arbitrary detention, torture, and racial discrimination.[11]

Although most historical summaries of the development of international law focus on its growth in Europe and the West,[12] the reality is more complex.

---

[9] BUERGENTHAL & MURPHY, *supra* note 8, at 15–16; MOORE, *supra* note 2, at 296; NUSSBAUM, *supra* note 7, at 186–87.

[10] *See, e.g.*, Vienna Convention on the Law of Treaties art. 53, May 23, 1969, 1155 U.N.T.S. 331:

> A treaty is void if... it conflicts with a peremptory norm of general international law....[A] peremptory norm of general international law is a norm accepted and recognized by the international community of States as a whole as a norm from which no derogation is permitted and which can be modified only by a subsequent norm of general international law having the same character.

[11] *See, e.g.*, Restatement of the Foreign Relations Law of the United States § 702 (3d ed. 1987).

[12] "Today's international law is a product of modern European civilization." Yasuoki Onuma, *Moderator's Introduction, in* JAPAN AND INTERNATIONAL LAW: PAST, PRESENT AND FUTURE (Nisuke Ando ed., 1999). "International law as it now stands is essentially the product of the European mind and has practically been 'received'... lock, stock and barrel by American and Asiatic states." J. H. W. Verzijl, *Western European Influence on the Foundations of International Law in* 1 J. H. W. VERZIJL, INTERNATIONAL LAW IN HISTORICAL PERSPECTIVE 442 (1968). "There is no doubt about it: the traditional law of nations is a law of European lineage." B. V. A. ROLING, INTERNATIONAL LAW IN AN EXPANDED WORLD 10 (Amsterdam 1960). Professor Nussbaum wrote that the international law of the Western states overwhelmed the views of East Asia rather than

Practices governing interactions among nations and peoples also developed in Asia and elsewhere,[13] and these norms have been merging with those that came to be accepted in the West.[14]

II. The Sino-Centric System in East Asia

"In contrast with the European World Order characterized by horizontal relations among sovereign States, the East Asian World Order was based on hierarchical relations with a Middle Kingdom at its apex."[15] Under this different approach,

---

merging with it, but added that Western concepts did later evolve as a result of the contact between the two systems:

> The expansion of the Western law of nations to the Far East did not involve a fusion of European and Asiatic ideas. The European conception prevailed as to substance and form. The Oriental nations had small success instilling their cherished notions regarding ranks and ceremonials into the new agreements. Nevertheless, the process of expansion in itself divested the law of nations more and more of its "European" character....

NUSSBAUM, *supra* note 7, at 196.

13 Various treaties covering a number of topics were entered into between European and Asian nations beginning in 1547. *See* Jeremy A. Thomas, *History and International Law in Asia: A Time for Review? in* ESSAYS IN HONOUR OF WANG TIEYA 813, 823 (Ronald St. John MacDonald ed., 1994) (*citing* ALEXANDROWICZ, AN INTRODUCTION TO THE HISTORY OF THE LAW OF NATIONS IN THE EAST INDIES (1967)).

14 Professor Onuma has explained that we need to look at "the history of international law from an intercivilizational perspective," because today's world is "a world of various civilizations' making which date back much further than modern European civilization." Onuma Yasuaki, *When Was the Law of International Society Born?—An Inquiry of the History of International Law from an Intercivilizational Perspective*, 2 J. HIST. INT'L L. 6, 7 (2000). He has explained that today's international law did not emerge until the end of the nineteenth century when global interaction became a reality. "What existed before were regional normative systems, each of which claimed its universal validity based on its universalistic world image. Sinocentric, Islamocentric, and Eurocentric systems were leading examples. Together with the subjugation of competing powers in other civilizations by European powers, European international law became the global standard." Onuma Yasuaki, *The Birth of International Law as the Law of International Society*, 94 AM. SOC'Y INT'L L. PROC. 44 (2000). Similarly, Georges Abi-Saab has explained that the European system had co-existed with other systems, which "it gradually managed to set aside or replace. Georges Abi-Saab, *International Law and The International Community: The Long Road to Universality, in* ESSAYS IN HONOUR OF WANG TIEYA 31, 32 (Ronald St. John MacDonald ed., 1994).

Professor Anand has written that the failure to appreciate "the contribution of Asian and African countries toward the development of modern international law... is more often than not based on ignorance of their history and lack of understanding of the cultures and cultural traditions." R. P. ANAND, ORIGIN AND DEVELOPMENT OF THE LAW OF THE SEA—HISTORY OF INTERNATIONAL LAW REVISITED 5 (1982).

15 Yoshiro Matsui, *Modern Japan, War and International Law in* Onuma, *supra* note 12, at 8.

the smaller nations around the periphery of China paid tributes to China and accepted China as the hegemonic power of the region. For the most part, China did not directly interfere with the internal affairs of its smaller neighbors, but the need to respect China and its role remained as a central feature of East Asian relationships.

A. *The Westernization of Law in East Asia*

After Commodore Matthew Perry came to Japan in 1853 with his "black ships," Japan entered into the 1854 Treaty of Peace and Amity with the United States.[16] This treaty was followed in 1858 with a Treaty of Commerce with the United States[17] and then similar treaties with other Western countries. These treaties were "unequal" and conveyed consular jurisdiction to the Western powers, established a conventional tariff, and gave to the Western country a unilateral most-favored-nation clause.[18] They also tended to restrict the movement of Westerners in Japan to identified treaty ports, and prohibited them from moving into the interior.[19]

On February 8, 1868, the new Meiji government in Japan declared that it would respect these treaties and conduct its foreign relations "according to the universal law of nations," but also indicated that it would seek to revise the burdensome unequal provisions of the earlier treaties.[20]

> Politically and psychologically galling, though not often called upon, were the extraterritoriality provisions that permitted foreigners accused of crimes on Japanese soil to be tried by foreigners resident in Japan. The impetus to design a Western style legal system developed in part from the desire to remove the unequal treaties, especially these extraterritorial provisions.[21]

The breakthrough occurred in 1894 with the Anglo-Japanese Treaty of Commerce and Navigation, signed 16 days before Japan's declaration of war against China.[22] This treaty recognized freedoms of residence, travel, property, trade, and navigation for each country's subjects on an equal basis,[23] and it marked Japan's entrance into the "Family of Nations" as a "Civilized Nation." Japan thus moved out of the

---

16 Clive Parry, 111 The Consolidated Treaty Series 377 (1969).

17 Clive Parry, 119 The Consolidated Treaty Series 254 (1969).

18 Matsui, *supra* note 15, at 9.

19 *Id.*

20 *Id.* at 10 (citing Gaimusho [Ministry of Foreign Affairs] ed., 1 *Nihon Gaiko Bunsho* [*Diplomatic Documents of Japan*] 227, Book 1 (1936).

21 Michael Young & Constance Hamilton, *Historical Introduction to the Japanese Legal System*, Japan Business Guide, ch. 1 (1988), *reprinted in* Curtis J. Milhaupt, J. Mark Ramseyer & Mark D. West, The Japanese Legal System: Cases, Codes, and Commentary 32 (2d rev. ed. 2012).

22 Clive Parry, 180 The Consolidated Treaty Series 257 (1969).

23 Matsui, *supra* note 15, at 10.

East Asian World Order and into the European sovereign state system, and it used force to bring an end to the Sino-Centric system that had operated in East Asia for centuries. Japan moved Ryukyu from being a tributary of China to being a part of Japan in 1874–79, and then defeated China in the Sino-Japanese War of 1894–95.[24] Japan also acted to break down Korea's tributary relationship with China in 1875–76, and then more decisively in the Sino-Japanese War of 1894–95, followed by the formal annexation of Korea in 1905–10 (after Japan defeated Russia in the Russo-Japanese War of 1904–05 and thereby secured Korea into its own sphere of influence).[25] The Japanese Association of International Law was established in 1897, nine years before the founding of the American Society of International Law in 1906.[26]

B. *Japanese Adherence to International Law Principles*

Japanese authors tend to emphasize that Japan engaged in "scrupulous observance of international law" from 1854 to the early 1930s.[27] This adherence was designed to earn acceptance into the "Family of Nations," and later to provide justification for Japan's expansionist activities.[28]

Some Japanese scholars found similarities between the natural law roots of international law principles and "their own neo-Confucian metaphysical concept of the 'principles of the universe (*ten ri* or *ten do*)' which were applicable to the human relations in society."[29] Japan participated in five international arbitrations between 1873 and 1903, more than any other country during that period, but became demoralized when it lost the 1903 *Yokohama House Tax Case* before the Permanent Court of Arbitration.[30] This defeat led many Japanese to view

---

24 *Id.* at 11–12.

25 *Id.* at 12–13.

26 Shigeru Oda, *Banquet Speech: One Hundred Years of the Japanese Association of International Law and Fifty Years of the International Court of Justice in* Onuma, *supra* note 12, at 235.

27 Matsui, *supra* note 15, at 10. *See also id.* at 27 ("Until about the time of First World War, Japan maintained a good record in observing international law."); Oda, *supra* note 26, at 236 ("It is worth mentioning that Japan was at that time regarded as a nation which most faithfully adhered to the rules of warfare....[I]n the first years of this century, Japan was regarded as a law-abiding nation."); Hisashi Owada, *Japan, International Law and the International Community, in* Onuma, *supra* note 12, at 347, 357 (referring to Japan's "faithful observance and application of international law"); *id.* at 359 ("with the exception of a comparatively brief period of less than twenty years from the beginning of the 1930s until the end of the Second World War in 1945...Japan tended to observe quite meticulously and scrupulously the norms of international law in her conduct of foreign relations.")

28 Matsui, *supra* note 15, at 27; Owada, *supra* note 27, at 359.

29 Owada, *supra* note 27, at 347, 351; *see also id.* at 352.

30 *Id.* at 355. This case was brought by France, Germany, and Britain against Japan, after the unequal treaties had been negotiated and concerned whether a building built upon

international law as "not so much a body of principles based on natural justice which the East could share in common with the West," but rather "as a bunch of technical rules to be manipulated."[31] Many Japanese scholars developed a conservative approach toward international law, viewing it as in a state "in which the evolutionary process of the law ceased to be in motion and those rules tended to be fixed in Japan then and there."[32] Japanese scholars and international lawyers now tend to "interpret and apply [international] law almost as a pure analytical process rather than as a process of testing the validity of the law in the context of the social reality in which the case in question has to be weighed," i.e., applying "formal logic, almost divorced from the context of societal values of the international community in which the case has to be examined."[33] This approach has been criticized as "an excessively legalistic and technical approach to international law"[34] by Hisahi Owada, former President of the International Court of Justice.

C. *The State of "Law" in Japan in the Early 1800s*

Many writers have observed that Japan (and other East Asian communities) did not in the early 1800s recognize and utilize "law" and the "rule of law" in same way these concepts were used in the West. "In traditional China law remained a small and not very significant department of ethics. It was not considered worthy of study in itself, nor was there any interest in systematizing it."[35] Similarly, in Tokugawa Japan, "the idea of law and legal philosophy itself were absent."[36]

The Tokugawa Shogunate governed through a feudal structure, forbidding Japanese to travel abroad and permitting foreigners little access to Japan.[37] Japan's feudal structure was different from Western feudalism in that "contract played no role in the feudal system" in Japan and "the 'glue' that held the feudal system together was a kind of family or kinship relationship together with Japanese notions of Neo-Confucianism."[38] Control was exercised through "the notion that the peasant (or any subordinate Lord) owed obligations to his higher Lord."[39]

---

land conveyed in an in-perpetuity lease under the previous treaty could be taxed. Japanese officials and scholars accepted that the conveyed lands would not be subject to taxation, but were flabbergasted when the arbitrators ruled that the subsequently built buildings were also exempt from taxation.

31 *Id.* at 356.

32 *Id.* at 361.

33 *Id.* at 364.

34 *Id.* at 367.

35 Richard H. Minear, Japanese Tradition and Western Law: Emperor, State, and Law in the Thought of Hozumi Yatsuka 155 (1970).

36 *Id.* at 157.

37 Carl F. Goodman, The Rule of Law in Japan: A Comparative Analysis 12 (2003).

38 *Id.* at 13.

39 *Id.*

Although rulers "had an obligation to justly rule," the primary concept connecting society was the concept of "obligation," and the ruler's subjects did not have "rights."[40] Throughout the Tokugawa period,

> Japan is still either following the commands of a centralized government with no formal legal system that would apply principled rules and allow persons to form their own governing law for their relationships or is following an informal system of dispute resolution which relies on compromise to re-establish harmony between the disputing parties.[41]

Some authors have explained that although "[d]uring the Tokugawa period there had been judicial law as well as standardized forms of action through which the government usually afforded remedies to parties whose legitimate interests were injured,... a legal science, analogous to the European legal science, with which Meiji scholars were confronted, had not emerged."[42] Although claims could be brought during the Tokugawa period, the concept of a "right" as it was understood in Europe was lacking and therefore "Meiji students of Western jurisprudence had to coin a new term, *ken ri* (power plus interest) in order to express the concept of a right."[43]

The hierarchical social structure was so rigid during the Tokugawa period that a dispute could not be taken to a higher level for resolution without the permission of the claimant's immediate superior. Officials were thus able to pressure potential litigants directly and could also "encourage other people, on whose good will the litigant were dependent, to discourage the litigant from continuing the dispute."[44] It was also difficult to pursue claims because it was challenging to identify "clear-cut rules" that applied to any given situation. "Personal entitlements and even duties were apparently intentionally kept hazy and hidden from the view of the population."[45] In addition, "[r]ights and entitlements, such as they were,... attached more to the group than to the individual."[46] Commentaries on legal principles were not generally published, and judges were not independent, but were rather "functionaries of the shogunate government and slipped easily and quickly from judge to administrator and back."[47]

---

[40] *Id.* at 14.

[41] *Id.* at 16.

[42] Kenzo Takayanagi, *A Century of Innovation: The Development of Japanese Law, 1868–1961, in* LAW IN JAPAN 15–40 (von Mehren ed., 1963), *reprinted in* THE JAPANESE LEGAL SYSTEM: INTRODUCTORY CASES AND MATERIALS 173 (Hideo Tanaka ed., 1976).

[43] *Id.* at 174.

[44] Young & Hamilton, *supra* note 21, at 31.

[45] *Id.*

[46] *Id.*

[47] *Id.*

With the beginning of the Meiji period, it became clear that "Japan needed a legal system"[48] to overcome the unequal treaties and the exercise of consular jurisdiction by the Western powers. "Western law" came to be viewed "as the embodiment of civilized justice."[49] The concept of "the law of nations" invoked by the U.S. Consul-General Townsend Harris when negotiating the 1858 Treaty of Amity and Commerce "was totally alien and new" to the Japanese negotiators, but they came to understand that it was "an essential prerequisite for a satisfactory conduct of intercourse with these barbarian Westerners."[50] Japanese scholars were, therefore, sent to the West,[51] and Western advisors came to Japan.[52] Japan was seeking to understand Western legal concepts in general at the same time that it was seeking to understand Western international law, and some have stated that Japan received its understanding of "law" through its understanding and practice of Western international law.

III. Western International Law Around 1900

In the late nineteenth century, Western international law was even more primitive than it is today. No global institutions existed, and only a few special-purpose regional organizations had been created. Some topics—such as diplomatic immunity—were fairly well defined, and consensus had also been reached on the important goals of stopping piracy and slavery. War was still viewed by many as an acceptable instrument of foreign policy, but the dramatic increase in destructive weaponry resulting from the industrial revolution caused many to realize that some constraints were needed on the use of force. Major international meetings were called, the most significant being the 1899 and 1907 Hague Conferences (which Japan participated in), which were designed to codify the laws of armed conflict and establish limits on certain types of military activities. The growth of daily newspapers in the industrialized countries had the effect of allowing common citizens to participate more fully in policy decisions, and led, in many countries, to a democratization of international politics.

Twenty-five nations attended the 1899 Hague Conference, which was convened by Czar Nicholas II of Russia, and a larger number ratified the documents produced by the meeting, which included conventions for the Peaceful Settlement of International Disputes, on the Laws and Customs of War on Land, for the Adaptation to Maritime Warfare of the Principles of the Geneva Convention of 1864, Prohibiting the Launching of Projectiles and Explosives from Balloons

---

48 Goodman, *supra* note 37, at 17.
49 Takayanagi, *supra* note 42, at 177.
50 Owada, *supra* note 27, at 347, 350.
51 *See, e.g.*, Minear, *supra* note 35.
52 Goodman, *supra* note 37, at 17.

and declarations on the use of projectiles to transmit poisonous gases, and on the prohibition of dum-dum bullets.[53] Although European nations dominated the negotiations, 19 Latin American nations signed or ratified one or more of the documents, as did China, Japan, Korea, Persia, Siam, and Turkey.[54]

The 1907 Hague conference, called again by the Russian Czar Nicholas II upon the initiative of Theodore Roosevelt, produced conventions on the Pacific Settlement of International Disputes, the Limitation of Employment of Force for Recovery of Contract Debts, the Opening of Hostilities, the Laws and Customs of War on Land, the Rights and Duties of Neutral Powers and Persons in Case of War on Land, the Status of Enemy Merchant Ships at the Outbreak of Hostilities, the Conversion of Merchant Ships into War-Ships, the Laying of Automatic Submarine Contact Mines, Bombardment by Naval Forces in Time of War, Adaptation to Maritime War of the Principles of the Geneva Convention, Certain Restrictions with Regard to the Exercise of the Right of Capture in Naval War, the Creation of an International Prize Court (never ratified), and the Rights and Duties of Neutral Powers in Naval War.[55] The European nations again dominated the negotiations, but 18 Latin American nations signed or ratified one or more of the conventions (Honduras was missing) as did China, Japan, Persia, Siam, and Turkey (with Korea missing because it had been placed under a protectorate by Japan). Liberia also adhered to many of the conventions.[56]

The nature of the international legal system that was being built was thought by many to be one of consent—or "positivism"—wherein only those norms agreed upon by the states could be enforced against them.[57] But perhaps because of the theocracies that had governed many parts of Europe in previous centuries, the

---

[53] *See generally* the website of The Avalon Project, http://www.yale.edu/lawweb/avalon/lawofwar/hague99/haguemen.htm.

[54] SIGNATURES, RATIFICATIONS, ADHESIONS AND RESERVATIONS TO THE CONVENTIONS AND DECLARATIONS OF THE FIRST AND SECOND HAGUE PEACE CONFERENCES (CLASSIC REPRINT) 2–4 (Forgotten Books 2012) (1914) [hereinafter SIGNATURES].

[55] The website of The Avalon Project, *supra* note 53.

[56] SIGNATURES, *supra* note 54, at 8–11.

[57] The Italian scholar Alberico Gentili (1552–1608) departed from the theological approach utilized by other writers of his time and "deduced the rules of the law not from some metaphysical source but from the practice of states and the writings of historians. He was thus the first representative of the 'positivists,' who argue that the law is created by humans for definite conditions and purposes rather than by some supreme being for all eternity." LEVI, *supra* note 1, at 10.

The next significant positivist was the British scholar Richard Zouche (1590–1660), who "was the first author to undertake a systematic treatment of the entire field of international law." His writings "simply set forth the controversial issues as such, without venturing to offer a decision...." "[W]ith him international law is based distinctly on custom—supposing it is reasonable—and on treaties. While Zouche mentions natural law, he considers it to be knowable from the actual attitudes of men. Of the traditional natural-law doctrine, his book shows practically no mark." NUSSBAUM, *supra* note 7,

canon law that had developed during that period, and the religious fervor that still burned brightly for many, others contended that certain inherent principles also governed nations. Tension emerged between this "natural law" formula for the basis of international law and the perspective of "positivism" promoted by others, and this tension still exists today.

The Dutch diplomat Hugo de Groot, who wrote under the Latin name Grotius, is often called the "father"[58] or "founder"[59] of international law because he tried to reconcile the conflicting sources of international law, believing "that the foundation of international law is a combination of natural and positive law."[60] His analysis of the laws of war, the law of the sea,[61] and the protection owed to diplomats laid the framework for modern thinking on these topics. He believed that a "law of nature" could be deduced by logical reasoning, rather than by resort to divine sources, and thus tried to formulate a law that could be "acceptable to all, conceivably even to 'infidels.'"[62]

Another continuing issue has been whether international law is incorporated into national legal systems, and is thus part of the law applied by national courts ("monism"), or whether it is a separate and distinct legal system governing the nations but not accessible by normal citizens in disputes in domestic courts ("dualism").

A. *Did Western States View International Law as Applying Equally Everywhere?*

European and U.S. scholars and judges viewed international law as applying only to "civilized nations,"[63] and this term referred almost exclusively to Christian nations.[64] Theodore Woolsey's influential *Introduction to the Study of International*

---

at 166–67 (discussing RICHARD ZOUCHE, JURIS ET JUDICII FECIALIS, SIVE JURIS INTER GENTES ET QUAESTIONUM DE EODEM EXPLICATIO (1650)).

58 W. S. M. KNIGHT, THE LIFE AND WORKS OF HUGO GROTIUS 112 (1925).

59 MOORE, *supra* note 2, at viii (1924).

60 LEVI, *supra* note 1, at 11.

61 Grotius was particularly influential in promoting free access to the oceans and their resources, and was undoubtedly influenced himself by the maritime practices of Asian nations in the East Indies and elsewhere. *See, e.g.*, ANAND, *supra* note 14, at 124.

62 LEVI, *supra* note 1, at 10.

63 *See, e.g.*, The Paquete Habana, 175 U.S. 677, 686, 700, 709 (1900); Hilton v. Guyot, U.S. 163, 228 (1895). This term remains in Article 38(1)(c) of the Statute of the International Court of Justice, T.S. No. 993, 59 Stat. 1055 (1945), which describes as one of the sources of international law "general principles of law recognized by civilized nations."

64 Oppenheim pointed out that "whenever a new Christian state made its appearance in Europe, it was received into the existing European community of states," but that until recently "international law was confined to those states." 1 OPPENHEIM'S INTERNATIONAL LAW 87 (Sir Robert Jennings & Sir Arthur Watts eds., 9th ed. 1997). Wheaton explained that the law of nations "has always been, and still is, limited to the civilized and Christian people of Europe or to those of European origin." HENRY WHEATON, ELEMENTS OF INTERNATIONAL LAW 15 (1866).

Law[65] contains a typical Eurocentric and politically-incorrect explanation of this phenomenon, explaining that Christians were "the first to elaborate a system of international law" for the same reasons that "have enabled Christian states to reach a higher point of civilization than any other."[66] These reasons include "the high moral standards of the religion... which cultivates alike the sentiments of justice and humanity" as well as the Roman law heritage.[67] Christian nations, he explained, had shared "religious and jural views" and "a similar historical development," but "[n]o such common feeling, but quite the opposite, existed between them and their Mohammedan neighbors; and hence the latter were long shut out from the pale of their international law."[68]

One of the major disputes of the early colonial period was whether the colonized peoples had any rights of any sort under international law. The generally accepted view was that "peoples overseas could be subjected to European rule and their territories annexed through effective occupation by the conquering state," and "[t]he territory then became subject to treatment or mistreatment without protection of international law or, indeed, with its approval. Rules legitimizing imperialism and its means... endured well into the twentieth century, until most colonies became independent."[69]

The first writer to oppose this view was a Spanish professor of theology Francisco Vitoria (1480–1546), who "defended Spain's right in principle to create overseas dependencies and to exploit them," but also "argued that Spain was obliged to treat the conquered Indians in the Americas humanely, and he even granted these Indians a limited right to conduct 'just wars' against their cruel conquerors."[70] He "considered that the Amerindians had a soul, and in consequence were part of the *societas gentium*, the expression of the fundamental unity of the human race, and were subjects of the *jus humane societatis* or *jus gentium*, derived from natural law."[71]

During the Tokugawa period, strenuous efforts had been made to keep Christianity out of Japan:

> It is a well-known historical fact that, fearful of the devastating effect of Christianity on the moral base of its political power, the Tokugawa Shogunate strictly banned the spread of the Gospel in Japan, and this ban on Christianity formed the cornerstone of the Shogunate's policy of national seclusion.[72]

---

65 Theodore D. Woolsey, Introduction to the Study of International Law (4th ed. 1874).

66 *Id.* at 22.

67 *Id.*

68 *Id.*

69 Levi, *supra* note 1, at 9.

70 *Id.* at 10.

71 Abi-Saab, *supra* note 14, at 33 (referring to de Vitoria, De Indis (1993)).

72 Yosiyuki Noda, *Nihon Ni Okeru Hikaku-Ho No Hatten To Genjo (Comparative Jurisprudence in Japan: Its Past and Present)*, 89 Hogaku Kyokai Zasshi 1244–87 (1972–73),

During the nineteenth century, Western states were forced to realize that non-Christian countries such as Turkey, Persia, Siam, Japan, and China needed to be included within the international legal structure. It was never exactly clear what was needed to be admitted to the family of nations. The British scholar T. J. Lawrence wrote in 1895 that "a certain degree of civilization is necessary, though it is difficult to define the exact amount."[73] "It would, for instance, be absurd to expect the king of Dahomey to establish a Prize Court, or to require the dwarfs of the central African forest to receive a permanent diplomatic mission."[74] In 1856, the European nations formally admitted Turkey into their "family of nations" in Clause 7 of the Treaty of Paris, after the Crimean War, which had been concluded to maintain the balance of power in Europe.[75] Western countries started dealing with China as a "state" for at least certain purposes because of the relationships that developed after China's defeats in the Opium Wars of 1840 and 1856.[76] Japan forced itself in by defeating China in 1894–95 and Russia in 1904–05.[77] In 1900, the U.S. Supreme Court referred to "the Empire of Japan" as "the last state admitted into the rank of civilized nations."[78] Africa continued to be completely excluded in a formal sense, and at the Berlin Conference on Africa in 1884–85, "where European powers agreed on rules for dividing between themselves territories which they had not yet occupied or even explored,"[79] no African representative was invited. But the colonial process forced Europeans to come to grips with the rest of world, and as Professor Anghie has explained, "[i]t was principally through colonial expansion in the nineteenth century that international law became universal. . . ."[80]

---

reprinted in THE JAPANESE LEGAL SYSTEM: INTRODUCTORY CASES AND MATERIALS 196–97 (Hideo Tanaka ed., 1976).

73 T. J. LAWRENCE, THE PRINCIPLES OF INTERNATIONAL LAW 58 (1895).

74 *Id.*

75 *See* Abi-Saab, *supra* note 14, at 37 and *see generally* SIR TRAVERS TWISS, THE LAW OF NATIONS CONSIDERED AS INDEPENDENT COMMUNITIES 88–124 (1884) (discussing in some detail the status of the Ottoman Empire under international law).

76 China was not enthusiastic about the Western international law "concept of a community of equal States adhering to a common code for intercourse," and preferred their own customs and world order. Thomas, *supra* note 13, at 826 (*quoting from* Wang Tieya, *International Law in China: Historical and Contemporary*, 221:2 HAGUE RECEUIL 203, 226 (1990)).

77 A Japanese diplomat was quoted as having said that "We show ourselves equal to you in scientific butchery, and at once we are admitted to your council tables as civilized men." ROLING, *supra* note 9, at 27.

78 *The Paquete Habana*, 175 U.S. 677, 700 (1900).

79 Abi-Saab, *supra* note 14, at 37.

80 Antony Anghie, *Colonialism and the Birth of International Institutions: Sovereignty, Economy, and the Mandate System of the League of Nations*, 34 N.Y.U. J. INT'L L. & POL. 513, 516 (2002).

Writing in 1905, Oppenheim declared that 72 European and 21 American states were in the family of nations, but that "in Asia only Japan is a full and real member of the Family of Nations, Persia, Korea, China, Siam and Tibet are, for some parts, only within the family."[81] The British scholar T. J. Lawrence was more positive with regard to China, writing in 1895 that "Turkey, China and Japan were formally placed under International Law as soon as they expressed a desire to submit themselves to it."[82]

The Western countries negotiated a wide series of multilateral treaties in the second half of the nineteenth century, but Asian countries were not centrally involved in any of these negotiations.[83] China "did not adhere to the Universal Postal Union until 1897, 20 years after its inception, and this was the first public international organisation in which she took part."[84]

B. *The Content of International Law at the Time*

Because international law was viewed as regulating activities among states, it covered only selected topics and left many issues unregulated. International law required that treaties be followed (*pacta sunt servanda*), it ensured the immunity of diplomats, it regulated the treatment of foreigners or aliens in some detail, it provided rules allowing for free use of the seas, and it had some principles governing the use of armed force. The Western books on international law that had the earliest impact in Asia were Henry Wheaton's 1836 book entitled *Elements of International Law*, which was translated into Chinese in 1864 and reprinted in Japan in 1865, Theodore D. Woolsey's *Introduction to the Study of International Law* (1864), James Kent's *Commentaries on International Law* (1826), and J. Bergeon's *Le Droit International de l'Europe* (1873).[85]

Woolsey was president of Yale College and his book was republished with editions several times.[86] His book begins with a discussion of the theoretical underpinnings of international law and then contains chapters on the sovereign rights of independent states, their rights in the oceans and rivers, the rights of aliens in foreign countries, the rights of diplomats to immunity, the law governing treaties, and the laws that apply in armed conflicts. The material on the use of force fills half of the volume, covering neutrality in some detail as well as the justifications for using force and the limitations on its use.

---

81 Thomas, *supra* note 13, at 822 (quoting from OPPENHEIM, INTERNATIONAL LAW 37 (1st ed. 1905)).

82 LAWRENCE, *supra* note 73, at 59.

83 Thomas, *supra* note 13, at 828.

84 *Id.*

85 R. P. Anand, *Family of "Civilized States and Japan: A Story of Humiliation, Assimilation, Defiance and Confrontation*, 5 J. HIST. INT'L L. 1, 19 (2003); Thomas, *supra* note 13, at 832.

86 *See, e.g.*, WOOLSEY, *supra* note 65.

Other international law treatises of the time were similarly sparse in the topics they covered. T. J. Lawrence's 1895 book[87] also devotes more than half its pages to the laws governing armed conflict, and otherwise covers diplomatic immunity, the equality of states, methods of acquiring territory, jurisdiction, maritime principles, and has brief references to piracy and slavery.

The late nineteenth century was a period of intense imperialism, with France, Britain, and Germany competing for colonies in Africa, Asia, and the Pacific, and the United States joining the fray with its acquisitions of the Philippines, Guam, and Puerto Rico in the Spanish-American War in 1898 and annexation of Hawaii that same year. Japan, in particular, learned the lesson that conquest of other territories was part of what it meant to be a "civilized nation."[88]

C. *Japan Becomes a "Civilized Nation"*

In 1900, Justice Horace Gray wrote the majority opinion for the U.S. Supreme Court in *The Paquete Habana*,[89] involving two small fishing vessels that were seized in 1898 as prizes of war during the Spanish-American War. President William McKinley had decreed that U.S. naval activities should be conducted consistently with "the law of nations applicable to such cases" and "upon principles in harmony with the present views of nations and sanctioned by their recent practice."[90] Justice Gray again explained that international law is part of U.S. law:

> International law is part of our law, and must be ascertained and administered by the courts of justice of appropriate jurisdiction as often as questions of right depending upon it are duly presented for their determination. For this purpose, where there is no treaty and no controlling executive or legislative act or judicial decision, resort must be had to the customs and usages of civilized nations, and as evidence of these, to the works of jurists and commentators who by years of labor, research, and experience have made themselves peculiarly well acquainted with the subjects of which they treat.[91]

He then engaged in an extensive survey of treatises, cases, and historical practices which led to the conclusion that:

> by the general consent of the civilized nations of the world, and independently of any express treaty or other public act, it is an established rule of international law, founded on considerations of humanity to a poor and industrious order of men, and of the mutual convenience of belligerent states, that coast fishing vessels, with their implements and supplies, cargoes and crews, unarmed and honestly pursuing their

---

87 Lawrence, *supra* note 73.
88 Anand, *supra* note 85, at 25–27.
89 *The Paquete Habana*, 175 U.S. 677 (1900).
90 *Id.* at 712 (quoting from President McKinley's decrees of April 22 and 26, 1898).
91 *Id.* at 700.

> peaceful calling of catching and bringing in fresh fish, are exempt from capture as prize of war.[92]

Again, Justice Gray's survey is primarily of European and U.S. scholars, cases, and events, but the Argentine writer Carlos Calvo is included,[93] as is the Japanese scholar Sakue Takahashi.[94]

D. *Twentieth-Century Developments*

The interaction between Western and Asian approaches toward international relations and international law caused both to rethink some of their assumptions and led to renewed efforts to develop international law. During the twentieth century, international law developed substantially, with Asian countries participating actively in that development. Enormous strides have been made in codifying the law governing maritime matters, private transactional disputes, public economic relations, and the human rights that belong to all individuals.

But some important differences still exist between Asian and Western approaches to this subject. Perhaps the most striking concerns dispute-resolution procedures. Numerous international and regional tribunals have been developed, but Asian nations have been reluctant to use them. Only three cases involving East Asian nations have been adjudicated by the International Court of Justice.[95] In 1909, China rejected a Portuguese suggestion that their dispute over Macao's boundary be submitted to the Permanent Court of Arbitration in The Hague for decision. "European and American countries have a bias against East Asian people," the Chinese negotiator is reported to have stated. "Hague arbitration will definitely defend Portugal's interest.... It is better for us to negotiate with Portugal directly so that we may yet have a fifty-fifty chance to succeed."[96] Japan apparently lost interest in utilizing international arbitration after it lost the *House Tax* arbitration in the Permanent Court of Arbitration in 1905. "It was suspected that the Western lawyers who made up the tribunal were strangers to Oriental ideas, principles and theories of jurisprudence and that they had little knowledge of legal and administrative concepts based on Oriental culture, and also that

---

92 *Id.* at 708.

93 *Id.* at 703–04, 708.

94 *Id.* at 700 (quoting SAKUE TAKAHASHI, INTERNATIONAL LAW 11, 178, where he explained that Japan had exempted coastal fishing vessels from seizure in its 1894 war with China).

95 Temple of Preah Vihear (Cambodia v. Thailand), 1962 I.C.J. 6 (June 15); Sovereignty over Pulau Ligitan and Pulau Sipadan (Indon./Malay.), 2002 I.C.J. 625 (Dec. 17); Sovereignty over Pedra Branca/Pulau Batu Puteh, Middle Rocks and South Ledge (Malay./Sing.), 2008 I.C.J. 12 (May 23).

96 Thomas, *supra* note 13, at 827 (*quoting from* JEROME COHEN AND HUNGDAH CHIU, PEOPLE'S CHINA AND INTERNATIONAL LAW 11 (1974)).

they might not be entirely free from racial or religious prejudices in dealing with disputes between European and Asiatic countries."[97]

This attitude and reluctance to use third-party adjudication remains today, and other differences between Western and Asian approaches toward international law can also be identified. Asian countries remain skeptical about certain aspects of customary international law, because they view it as being formed by the practices and expectations of Western countries without active attention to Asian perspectives. They view international law as essentially instrumental in nature rather than normative and are skeptical that international law norms can be viewed as being neutral. They sometimes express skepticism about the "sovereign equality of states," because they are familiar historically with a sense of hierarchy among political communities, and they may believe that such hierarchies can still be found today. They view human rights through a different lens, and are more comfortable than Westerners with notions of "group rights."

But despite these important differences in perspective, international law has become part of the thinking and planning of East Asian nations. "Thus international law . . . , having started its life as a stranger to the country towards the end of the Tokugawa era, has come through some vicissitudes of sunny and rainy days to an age when it is treated [in Japan] as a matter of course by government officials and lawyers in general."[98]

IV. Conclusion

Japan's orderly but cautious bureaucracy has meant that Japan has in recent years rarely taken bold initiatives in its foreign relations. Participants in the Third United Nations Conference on the Law of the Sea (1974–82) sometimes commented that Japan's delegates seemed to be about a year behind the other delegations with regard to the issues being discussed. Japan has made broad claims to extended maritime zones under the 1982 Law of the Sea Convention, which seem to many to go beyond the language in the Convention, and it has significant maritime delimitation disputes with its neighbors.[99]

When Japan's unilateral increase in the harvesting of blue fin tuna was challenged under the dispute-resolution procedures created by the Law of the Sea Convention by New Zealand and Australia in the late 1990s, Japan was able to avoid a decision on the merits by raising formalistic procedural objections to the

---

97 Miyoshi Masahiro, *International Law in the Modern History of Japan*, Hohkei Ronshu [Journal of Legal and Political Studies] 15, n. 136 (Dec. 1994).

98 *Id.* at 20.

99 *See generally* Jon M. Van Dyke, *Disputes Over Islands and Maritime Boundaries in East Asia, in* Maritime Boundary Disputes, Settlement Processes, and the Law of the Sea 39–75 (Seoung-Yong Hong & Jon M. Van Dyke eds., 2009).

proceeding.[100] More recently, however, Japan filed two prompt-release claims in the International Tribunal for the Law of the Sea in 2007 against the Russian Federation, thus trying to take advantage of these new procedures.[101] And in 2010, Australia filed a proceeding against Japan in the International Court of Justice arguing that Japan's "scientific whaling" violates the International Whaling Convention, the Southern Ocean Whale Sanctuary, the Convention on International Trade in Endangered Species of Wild Fauna and Flora, and the Convention on Biological Diversity.[102] This proceeding will test Japan's commitment to third-party dispute resolution procedures and will help define how Japan approaches international law in the coming generations.

---

100 *The Blue Fin Tuna Arbitration* adjudicated under the dispute-resolution procedures of the United Nations Law of the Sea Convention was dismissed on procedural grounds. Southern Bluefin Tuna (Australia and New Zealand v. Japan), ITLOS Case Nos. 3 and 4, Provisional Measures Order (Aug. 27, 1999), *available at* http://www.un.org/Depts/los/ITLOS/Order-tuna34.htm; Award on Jurisdiction and Admissibility (Aug. 4, 2000), *available at* http://www.worldbank.org/icsid/bluefintuna/award080400.pdf. *See* Jon M. Van Dyke, *Louis B. Sohn and the Settlement of Ocean Disputes*, 33 GEO. WASH. INT'L L. REV. 31 (2000).

101 Honshinmaru (Japan v. Russian Federation), Judgment of ITLOS Case No. 14 (Aug. 6, 2007); Tomimaru (Japan v. Russian Federation), Judgment of ITLOS Case No. 15 (Aug. 6, 2007).

102 Whaling in the Antarctic (Australia v. Japan), 2010 I.C.J. 16 (filed June 1, 2010), *available at* http://www.icj-cij.org/docket/files/148/15953.pdf.

CHAPTER EIGHT

JAPAN'S EFFORTS IN UNITED NATIONS PEACEKEEPING OPERATIONS: FROM THE PERSPECTIVES OF INTERNATIONAL LAW AND FOREIGN POLICY-MAKING

Osamu Yoshida*

I. International Law in Diplomacy and Foreign Policy-Making

Since the eighteenth century, the term "diplomacy" has been used with a technical and special meaning, indicating for example, "the art of managing the intercourse and adjusting the relations between states by negotiations"[1] or "la science et l'art de la représentation des États, et des négociations."[2] Today, "foreign policy," a more widely used term in academic discourse, frequently involves goals, strategies, measures, methods, guidelines, directives, understandings, and agreements by which national governments conduct international relations with one another and with other international and non-governmental organizations.[3] Further, "foreign policy-making," a related term, is concerned primarily with a means-end way of considering the goals and actions of the

* Professor of Public International Law and International Organisations at the University of Tsukuba.

1 Edmund A. Walsh, The History and Nature of International Relations 1 (1922).

2 Alphonse Rivier, Principes du droit des gens 432 (1896). *See also* Dictionnaire de la terminologie du droit international 214–15 (1960); Masataka Banno, Gendai Gaikō no Bunseki [Analysis of Modern Diplomacy] 6–11 (1971).

3 *See* Robert Jackson & Georg Sørensen, Introduction to International Relations: Theories and Approaches 226 *et seq.* (4th ed. 2010). According to Morgenthau, "[a] foreign policy, to be successful, must be commensurate with the power available to carry it out." Hans J. Morgenthau, American Foreign Policy: A Critical Examination 117 (1952). *See also* Hideo Sato, Taigai Seisaku [Foreign Policy] 5–6 (1989). On the differences between "diplomacy" and "foreign policy," *see, e.g.*, Gendai Nihon no Kokusai Seisaku [International Policy in Modern Japan] 1–7 (Akio Watanabe ed., 1997).

government.[4] While it could be suggested that international law may frequently have a limited influence on inter-state relations,[5] in the growth of the so-called "legalization of world politics,"[6] namely the legalization of global environmental protection, international economic relations, and so forth, the role and function of international law has greatly increased. In addition, in Japan, it is said that the Treaties Bureau of the Ministry of Foreign Affairs (currently the Bureau of International Legal Affairs), which functions as treaty drafter and interpreter of international law, has exerted a strong influence over its diplomatic policy.[7]

This chapter deals with Japan's efforts in United Nations (UN) peacekeeping operations. After the Gulf Crisis of 1990–1991, Japan has come to recognize the need to contribute actively, while being within its constitutional framework, to UN peacekeeping operations.[8] As will be mentioned below, UN peacekeeping operations are peculiar international systems developed within the framework of the UN Charter, and Japan's efforts towards and contributions to peacekeeping operations can be considered as a unique legal process and development involving some elements of foreign policy-making. Japan has created a legal framework that enables it to participate in UN peacekeeping operations and other international activities.[9] The compatibility between the domestic framework and the practice of UN peacekeeping operations is one of the issues highlighted in this chapter.[10]

---

[4] JACKSON & SØRENSEN, *supra* note 3, at 226. On the essentials of foreign policy-making, *see* GRAHAM ALLISON & PHILIP ZELIKOW, ESSENCE OF DECISION: EXPLAINING THE CUBAN MISSILE CRISIS (2d ed. 1999).

[5] On this point, *see, e.g.*, Arthur Watts, *The Importance of International Law, in* THE ROLE OF LAW IN INTERNATIONAL POLITICS 5 (Michael Byers ed. 2000); R. St. J. Macdonald, *Influence of Legal Considerations upon Foreign Policy, in* 2 ENCYCLOPEDIA OF PUBLIC INTERNATIONAL LAW 442–46 (1995).

[6] *See, e.g.*, LEGALIZATION OF WORLD POLITICS (Judith L. Goldstein et al. eds., 2001).

[7] Shotaro Yachi, *The Role of the Treaties Bureau of the Ministry of the Foreign Affairs in Japan's Foreign Policy Decision-Making Process*, 31 JAPANESE ANN. INT'L L. 82 (1988).

[8] *See generally* UN PEACE-KEEPING OPERATIONS: JAPANESE POLICY AND PRACTICE (Ministry of Foreign Affairs of Japan ed., Apr. 1997).

[9] This paper does *not* deal with issues directly concerning Article 9 of the Japanese Constitution. On this subject, *see* Toshiya Ueki, *9 Jō to Anzenhoshō Taisei: Kokusaihōgaku no Shiten kara* [*Article 9 and Security System: From the Perspective of the Science of International Law*], 1260 JURISUTO 82 (2004); Yoshiro Matsui, *United Nations' Activities for Peace and the Constitution of Japan, in* TRILATERAL PERSPECTIVES ON INTERNATIONAL LEGAL ISSUES: RELEVANCE OF DOMESTIC LAW AND POLICY 495 (Michael K. Young & Yuji Iwasawa eds., 1996).

[10] On the significance of international law in the area of Japan's diplomacy, *see* Shunji Yanai, *International Law in Japanese Diplomacy*, KOKUSAI SHAKAI NO HŌ TO SEIJI [L. & POLITICS IN INT'L SOC'Y] 156 (Japanese Soc'y of Int'l L. ed., 2001).

II. United Nations Peacekeeping Operations

In light of the series of various activities since the General Assembly's establishment of the United Nations Emergency Forces (UNEF I) in 1956,[11] although there is no universally accepted definition of peacekeeping operations,[12] they may be defined generally as

> the deployment of a United Nations presence in the field, hitherto with the consent of all the parties concerned, normally involving United Nations military and/or police personnel and frequently civilians as well. Peacekeeping is a technique that expands the possibilities for both the prevention of conflict and the making of peace.[13]

While the UN Charter of 1945 in itself contains no explicit provisions or written principles and rules for peacekeeping operations, its international legal basis was in effect subsequently confirmed by the *Advisory Opinion concerning Certain Expenses of the United Nations*[14] by the International Court of Justice (ICJ). The Court stated that actions appropriate for the fulfillment of the purposes mentioned in Article 2 of the UN Charter could not be considered *ultra vires* and did not transgress the competency of the UN.[15] In this case, the Court referred to Articles 11, 14, and 22 of the Charter as specific provisions on which peacekeeping operations organized by the General Assembly can be based.[16] Further, at

---

[11] G.A. Res. 998 (ES-1), 563d plen. mtg, (Nov. 4, 1956), G.A. Res. 1000 (ES-1), 565th plen. mtg, (Nov. 5, 1956), G.A. Res. 998 (ES-1), 567th plen. mtg, (Nov. 7, 1956), *reproduced in* Basic Documents on United Nations and Related Peace-Keeping Forces: With an Appendix on UN Military Observer Missions 3–6 (Robert C.R. Siekmann ed., 2d ed. 1989). On UNEF I, *see, e.g.*, 1 Rosalyn Higgins, united nations peacekeeping 1946–1967, 219 *et seq.* (1969); Abdel-Latif M. Zeidan, The United Nations Emergency Force 1956–67 (1976).

[12] *See* Boris Kondoch, International Peacekeeping 13–14 (2007).

[13] The Secretary-General, *Report of the Secretary-General on An Agenda for Peace: Preventive Diplomacy, Peacemaking and Peace-keeping*, pursuant to the statement *adopted by the Summit Meeting of the Security Council on 31 January 1992*, U.N. Doc. A/47/277–S/24111 (June 17, 1992). It is said that the term "peace operations" includes activities of peacekeeping, conflict prevention and peace-making, and peace-building. Kondoch, *supra* note 12, at 16. *See also* Shigeru Kozai, Kokuren no Heiwaiji Katsudō [United Nations Peacekeeping Operations] 1–7 (1991).

[14] Certain expenses of the United Nations art. 17, para. 2 of the Charter, Advisory Opinion, 1962 I.C.J. 151 (July 20). On this case, *see, e.g.*, Akio Morita, *Kokuren Keihi Jiken* [*Case concerning Certain Expenses of the United Nations*], *in* Kokusaihō Kihon Hanrei [Basic Cases of International Law] 170 (Takane Sugihara & Hironobu Sakai eds., 2010).

[15] Certain expenses of the United Nations, *supra* note 14, at 168; Leo Gross, *Expenses of the United Nations for Peace-Keeping Operations: The Advisory Opinion of the International Court of Justice*, 17 Int'l Orgs. 1 (1963).

[16] With regard to the legal basis of UN peacekeeping operations, *see* Nigel D. White, *The UN Charter and Peacekeeping Forces: Constitutional Issues*, 3 International

present, most peacekeeping operations are established by the UN Security Council as sub-organs under Article 29 of the Charter. Thus, it may be safe to say that peacekeeping operations have gradually formed as a matter of "subsequent practice"[17] as an important aspect of so-called UN Law. Member states' participation in these peacekeeping activities could be regarded as the partial implementation of the developing legal system as a "constitution" of the international community.[18]

Based on the experience gained from early peacekeeping operations, particularly UNEF-I and ONUC (Opération des Nations Unies au Congo),[19] the following requirements and guiding principles were developed for the establishment of peacekeeping operations:[20]

(i) existence of a truce or cease-fire;[21]
(ii) consent of all parties to the conflict (UNEF-I) or establishment of the operation at the request of the parties (ONUC);[22]
(iii) impartiality or neutrality (no involvement in the conflict, no favouring of one party over the other);[23]

PEACEKEEPING 43 (1996): ALEXANDER ORAKHELASHVILI, *The Legal Basis of the United Nations Peace-keeping Operations*, 43 VA. J. INT'L L. 485 (2003).

17 *See* KOKUSAIHŌ KŌGI [LECTURES ON INTERNATIONAL LAW PRACTICE] 383–84 (Masaharu Yanagihara, Koichi Morikawa & Atsuko Kanehara eds., 2010); Shinya Murase, 2 *Anzenhoshō ni kansuru Kokusaihōto Nihonhō* [*International Law relating to Security and Japanese Law*] 1350 JURISUTO 61 (2008); SHINYA MURASE, *Security Council Resolutions and Japanese Law*, *in* KOKUREN ANPORI NO KINŌ HENKA [CHANGING FUNCTIONS OF THE UN SECURITY COUNCIL] 149, 155 (Shinya Murase ed., 2009).

18 On this subject, *see, e.g.*, JAN KLABBERS, ANNE PETERS & GEIR ULFSTEIN, THE CONSTITUTIONALIZATION OF INTERNATIONAL LAW 19–25 (2009).

19 *See generally* GEORGES ABI-SAAB, THE UNITED NATIONS OPERATION IN THE CONGO 1960–64 (1978).

20 *See* The Secretary-General, *Report of the Secretary-General on Summary Study of the Experience derived from the Establishment and Operation of the Force*, UN Doc. A/3943 (Oct. 9, 1958). *See also* Lilly Sucharipa-Behrmann, *Peace-Keeping Operations of the United Nations*, *in* THE UNITED NATIONS: LAW AND PRACTICE 91–92 (Franz Cede & Lilly Sucharipa-Behrmann eds., 2001); YANAGIHARA, MORIKAWA & KANEHARA, *supra* note 17, at 383; TAKAHIRO SHINYO, SHIN KOKUREN RON [NEW THEORY OF THE UNITED NATIONS] 140–41 (1995). *Cf.* KOKUSAI HEIWA KYŌRYOKU NYŪMON [INTRODUCTION TO INTERNATIONAL PEACE COOPERATION] 192–96 (Takahiro Shinyo ed., 1995).

21 This principle is intended to reduce the chances that Japanese personnel would face situations in which they would need to use their weapons. *See* L. WILLIAM HEINRICH JR., AKIHO SHIBATA & YOSHIHIDE SOEYA, UN PEACEKEEPING OPERATIONS: A GUIDE TO JAPANESE POLICIES 96 (1999).

22 *See* HILAIRE MCCOUBREY & NIGEL D. WHITE, THE BLUE HELMETS: LEGAL REGULATION OF UNITED NATIONS MILITARY OPERATIONS 69–75 (1996).

23 *See* MCCOUBREY & WHITE, *supra* note 22, at 75–84; Shyla Vohra, *Impartiality in United Nations Peace-Keeping*, 9 LEIDEN J. INT'L L. 63 (1996).

(iv) use of force only in self-defense or if hindered by force to fulfill the mandate;[24] and

(v) personnel of peacekeeping operations must take orders only from the commander of the operation and not from the organs of the sending state.

Traditional peace operations (first generation) were mostly designed to respond to inter-state conflicts by stationing unarmed or lightly armed UN forces between hostile parties to monitor a truce, troop withdrawal, or buffer zone while political negotiations proceeded. After the Cold War ended, peace operations were involved in intra-state conflicts, and they came to assume not only a military function but police and administrative functions as well (multi-functional operations or second generation peace operations).[25] Third generation peace operations extend from low-level military operations to protect the delivery of humanitarian assistance to the enforcement of cease-fire and authoritative assistance in the rebuilding of failed states. It is suggested that their distinct characteristics lay in the lack of strict consent by one or more parties to some or all of the United Nations mandates.[26]

---

[24] *See* Basic Principles on the Use of Force and Firearms by Law Enforcement Officials, paras. 9–11, U.N. Doc. A/CONF.144/28/Rev. 1, at 110, *reproduced in* DOCUMENTS ON THE LAW OF UN PEACE OPERATIONS 444–48 (Bruce Oswald, Helen Durham & Adrian Bates eds., 2010); Article 21 of the Convention on the Safety of United Nations and Associated Personnel (New York), U.N. Treaty Series, Vol. 2051, at 363 (Dec. 9, 1994), *reproduced in id.* at 188–93. *See generally* MCCOUBREY & WHITE, *supra* note 22, at 84–88. For example, in the case of the United Nations Peacekeeping Force in Cyprus (UNFICYP), the Aide-mémoire concerning some questions relating to the function and operation of the UNFICYP states that "[w]hen acting in self-defense, the principle of minimum force shall always be applied, and armed force will be used only when all peaceful means of persuasion have failed. The decision as to when force may be used under these circumstances rests with the commander on the spot whose main concern will be to distinguish between an incident which does not require fire to be opened and those situations in which troops may be authorized to use force. Examples in which troops may be so authorised are: (a) attempts by force to compel them to withdraw from a position, which they occupy under orders from their commanders, or to infiltrate and envelop such positions as are deemed necessary by their commanders for them to hold, thus jeopardizing their safety; (b) attempts by force to disarm them; (c) attempts by force to prevent them from carrying out their responsibilities as ordered by their commanders." *See* S.C. Res. S/5653, at 4, ¶ 18, U.N. Doc. S/5653 (Apr. 11, 1964).

[25] *See, e.g.*, JAMES COCKAYNE & DAVID MALONE, *United Nations Peace Operations Then and Now*, 9 INTERNATIONAL PEACEKEEPING 1 (2004).

[26] *See* Michael W. Doyle & Nicholas Sambanis, *Peacekeeping Operations*, *in* THE OXFORD HANDBOOK ON THE UNITED NATIONS 327 *et seq.* (Thomas G. Weiss & Sam Daws eds., 2007).

III. Law concerning Cooperation for United Nations Peacekeeping Operations and Other Operations

During the so-called Cold War period, Japan's personnel contribution to the UN sponsored peacekeeping activities was severely limited, and Japan never sent abroad any personnel from the Japan Self-Defense Forces (SDF) to act as peacekeepers.[27] Due to a highly sensitive issue surrounding constitutional controversies, sending the SDF abroad was considered to require explicit provisions for allowing such activities.[28]

In September 1991, the International Peace Cooperation Bill was presented to the Diet. After a controversial parliamentary debate, the Law concerning Cooperation for United Nations Peacekeeping Operations and Other Operations (International Peace Cooperation Law or PKO law) was passed on June 15, 1992 and came into effect on August 10 that year (Act No. 79 of June 19, 1992).[29] It aims to enable Japan to participate in UN peacekeeping operations, international humanitarian relief operations, and international election observer operations[30] and is based on the following "Five Principles" that provided the basis for the Bill's drafting:[31]

1. Agreement on a cease-fire shall have been reached among the parties to the conflict.[32]
2. Consent for the undertaking of United Nations peacekeeping operations as well as Japan's participation in such operations shall have been obtained from the host countries as well as the parties to armed conflicts.[33]

---

[27] However, in 1989, twenty-seven Japanese election monitors (civilian personnel) participated in the United Nations Transition Assistance Group (UNTAG) and six election monitors in the United Nations Observer Mission to Verify the Electoral Process in Nicaragua (ONUVEN). *See* Shunji Yanai, *Law concerning Cooperation for United Nations Peace-keeping Operations and Other Operations: Japanese PKO Experience*, 36 Japanese Ann. Int'l L. 33 (1993); Hugo Dobson, Japan and United Nations Peacekeeping: New pressures, New Responses 56–57 (2003).

[28] *See* Yanai, *supra* note 27, at 33–34.

[29] Text of unofficial English translation *in* 36 Japanese Ann. Int'l L. 272–89 (1993). A revised text is available at http://www.pko.go.jp/PKO_E/pko_main_e.html. On a detailed analysis of the legislation process, *see* Yanai, *supra* note 27, at 37 *et seq.*

[30] Preamble of the Act on Cooperation for United Nations Peacekeeping Operations and Other Operations. The term "international election observer operations" was added in 1998 amendments (discussed below).

[31] For the significance and background of the Principles, *see* Yanai, *supra* note 27, at 41 *et seq.*; Gaikō Gekihen—Drastic Changes in Japan's Diplomacy: Yanai Shunji—Moto Gaimushō Jimujikan [Administrative Vice-Minister of the Ministry of Foreign Affairs] 85–88 (Makoto Iokibe, Motoshige Ito & Katsuyuki Yakushiji eds., 2007).

[32] Act on Cooperation for United Nations Peacekeeping Operations and Other Operations, No. 79 (June 19, 1992), art. III(1).

[33] *Id.* arts. III(1) and VI.1(1).

3. The peacekeeping force shall strictly maintain impartiality, not favoring any party to the conflict.[34]
4. Should any of the requirements in the above-mentioned guideline cease to be satisfied, the international peace cooperation corps may suspend international peace cooperation assignments. Unless the requirements are satisfied again in the short term, the Government of Japan may terminate the dispatch of the personnel engaged in international peace cooperation assignments.[35]
5. Use of weapons shall be limited to the minimum necessary to protect the lives of personnel.[36]

The Five Principles were largely conformable to the already established principles of UN peacekeeping operations, and it is thus said that Japan intended to limit its participation to the traditional type of peacekeeping.[37] With regard to the last point, namely, the minimal use of weapons by SDF units, Shunji Yanai, former Director-General of the Treaties Bureau of the Ministry of Foreign Affairs, stated the following in the Special Committee on Peace Cooperation with the United Nations at the House of Councillors:

> In any case, it is observed that the minimum use of weapons by contingents of the Member States, participating in United Nations peacekeeping operations, in order to protect the lives of such personnel do not constitute the use of force prohibited in international law.[38]

The specific assignments undertaken by Japan for peacekeeping operations are provided for in Article III(1).[39] The so-called "core" missions such as "monitoring

---

34 *Id.* art. III(1).
35 *Id.* arts. VI.13 and VIII.1(6).
36 *Id.* art. XXIV.
37 Shigeru Kozai, *UN Peace-Keeping and Japan: Problems and Prospects*, *in* Japan and International Law: Past, Present and Future, International Symposium to mark the Centennial of the Japanese Association of International Law 35 (Nisuke Ando ed., 1999); Yanai, *supra* note 27, at 49.
38 *See* the Minutes of the Special Committee on Peace Cooperation with the United Nations at the House of Councillors, 122d Sess., No. 4, at 22 (Dec. 6, 1991) (quoted in Ryo Yamamoto, *Legal Issues concerning Japan's Participation in United Nations Peace-Keeping Operations*, 47 Japanese Ann. Int'l L. 136, 152 (2005)).
39 They include:
- Monitoring the observance of cessation of armed conflicts and demobilization of armed forces;
- Stationing and patrol in areas demarcated for preventing the occurrence of armed conflicts;
- Inspection or identification of the carrying in or out of weapons;
- Collection, storage, or disposal of abandoned weapons;
- Assistance for the designation of cease-fire lines and other boundaries;
- Assistance for the exchange of prisoners-of-war;
- Observation or management of fair execution of elections or plebiscites;
- Advice or guidance for and supervision of police administrative matters;

the observance of cessation of armed conflict or the implementation of relocation, withdrawal, or demobilization of armed forces as agreed upon among the parties to armed conflict" undertaken by SDF units[40] are subject to *prior approval* by the Diet,[41] and the dispatch of a contingent to these peacekeeping activities—going beyond a logistical nature—are to be "frozen" until a new legislation is enacted.[42]

Subsequently, in 1995, a review process of the law was initiated in accordance with Article III of the Additional Provisions, and in June 1998, the amended law was passed and promulgated (Act No. 102 of June 12, 1998). The following three amendments were made to allow the government to contribute more effectively to the effort towards international peace by the UN and other bodies:

1. Japan can cooperate in international election monitoring activities which are conducted with the involvement of the United Nations and/or certain regional organizations, and which do not take the form of UN peacekeeping operations.[43]
2. Japan can provide cooperation in kind to humanitarian international relief operations undertaken by certain international organizations even where no formal ceasefire agreement has been reached.[44]
3. Use of weapons by members of the Self-Defense Forces and other staff participating as a unit must, in principle, be at the order of the senior officer present at the scene.[45]

- Advice or guidance for administrative matters;
- Medical care, including sanitary measures;
- Search or rescue of afflicted people or assistance for their repatriation;
- Distribution of food, clothing, medical supplies, and other commodities to afflicted people;
- Installation of facilities or equipment to accommodate afflicted people;
- Repair or maintenance of facilities or equipment damaged by conflicts that are necessary for the daily life of afflicted people;
- Restoration of natural environment subjected to pollution and other damage by conflicts; and
- Transportation, storage, communication, construction, and installation of machines and apparatus.

40 These "core" missions are provided for in (a) to (f) of Article III(3) and the tasks in (q) of Article III(3) as prescribed by Cabinet Order.

41 Act on Cooperation for United Nations Peacekeeping Operations and Other Operations, *supra* note 32, art. VI(7).

42 *Id.* art. II of the Additional Provisions.

43 *Id.* art. III.2(2).

44 *Id.* art. III.4.

45 *Id.* art. XXIV.

The amended law paved the way for the Japanese government's cooperation in the OSCE's (Organization for Security and Co-operation in Europe) election monitoring operation in Bosnia-Herzegovina in September 1999, and Japan dispatched twenty-five election management and five monitoring staff members to participate in this operation.[46]

As of December 31, 2009, although Japan is second in terms of financial contributions, accounting for 12.5 percent of the peacekeeping budget (after the United States' 27.17 percent—see Figure 2), it only ranks 84th in the total number of participants (police, military experts on mission and troops).[47]

IV. Compatibility of the Peacekeeping Law with the Practice of the United Nations and Relevant International Legal Norms

As Minoru Tanba, former Director-General of the United Nations Bureau of the Ministry of Foreign Affairs, remarked in the Special Committee on Peace Cooperation with the United Nations at the House of Councillors, "self-defense" under UN peace operations is divided into two types:

> According to the practices and documentation of the United Nations, it is permitted for personnel participating in United Nations peacekeeping forces to carry small-sized weapons. They may use these weapons only for self-defense, including in the following situations. First, they may use weapons in order to safeguard their own lives. Second, they may use these weapons to prevent possible obstruction of their mission by an aggressive party to the conflict. While it is crystal clear that the use of weapons would be permitted, as *a natural law right* in the former case, it is not necessarily so in the latter case. It cannot be totally overlooked that in the same situations the use of weapons would constitute the use of force prohibited by the Constitution.[48]

Consequently, the SDF units' resorting to self-defense has been restricted to only the first type of self-defense for safeguarding their lives. In this respect, however, an amendment was made in 2001 to the PKO law, which permits the use of weapons by the SDF to protect "the lives or bodies of themselves, other Corps Personnel who are with them on the scene, or individuals who have come under their

---

46 Ministry of the Foreign Affairs of Japan, Diplomatic Bluebook 1999, Ch. II: Sectoral Analysis of the International Situation and Japan's Foreign Policy, Sec. 1: Ensuring Peace and Stability, Efforts toward the Realization of World Peace (1999), *available at* http://www.mofa.go.jp/policy/other/bluebook/1999/index.html.

47 *See* Peace and Security Section of the United Nations, Department of Public Information, *Year in Review: United Nations Peace Operations 2009*, 67, 72 (Jan. 2010).

48 *See* Minutes of the Special Committee on Peace Cooperation with the United Nations at the House of Councillors, 123d Sess., No. 14, at 24 (June 1, 1992), *quoted in* Yamamoto, *supra* note 38, at 153 (translation partly modified) [Minutes of the Special Committee on Peace Cooperation].

control during the performance of duties."[49] This largely resembles the related provisions of the Antiterrorism Special Measures Law.[50] Further, the amendment lifted the freeze on SDF participation in the United Nations peacekeeping forces that are engaged in activities such as monitoring ceasefires and disarming local forces,[51] and it also lifted the ban on the application of Article 95 of the SDF law which provided that weapons may be used to protect weapons stores.[52]

What was the background of this amendment? It may be safe to assume that there was general agreement that the International Peace Cooperation Law was not necessarily compatible with the practice of UN peacekeeping operations.[53] In previous peacekeeping experiences, SDF units had been engaged in various activities (i.e., transport of personnel) with other UN personnel, UN officials, and non-governmental agencies.[54] For instance, some former Japanese peacekeepers who participated in UNDOF took a stand, stating that the current policy negatively affected Japanese SDF cooperation with forces from other states (see Figure 1). In addition, a director from the Department of Peacekeeping Operations (DPKO) in the UN urged the amendment of the International Peace Cooperation Law.[55] Despite a series of amendments, however, some problems still remain unresolved.

As described above, the use of weapons is strictly limited to self-defense as "a natural law right" for self-preservation, while at present the SDF or Japanese peacekeepers can protect "other corps personnel who are with them on the scene, or individuals who have come under their control during the performance of duties." In other words, under such domestic law requirements, it cannot be expected that they are able to directly protect other UN personnel who are not present with them at the same spot or who are attacked while performing their peace operations, nor can they be dispatched to other areas to protect other

---

49 *Id.* Article XXIV (1–3) (emphasis added).

50 Article 12 of the Antiterrorism Special Measures Law reads:

> Members of the Self-Defense Forces in charge of Cooperation and Support Activities, Search and Rescue Activities or Assistance to Affected People, may proportionately use weapons when an unavoidable and reasonable cause exists for use of weapons to protect lives and bodies of themselves, other members of the Self Defense Forces who are with them on the scene, or those who are with them on the scene and have come under their control while conducting their duties.

51 Minutes of the Special Committee on Peace Cooperation, *supra* note 48. Article II of the Additional Provisions was deleted.

52 *Id.* Article VIII(8) was deleted.

53 Masahiko Asada, *PKO/PKO Kyōryoku Hō [PKO/PKO Cooperation Law]*, 257 Hōgaku Kyōshitsu 3 (2002).

54 *See in detail* Nihon no Bōei Hōsei [Japan's Defense Law System] 431–32 (Shigenobu Tamura, Kenichi Takahashi & Kazuhisa Shimada eds., 2008).

55 Katsumi Ishizuka, *Japan's Policy towards UN Peacekeeping Operations*, *in* UN Peace Operations and Asian Security 62 (Mely Caballero-Anthony & Amitav Acharya eds., 2005).

non-Japanese corps personnel (i.e., *kaketsuke-keigo*[56] or the use of weapons for "rushing to and guarding" military personnel of other countries participating in the same UN activity and executing duties).[57] With regard to this point, Gen Nakatani, former Defense Agency head, stated at the plenary session of the House of Councilors that "as a generalization, other states armed PKO corps, which act as a unit, will not become an object of defense."[58]

Importantly, with regard to self-defense, the Secretariat of the United Nations insists that '[t]he right of self-defense is not limited to States and applies as an inherent right also to the United Nations. United Nations forces have, accordingly, always been regarded as entitled to the right of self-defense and, expressly for this purpose, have been provided with light infantry weapons. This right has been consistently provided for in the rules of engagement established for each peacekeeping operation since their inception."[59] Perhaps more significantly, after the Cold War ended, in light of the changing situation in a conflict, the UN Security Council has often tended to expand the operations' original self-defense mandate.[60] For instance, UNPROFOR (United Nations Protection Force) was specifically authorized under Chapter VII of the Charter "in carrying out its mandate

---

56 *See* MURASE, *supra* note 17, at 58–59; YUICHI MARUMO, BŌEI HŌSEI [DEFENSE LAW SYSTEM] 66–67 (2007).

57 *See also Report of the Council on Reconstruction of a Legal Basis for Security, reproduced partly in* MINISTRY OF DEFENSE OF JAPAN, DEFENSE OF JAPAN 2009, 400–01 (2009) (saying that "[c]onsequently the Self-Defense Forces have participated in such activities based on a standard different from the international one that allows the use of weapons for 'rushing to and guarding' troops and military personnel of other countries participating in the same UN PKO activity and/or eliminating obstacles to the execution of UN PKO duties. This situation runs counter to common sense and could be criticized by the world community."). In 2007, the Council on Reconstruction of a Legal Basis for Security was established under Prime Minister Shinzo Abe in order to examine possible security policy changes. The full report is *available at* http://www.kantei.go.jp/jp/singi/anzenhosyou/index.html.

58 *See* Minutes of the plenary session of the House of Councilors, 153d Sess., No. 16, at 3 (Dec. 3, 2001) (author's translation).

59 *See* The Right of Self-Defense of United Nations Peacekeeping Forces and the Exercise of This Right, U.N. Charter art. 51 (July 19, 1993), Part Two. Legal Activities of the United Nations and Related Intergovernmental Organizations, Chapter VI. SELECTED LEGAL OPINIONS OF THE SECRETARIATS OF THE UNITED NATIONS AND RELATED INTERGOVERNMENTAL ORGANIZATIONS, UNITED NATIONS JURIDICAL YEARBOOK 1993, 371 (1993) [this extract is referred to *in* Hironobu Sakai, *Kokuren Heiwa Iji Katsudō no aratana Tenkai to Nihon* [*New Development of Peacekeeping Operations and Japan*], 105 KOKUSAIHŌ GAIKŌ ZASSI [J. OF INT'L L. AND DIPL.] 145, 154 (2006).

60 *See* Katherine E. Cox, *Beyond Self-Defense: United Nations Peacekeeping Operations & the Use of Force*, 27 DENV. J. INT'L L. & POL'Y. 239 (1999) (noting that "[u]ltimately it is not clear on what basis force can and cannot be used by peacekeeping operations. Nor is it clear how far the concept of self-defense can be pushed. At the moment it is apparently limitless, able to encompass even the defense of others so long as a legitimate mandate is being pursed.").

in the Republic of Croatia, acting in self-defense, to take the necessary measures, including the use of force, to ensure its security and its freedom of movement."[61] The continued expansion of such notions of self-defense would not be ideal or acceptable from legal, political, and military viewpoints, and it might soon be likely to become incompatible with Japan's Peace Cooperation Law.

The government of Japan takes the stand that, in accordance with the PKO law, while SDF units participating in UN peacekeeping operations are under the operational command (*sashizu*) of the UN, it continues to retain national and general supervision or direction (*shiki* or *shiki-kantoku*) over the SDF units as public servants of the Japanese government.[62] Here, the term supervision or *shiki-kantoku* implies a supervisory authority that includes certain types of disciplinary measures in the national legal system of Japan.[63]

According to government views concerning this issue, it is stated that the exercise of UN command must be compatible with the requirements of the Five Principles.[64] In this context, it appears that emphasis is inevitably laid upon the national character of the SDF units in UN peacekeeping operations, and this leads to the conclusion that Article 9 of the Japanese Constitution[65] would apply directly to these personnel acting as a national organ as well as an international agency.[66]

As Michael Bothe has expressed, it must be noted that, generally speaking, the authority of contributing states has to be exercised in a way that does not jeopardize the exclusive authority of the UN over its entire operations.[67] On this point, the Memorandum of Understanding between the United Nations and [Participating State] contributing Resources to [the United Nations Peacekeeping

---

61 S.C. Res.871, ¶ 9, U.N. Doc. S/RES/871 (Oct. 4, 1993).

62 *See, e.g.*, Statements by Prime Minister Kiichi Miyazawa, Minutes of the Plenary Session at the House of Councillors, 122d Session, No. 5, at 9 (Dec. 4, 1991), also *quoted in* YAMAMOTO, *supra* note 38, at 159. *See also* SHINYA MURASE, *Anzen Hoshō ni kansuru Kokusaihō to Nihon Hō* [*International Law concerning Security and Japan*], 1350 JURISUTO 57 (2008).

63 *See* Statements by Mr. I. Nomura, Deputy Minister of the Cabinet Office, Minutes of the Special Committee on Peace Cooperation with the United Nations at the House of Councillors, 123d Sess., No. 3, at 8 (Apr. 28, 1992), *quoted in* YAMAMOTO, *supra* note 38, at 160.

64 *See* YAMAMOTO, *supra* note 38, at 158; MURASE, *supra* note 17, at 57.

65 Article 9 is as follows:

> Aspiring sincerely to an international peace based on justice and order, the Japanese people forever renounce war as a sovereign right of the nation and the threat or use of force as means of settling international disputes. To accomplish the aim of the preceding paragraph, land, sea, and air forces, as well as other war potential, will never be maintained. The right of belligerency of the state will not be recognized.

66 *See* SAKAI, *supra* note 59, at 152 *et seq.*

67 UN PEACEKEEPING: A DOCUMENTARY INTRODUCTION at xv. (Michael Bothe & Thomas Dörchel eds., 1999). *Cf.* ASADA, *supra* note 53, at 3.

Operation] of 2007 provides that "the Government undertakes to ensure that the Commander of its national contingent is vested with the necessary authority and takes all reasonable measures to maintain discipline and good order among all members of the national contingent to ensure compliance with the United Nations standards of conduct, mission-specific rules and regulations and the obligations towards national and local laws and regulations in accordance with the status-of-forces agreement."[68] Further, Resolution 49/37 of the UN General Assembly stresses "the need for a unified and well-defined United Nation command and control structure, incorporating a clear delineation of functions between United Nations Headquarters and the field, and notes that while operational matters should essentially be the responsibility of the Force Commander, Headquarters is responsible for overall control and political direction."[69] Here, there is a possibility that the compatibility between the conduct of SDF units and the practice of peace operations as an evolving system of the UN law may matter in the near future.[70]

V. Outlook and the Present Situation

As the Japanese government has often reiterated since its admission to the UN in 1956, one of the basic "pillars" of Japanese foreign policy is international cooperation that is centred on, or under the auspice of, the UN (*Kokuren Chūshin Shugi Gaikō*).[71] The *Diplomatic Bluebook 2009* states that "[as] the understanding of the

---

68 Art. 7 (Discipline), 7.5, at 165, UN Doc. A/C.5/63/18 (Jan. 29, 2009). *See also* the 1991 Model Agreement between the United Nations and Member States contributing Personnel and Equipment to United Nations Peace-Keeping Operations (stating that the functions of the United Nations peacekeeping operation are exclusively international and the personnel made available by the participating state shall regulate their conduct with the interests of the United Nations only in view, and except on national administrative matters, they shall not seek or accept instructions in respect of the performance of their duties from any authority external to the United Nations, nor shall the Government of participating state give such instructions to them) [G.A. Res. 46/185, ¶ 9, U.N. Doc. A/RES/46/185, Annex, at 2 (May 23, 1991)].

69 G.A. Res. 49/37, ¶16, U.N. Doc. A/RES/49/37 (Feb. 9, 1995).

70 *See also* Toshiya Ueki, *Buki no Shiyō' no Kokusaihō jō no Konkyo wa Nani ka?* [*What is the Basis of "Use of Weapons" under International Law*], 445 Hōgaku Seminā 56 (1992).

71 In the 1957 edition of the Diplomatic Bluebook, the "UN-centered principle" (Kokuren Chūshin Shugi Gaikō) was defined as a kind of supreme law of the international community, whose compliance should be ensured by all states. *See* Gaiko Seisho [Diplomatic Bluebook] 1957 (Sept. 1957), ch. 3 on "Activities in the United Nations," *available at* http://www.mofa.go.jp/mofaj/gaiko/bluebook/index.html. *See also* Ko Nakamura, *Japan's Role in the United Nations*, 3 Japanese Ann. Int'l L. 93 (1959) (referring to Japan's three principles, i.e., (i) acting in concert with and through the United Nations, (ii) cooperation with the free nations of the West and (iii) collaboration with the countries of Asia and Africa).

Table 1. International peace cooperation activities by the self-defense forces.

Operations	Type of activities	Period of dispatch	Number of personnel
United Nations Transitional Authority in Cambodia (UNTAC)	Ceasefire monitors	Sep. 1992–Sep. 1993	8
	Engineering unit	Sep. 1992–Sep. 1993	600
United Nations Operation in Mozambique (ONUMOZ)	Headquarters staff	May 1993–Jan. 1995	5
	Transport coordination unit	May 1993–Jan. 1995	48
Humanitarian Relief Operations for Rwandan Refugees	Rwandan refugee relief unit	Sep. 1994–Dec. 1994	260
	Air transport unit	Sep. 1994–Dec. 1994	118
United Nations Disengagement Observer Force (UNDOF)*	Headquarters staff	Feb. 1996–Feb. 2009	2
		Feb. 2009	3
	Transport unit	Feb. 1996–	43
Humanitarian Relief Operations to Timor Leste	Air transport unit	Nov. 1999–Feb. 2000	113
Humanitarian Relief Operations for Afghanistan Refugees	Air transport unit	Oct. 2001–	138
United Nations Transitional Administration in Timor Leste (UNTAET) (United Nations Mission in Timor Leste (UNMISET))	Headquarters staff	Feb. 2002–Jun. 2004	7
	Engineering unit	Mar. 2002–Jun. 2004	405
Humanitarian Relief Operations for Iraqi Refugees	Air transport unit	Mar. 2002–Apr. 2003	50
Humanitarian Relief Operations for Iraqi Victims	Air transport unit	Jul. 2003–Aug. 2003	98
United Nations Mission in Nepal (UNMIN)*	Arms monitors	Mar. 2007–	6
United Nations Mission in Sudan*	Headquarters staff	Oct. 2008–	2
United Nations Stabilization Mission in Haiti (MINUSTAH)*	Headquarters staff	Feb. 2010–	2
	Engineering unit	Feb. 2010–	Approx. 350

* Ongoing international peace cooperation activities.

SOURCE: MINISTRY OF DEFENSE OF JAPAN, DEFENSE OF JAPAN 2010, at 564–5 (2010), website of the Secretariat of the International Cooperation Headquarters, Cabinet Office *available at* http://www.pko.go.jp/PKO_E/pko_main_e.html and interview with the Secretariat of the International Cooperation Headquarters, Cabinet Office.

Table 2. Top 10 Providers of assessed financial contributors to United Nations peacekeeping operations.

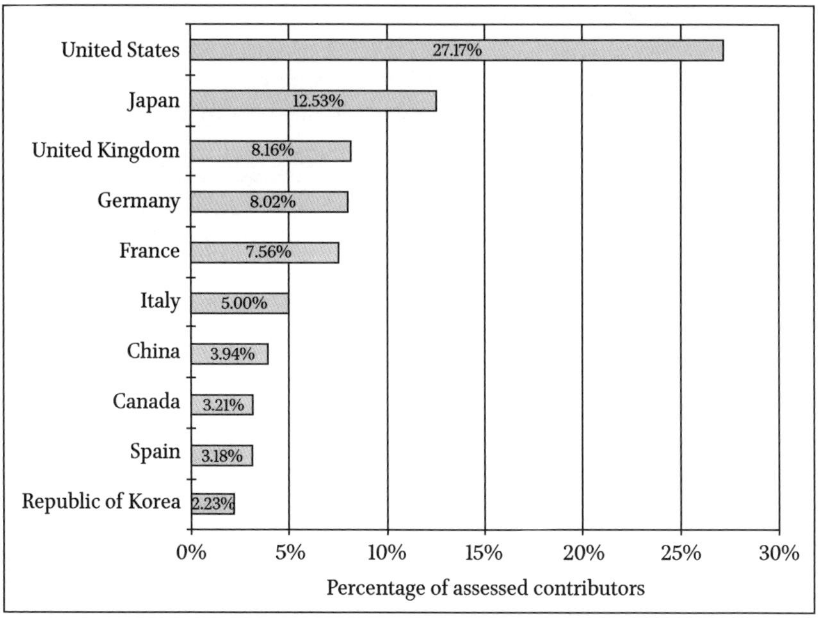

Source: Peace and Security Section of the United Nations, Department of Public Information, Year in Review: United Nations Peace Operations 2009, at 67 (2010).

Japanese people regarding the role of the UN and Japan's efforts is essential for Japan to advance its diplomacy robustly through the UN and other international organizations, Japan will also actively undertake public relations activities."[72] In this respect, voluntary-based international participation in United Nations peacekeeping operations would be likely to help the government realize its stated foreign policy objective.[73] However, it may be suggested, at the same time, that such international cooperation should be consistent with another important pillar of Japanese foreign policy, namely, enhancing relationships with neighboring

---

[72] Ministry of Foreign Affairs of Japan, Diplomatic Bluebook 2009, Ch. 3: Japan's Foreign Policy in Major Diplomatic Field, 25, *also available at* http://www.mofa.go.jp/policy/other/bluebook/index.html.

[73] It is said that, according to a government poll on diplomacy, out of 1,850 people, more than eighty percent supported Japan's participation in UN peacekeeping operations. Masami Ito, *Greater Peacekeeping Role OK, not Truce Enforcement*, Japan Times, Mar. 23, 2010.

countries such as China and the Republic of Korea.[74] Further, while this is not a subject to be dealt with in this chapter, it may be important to bear in mind that the individuals behind UN peacekeeping operations do not always achieve the reputation of being respectable persons holding good character.[75] As the personnel of UN peace operations frequently interact with the local population of the host state, civilian populations or individuals in that country are often subject to unexpected damage or injury from the operations' activities.[76]

The Democratic Party of Japan (DPJ), which became the ruling party in the general elections of August 30, 2009, aims to play a role in building peace by participating in UN peacekeeping operations and related efforts.[77] On November 20, 2009, with a view to rectify Japan's limitations in joining UN peacekeeping operations, Foreign Minister Katsuya Okada called for a review of Japan's Five Principles on PKO participation.[78] With regard to this statement, Deputy Press Secretary Yasuhisa Kawamura explained that:

> The Minister's instruction to review the current PKO principles came out from the recent changes surrounding the United Nations' peacekeeping activities which have become larger in magnitude and more complex in terms of functions. It is indeed a big change, so we need to adapt ourselves better to the newly arriving situations

---

74 On this point, the role of international should be emphasised. *See* in particular collected articles in CHOONG-HYUN PAIK, INTERNATIONAL LAW IN KOREAN PERSPECTIVE (2004).

75 For instance, on Jan. 3, 2007, the Daily Telegraph reported that UN peacekeepers and civilian staff were raping and abusing children as young as 12 in southern Sudan. *Kokuren Yōin, Seiteki Gyakutai ka [United Nations Personnel, Sexual Abuse?]*, ASAHI SHIMBUN, Jan. 5, 2007. *See also* Report of the UN Security Council, *Sexual Exploitation and Abuse by UN Peacekeeping Personnel*, No. 3, 1–6 (Feb. 20, 2006); Muna Ndulo, *The United Nations Responses to the Sexual Abuse and Exploitation of Women and Girls by Peacekeepers During Peacekeeping Missions*, 27 BERKELEY J. INT'L L. 127 (2009).

76 On this topic, *see, e.g.*, UNINTENDED CONSEQUENCES OF PEACEKEEPING OPERATIONS (Chiyuki Aoi, Cedric de Coning & Ramesh Thakur eds., 2007); Marten Zwanenburg, *UN Peace Operations between Independence and Accountability*, 5 INT'L ORG. L. REV. 23 (2008); Daphna Shraga, *UN Peacekeeping Operations: Accountability of International Humanitarian Law and Responsibility for Operations-Related Damage*, 94 AM. J. INT'L L. 406 (2000); Kirsten Schmalenbach, *Third Party Liability of International Organizations: A Study on Claim Settlement in the Course of Military Operations and International Administrations*, 10 INTERNATIONAL PEACEKEEPING 33 (2006); KIRSTEN SCHMALENBACH, DIE HAFTUNG INTERNATIONALER ORGANISATIONEN (2004).

77 *See* Democratic Party of Japan's Platform for Government, 2009 Change of Government, *Putting People's Lives First*, para. 54 (Aug. 18, 2009) at 29, *available at* http://www.dpj.or.jp/english/manifesto/manifesto2009.pdf.

78 *See Japan should seek Ways to join U.N. PKO Operations more actively*, JAPAN TIMES WEEKLY, Nov. 28, 2009. *See also PKO 5-Gensoku, Minaoshi wo Kentō [Considering the Review of the PKO Five Principles]*, ASAHI SHIMBUN, Oct. 22, 2009.

> surrounding PKOs. In that sense, our actions should be taken in an appropriate timing.[79]

In addition, on March 16, 2010, during the meeting of the House of Councillors' Foreign Affairs and Defense Committee, Okada expressed the view that, given the fact that a UN resolution had been adopted, Japan could make it easier for the SDF units to use weapons when they participated in United Nations peace operations abroad.[80]

On January 25, 2010, the Japanese government decided to send an SDF unit to join a UN peacekeeping operation in Haiti with a view to provide humanitarian and reconstruction aid following the earthquake on January 12,[81] and the UN accepted this offer.[82] Since 1993, although the UN has deployed five missions in Haiti, including the present multidimensional UN Stabilization Mission in Haiti (MINUSTAH), none of them have been successful.[83] In the case of Haiti, unlike UNTAC or UNMIS, a formal cease-fire agreement did not exist, and after the earthquake, security and public order deteriorated. It might be said that dispatching the SDF could clash with the government's Five Principles.[84] Further, in order to study the feasibility of dispatching military helicopters to participate in the UN peacekeeping mission in southern Sudan, Japanese experts travelled to Sudan.[85] Since June 2008, UN Secretary-General Ban Ki Moon requested that the SDF join in peacekeeping operations in Sudan.[86] Foreign Minister Okada stated in the Diet that "Japan has made wonderful achievements in Cambodia and East Timor, but it cannot be said that Japan's recent contribution is enough. In order to play a larger role in maintaining and building peace, I will consider further contributions in addition to Haiti."[87]

---

79 Press Conference, Deputy Press Sec'y, Ministry of Foreign Affairs of Japan (Oct. 22, 2009) (on file with author).

80 Minutes of the Committee on Foreign Affairs and Defense, House of Councillors, 174th Sess., No. 3 (Mar. 16, 2010).

81 *Haichi PKO, 300-nin Haken [Dispatching 300 personnel to the PKO in Haiti]*, ASAHI SHIMBUN, Jan. 26, 2010. *See also* S.C. Res. 1908, U.N. Doc. S/RES/1908 (Jan. 19, 2010) regarding Haiti and MINUSSTAH).

82 *Jieitai-PKO, Kokuren ga Ryōshō [UN "approves" a SDF PKO mission]*, ASAHI SHIMBUN, Jan. 30, 2010.

83 *See* LISE MORJÉ HOWARD, UN PEACEKEEPING IN CIVIL WARS 319–21 (2008).

84 *Japan to send Peacekeeping Troops to Haiti*, BBC MONITORING ASIA PAC., Jan. 25, 2010; *PKO 5-Gensoku, hatsu no Reigai [The First Exception of the PKO Five Principles]*, ASAHI SHIMBUN, Feb. 7, 2010.

85 *Sūdan PKO, Heri Haken wo Kentō [Considering to send Helicopters to the PKO in Sudan]*, ASAHI SHIMBUN, May 7, 2010.

86 *Japan considers sending peacekeeping helicopters to Sudan*, SUDAN TRIBUNE, 7 May 2010.

87 Minutes of the Plenary Session of the House of Representatives, 174th Sess., No. 4 (Jan. 29, 2010).

Whatever the measures taken to facilitate Japan's participation in UN peacekeeping operations, the Japanese people should bear in mind what the Deputy Prime Minister and Foreign Minister of Japan declared before the UN General Assembly on the occasion of Japan's entry to the UN on December 18, 1956:

> The people of Japan today desire peace for all time and are deeply conscious of the high ideals controlling human relationships. We have determined to preserve our security and existence, trusting in the justice and faith of the peace-loving peoples of the world. We recognize that all peoples of the world have the right to live in peace, free from fear and want. We desire to occupy an honoured place in an international society striving for the preservation of peace, and the banishment of tyranny and slavery, oppression and intolerance, for all time from the earth. We believe that no nation is responsible to itself alone, but that the laws of political morality are universal; and that obedience to such laws is incumbent upon all nations who would sustain their own sovereignty and justify their sovereign relationship with other nations.[88]

[88] Mamoru Shigemitsu, Deputy Prime Minister and Foreign Minister of Japan, Address before the United Nations General Assembly on the occasion of Japan's admission to the United Nations (Dec. 18, 1956). The whole speech is available in English at the ministry's website, http://www.mofa.go.jp/policy/un/address5612.html. For Shigemitsu's speech, *see also* Yasushi Akashi, *Japan in the United Nations*, 15 JAPANESE ANN. INT'L L. 23, 26–27 (1971).

CHAPTER NINE

THE CHEONAN INCIDENT: A PERSPECTIVE FROM INTERNATIONAL LAW AND POLITICS

Seokwoo Lee and Hee Eun Lee

I. Introduction

On March 26, 2010, the South Korean corvette, *Cheonan*, tragically sank near the Northern Limit Line (NLL), the disputed maritime border between North and South Korea in the West Sea (Yellow Sea) on the South Korean side killing 46 sailors. News of the ship's sinking dominated coverage from the South Korean news media for weeks and included videos of anguished relatives of the young men who lost their lives. At the time, President Lee Myung-bak vowed to find the cause of Cheonan's sinking. In a show of restraint, there was no immediate indication from the South Korean government as to who was to blame though there was widespread speculation that the sinking was caused by North Korea. Calling for a thorough investigation, the South Korean government commissioned the Joint Civilian-Military Investigation Group comprised of investigators from South Korea, the United States, Australia, the United Kingdom and the Kingdom of Sweden. On May 20, 2010 the group issued its final report and laid responsibility for the attack on *Cheonan* solely with North Korea. It concluded that the " '*Cheonan*' was sunk as the result of an external underwater explosion caused by a torpedo made in North Korea."[1] The reaction of the South Korean government was swift. In his speech to the South Korean people several days later on May 24, President Lee enumerated specific steps his government would take in response to the incident which included closing off South Korean waterways to North Korean vessels

[1] Investigation Result on the Sinking of ROKS "Cheonan," Ministry of Nat'l Def. (May 20, 2010), *available at* http://www.mnd.go.kr/webmodule/htsboard/template/read/engbdread.jsp?typeID=16&boardid=88&seqno=871&c=TITLE&t=&pagenum=3&tableName=ENGBASIC&pc=undefined&dc=&wc=&lu=&vu=&iu=&du=&st=.

along with halting all inter-Korean trade with the notable exception of South Korean business activities in the North Korean city of Kaeseong.[2]

Beyond the measures taken by the South Korean government, President Lee also indicated that he would refer the matter to the Security Council with the hope that the member states of the United Nations would hold North Korea accountable. Additionally, in a show of resolve against the North, working in consultation and cooperation with the United States, the two countries conducted a series of joint naval exercises in the East Sea (Sea of Japan). Nevertheless, despite the efforts of the South Korean administration to "internationalize" the incident by attempting to secure a Security Council resolution and to involve US naval forces to pressure North Korea, there appears to be no tangible payoff in South Korea's attempt to magnify the incident. In fact, South Korean efforts seemed to have backfired.

On November 23, less than seven months after the *Cheonan* incident, North Korean artillery shells exploded on Yeonpyeong Island just south of the NLL, not far from the site where *Cheonan* sank, leaving 4 South Koreans dead and 19 injured. South Korea counterattacked with shelling of its own, which according to the South Korean media largely missed their intended targets. Soon afterwards, consistent with its response to the sinking of *Cheonan*, South Korea responded with stern words and naval drills. President Lee declared in a nationally televised address on November 29 that "Now is the time we have to demonstrate our determination with actions rather than many words." From November 28 to December 1, the South Korean navy conducted joint naval drills with the USS George Washington carrier fleet in the West Sea (Yellow Sea).

The domestic and foreign policy decisions made by the South Korean government in response to these attacks revealed the failure of the administration to appreciate the complexities of inter-Korean relations which includes the outstanding and ongoing maritime border issue over the NLL. Needless to say, the relationship between North and South is complicated. It cannot be viewed simply from a political or legal perspective given that the formal relationship between the two countries is defined by the armistice that was concluded at the end of the Korean War. Because the armistice is not a peace treaty, both countries are technically in a state of war even though at the same time, many in the South cannot fathom a return to all out armed conflict. It is quite difficult to assess on the ground whether the situation South Korea finds itself in is a time of war or peace.

Adding to this confusion is the perspective taken from the South Korean Constitution which provides in Article 3 that, "[t]he territory of the Republic of Korea shall consist of the Korean peninsula and its adjacent islands."[3] This leads to the

[2] Lee, Myung-bak, President of Republic of Korea, National Address on Sinking of the Cheonan (May 24, 2010), *available at* http://www.koreatimes.co.kr/www/news/nation/2010/05/113_66392.html.

[3] Const. of the Republic of Korea art. 3 (S. Korea), *available at* http://english.ccourt.go.kr/home/att_file/download/Constitution_of_the_Republic_of_Korea.pdf.

conclusion that the North Korean government is illegitimate and in illegal occupation, and thus the conflict with the North is entirely an internal matter. Yet despite this domestic legal understanding in the South, both countries are members of the United Nations and North Korea is considered to have legal personality under international law as a legitimate state.

This apparent tension that exists between the internal political and legal perspective of South Korea towards the North as a renegade, and the realities of North Korea's international legitimacy have not hampered both countries abilities to manage their relationship. In fact, it could be said that both North and South have been relatively successful in avoiding all out armed conflict through the use of dispute management mechanisms that were put in place after the signing of the armistice. This ability to keep a relative peace shows that inter-Korean relations have a special nature unlike those between other states and that inter-Korean issues should be approached in a sensitive way. However, the Lee administration's handling of *Cheonan* and Yeonpyeong incidents revealed an inability to appreciate this special relationship and brought to the surface a number of unsettled issues that have seemingly confounded the administration's response. These include the question of state recognition of North Korea by the South, along with the related conflict of law between the South Korean Constitution and international law, and the South's foreign policy position on dispute settlement. With no apparent resolution of these issues or clear direction on how to approach these open questions, the administration pressed forward leading towards a series of mistakes, miscalculations, and missed opportunities on the domestic and international fronts complicating the administration's position on dealing with the North.

II. Mistakes, Miscalculation, and Missed Opportunities: Back to the Cold War?

With respect to the *Cheonan* incident, an examination of the domestic actions taken by the Korean government reveal parallels with the administration's response towards the candlelight vigils that took place in reaction to the decision to resume US beef imports at the beginning of Lee Myung-bak's presidency. The administration failed to exercise leadership to shore up public opinion on the issue before it mandated its policies. The result was a deepened ideological gap and doubt within a key segment of the Korean populace because of a lack of transparency in the decision-making process and insufficient explanations given to the public on what precipitated the policy decision. The National Bureau of Audit (the Korean equivalent to the United States' Government Office of Accountability) that examined the government's handling of the incident found that the initial briefing provided by the South Korean military concealed and manipulated crucial evidence and the timeline of events that led up to the sinking of *Cheonan*. While it was quite understandable for the South Korean government keep certain information classified, the kinds of mistakes that were made in this case resulted in a crisis of confidence in the government's handling of the investigation and the subsequent conclusions that were released by the international investigation. There were a significant number of South Koreans who still believe in various conspiracy theories that argue essentially that the Lee administration with assistance from the United States sank *Cheonan* in an effort to shore up public support before crucial local elections that year and to justify the administration's hard line policies toward the North.

On the international front, the administration faced a similar attitude among key neighbors, namely China and Russia, who expressed doubt at the time as to North Korea's culpability. Given the Lee administration's efforts to strengthen strategic ties with the United States, it was not surprising that China and Russia were wary of South Korea's efforts to lay blame on the North. Despite this obvious position, the South Korean government failed to adequately engage both members of the "Permanent Five," to ensure widespread support for Korea's international effort to punish North Korea. Both China and Russia were left off of the Joint Civilian-Military Investigation Group whose conclusions were called into question by both nations. It was under these circumstances that South Korea sought to bring the *Cheonan* incident to the Security Council seeking a resolution that would clearly lay state responsibility of the tragedy on North Korea.

This begs the question of what gave the South Korean government the apparent confidence to bring this matter before the Security Council? More specifically, why did South Korea think that China and Russia would be sympathetic to its cause? Economic relations between South Korea and China and Russia have improved in quantity and quality, but that does not mean that security issues would be positively impacted by improved economic relations. Most notably, despite the magnitude of the incident, the South was unable to get an actual resolution put up for a vote due to the strong initial opposition from China. The resulting presidential statement from the Security Council failed to even mention North Korea specifically by name. While it provided that "the Security Council condemns the attack" and that it "underscores the importance of preventing further such attacks or hostilities against the Republic of Korea,"[4] it essentially did nothing as both North and South claimed victory after it was issued. The North argued that the statement showed that the South failed to prove that it was the culprit for the sinking while the spin from the South was that it showed that the international community was steadfast in its condemnation of North Korea.

All of this revealed that the South Korean government did not have clear minimum standards in terms of the kind of outcome it desired from its efforts at the Security Council. The failure to garner a clear statement attributing responsibility

---

4 President of the Security Council, Statement made on behalf of the Council on Attack on Republic of Korea Naval Ship "Cheonan," U.N. Doc. S/PRST/2010/13 (July 9, 2010), *available at* http://www.un.org/Docs/sc/unsc_pres_statements10.htm.

to North Korea only fueled domestic conspiracy theories that the South Korean government and the United States were somehow responsible for the tragedy. In short, the South Korean government desired to show the North that there was a price to pay for attacking *Cheonan*; however, its effort to bring the international community to punish North Korea resulted in failure and put the South Korean government in the uncomfortable position of having no apparent exit strategy. It revealed a naivety on the part of the South as to the realities of the regional political dynamics at play. By putting forth a resolution in the Security Council that would force China and Russia to reveal their hands on North Korea was hasty and unwise and threatened South Korea's immediate future relations with both countries.

With the course of action set by the Lee administration, the Korean peninsula continues to replay the Cold War bipolar order where the dominance of two hegemonic forces in Northeast Asia largely determined international relations in the region. Where Moscow once was, Beijing has now filled the vacuum created by the collapse of the Soviet Union. The administration's approach in this situation pitted China, along with North Korea and Russia on one side against the United States, Japan, and South Korea on the other. In doing so, it created a sense that the administration failed to manage and take control of the crisis on its own terms by setting a course of action that has essentially taken the political initiative out of South Korean hands and passing it on to the United States which had the risk of further escalating an already delicate situation. At the time, the United States indicated that it would seize North Korean bank accounts in foreign banks that the Treasury Department kept under surveillance. While asserting that it has authority to do so under Security Council Resolution 1874 which was adopted in June of 2009, the timing of this effort seemed to suggest that the United States was signaling that the freezing of North Korean assets was due to the *Cheonan* incident. The timing of this action led to the appearance that the United States was using the matter as a pretext for further action against North Korea.

III. Losing China?

The end result of such an approach was that South Korea likely lost an opportunity to engage the one state that has the most influence over North Korea, that is China. What was particularly troubling was the Lee administration's miscalculated efforts to force China's hand on North Korea. To achieve a Security Council resolution condemning North Korea required the support or neutrality of the Permanent Five. The administration failed to fully engage China and Russia leaving both off the international team investigating the cause of the sinking of *Cheonan*. China's public skepticism of the results of the international investigation despite the overwhelming evidence of North Korean culpability and their apparent opposition to South Korea's efforts to secure a Security Council resolution revealed that the South Korean government failed to take into account China's strategic interests in supporting North Korea.

By referring the case to the Security Council, the South Korean government gave over any diplomatic initiative and control it had in managing its relations with North Korea. By effectively ignoring one hegemon, China, and involving another, the United States, South Korea was no longer in a position to independently deal with North Korea on its own terms. This further complicated the development of an exit strategy that might have been contemplated by the South. A far better approach would have been and continues to be for the South to take the initiative to deal bilaterally with the North on the serious issues that directly impact both sides and are the obvious source of conflict, namely, the problem of the Northern Limit Line.

IV. Northern Limit Line

The United Nations Command and the North Korean army established a Military Demarcation Line on land at the time they signed the Inter-Korean Armistice Agreement on May 27, 1953, but did not extend it into maritime areas. The seaward extension, which became known as the Northern Limit Line (NLL), was drawn by UN Commander General Mark Clarke on August 3, 1958,[5] and is a line that is roughly equidistant between the North Korean coastline and five tiny South Korean islands (Paengnyongdo, Taechongdo, Sochongdo, Yongpyo-Yolto, and Udo, which taken together, contain five square miles of land) that hug the North Korean coast but are controlled by and claimed by South Korea.[6] Its purpose was to prevent a clash between military vessels and aircraft of both sides, and seems originally to have been designed to prevent South Korean naval vessels and aircraft from going north. It has been challenged by North Korea ever

---

5 The fact that General Clarke drew this line on Aug. 30, 1953 has been widely reported, but the document itself does not seem to exist any longer. Interview with Alice Juda, Reference Librarian, U.S. Naval War Coll., in R.I. (July 29, 2009).

6 Some commentators have suggested that North Korea claims these five islands or some of them, *see, e.g.*, Victor Prescott, Maritime Political Boundaries of the World 445 (2004), and Jonathan I. Charney, *Central East Asian Maritime Boundaries and the Law of the Sea*, 89 Am. J. Int'l L. 724, 729 (1995). Recent statements from North Korea indicate, however, that it accepts South Korean sovereignty over the islands, but argues that they should be ignored or enclaved and that the maritime boundary between North and South Korea should be the equidistance line between the two Koreas, drawn without regard to the five islands. *See, e.g., S. Korea Proposes Defense Chiefs' Talks on New Sea Boarder*, Yonhap News Agency of Korea, May 17, 2006 (stating that a North Korean news agency had reported that North Korea "acknowledges South Korea's sovereignty over the five islands in the West Sea and is willing to establish a joint fishing area at the sea border").

since, because it was declared unilaterally and because North Korea views it as an infringement on its sovereignty and its legitimate access to the sea. Because the NLL is not mentioned in the Armistice Agreement itself, its status and that of the waters around it remain contentious.

South Korea acknowledges that the NLL declaration was not officially part of the agreement that marked the cessation of hostilities between the two countries, but argues that the NLL has become the *de facto* border because (1) North Korea did not object to the NLL until October 1973;[7] (2) North Korea implicitly recognized the NLL several times; and (3) the 1991 Basic Agreement stipulates (in Article 11) that "the South-North demarcation line and areas for non-aggression shall be identical with areas that have been under the jurisdiction of each side until the present time" and that the Protocol on Non-Aggression states (in Article 10) that "the South-North sea non-aggression demarcation line shall continue to be discussed in the future. Until the sea non-aggression demarcation has been settled, the sea non-aggression zones shall be identical with those that have been under the jurisdiction of each side until the present time." South Korea thus argues that the NLL cannot be unilaterally challenged or discussed except in a comprehensive agreement to bring permanent peace to the Korean peninsula, and South Korean conservatives view alterations to the NLL as a violation of the Korean Constitution which requires the government to maintain the integrity of the nation's borders. South Korean resistance to creating a joint development zone encompassing territory on both sides of the NLL is based partially on the concern that such an agreement would nullify the line and cede territory to North Korea. The United States concurs that the 1992 Basic Agreement between North and South Korea stipulates that both Koreas must respect the line until a new agreement can be reached.

North Korea counters that when the NLL was drawn, the UN command did not inform Pyongyang, which neither acknowledged nor accepted it. It argues that the NLL illegally restricts its access to the open sea and should be redrawn further to the south to more closely reflect the land demarcation between the two countries.[8] North Korea asserts that it has challenged the line on many occasions during the past 55 years, particularly as the value of the blue crab catch in the area has become more apparent.[9] It also argues that its vessels have regularly

---

7 Republic of Korea Ministry of Nat'l Def., The Republic of Korea Position Regarding the Northern Limit Line (Aug. 2002). "North Korea had observed the NLL for a couple of decades until it challenged the Line in the wake of a series of clashes in the West Sea (or Yellow Sea) in 1973." Suk Kyoon Kim, *Understanding Maritime Disputes in Northeast Asia: Issues and Nature*, 23 Int'l J. of Marine & Coastal L. 213, 220 (2008).

8 *Inter-Korean Generals' Talks Bogged Down over Sea Boarder*, Korea Times, Dec. 14, 2007.

9 DPRK Committee for Peaceful Reunification of Fatherland Secretariat Issues White Paper Rejecting NLL (Aug. 1, 2002). It does not seem to be appropriate to conclude that

fished in the waters claimed by the South, and that since March 1955 it has claimed under customary international law a 12-nautical-mile territorial sea from its coast, which extends well south of the NLL. Because the NLL hugs the North Korean coastline, Pyongyang claims that it unfairly gives too much ocean space to South Korea.

V. A Way Forward: Abandon the Cold War Paradigm and Take the Initiative

If the goal of the South Korean government was to hold North Korea responsible for the 46 innocent lives lost on *Cheonan* and to respond effectively to the attack on Yeonpyeong Island, it had to have better appreciated the realities of a post-Cold War Northeast Asia where economic relations with China are separate from security considerations in the region. It should also have given priority to taking the initiative to settle the outstanding boundary issue over the NLL. Despite the fact that the Lee administration decidedly took a harder line against the North in an about face from the "Sunshine Policy" pursued by his predecessors in the Blue House, South Korea should have addressed the territorial and boundary issues that contextualized the sinking of *Cheonan* and the shelling of Yeonpyeong. Because the sinking of *Cheonan* and the shelling of Yeonpyeong occurred near the NLL, and from the North Korean perspective, within its maritime border, any movement towards resolution will require both sides to resolve this outstanding territorial and boundary issue. Prior to the sinking of *Cheonan*, both sides have lost sailors and ships in 1999 and 2002 due to naval skirmishes near the NLL with each side claiming that the other was in violation of the maritime border. Failure to deal with this contentious maritime border issue will likely lead to future violent conflict which risks further escalation on the peninsula.

South Korea also needs to give proper weight to the critical role that China and Russia play in the region and especially in matters of importance to South Korea. In this regard, it appears that South's economic prosperity and dependence on the United States has caused it to neglect the relative political importance of China and Russia. Seoul must put aside the outdated strategy of pitting former Cold War allies and enemies against each other. Over the years, South Korea has sought to engage China through closer economic ties,[10] yet South Korean policymakers have seemingly forced China into the position of having to choose

North Korea "acquiesced" to the NLL by not protesting more vigorously prior to 1973, since it was not until the early 1970s that the countries of the world began the serious discussions that led to global recognition that coastal countries are entitled to extended maritime zones.

10 China is Korea's largest trading partner with the total volume of trade between the two countries amounting to $140 billion USD.

between improved relations with South Korea or risk destabilizing the North which could lead to thousands if not millions of North Koreans to flee across its largely unmanaged border between the two countries. China chose to side with the North maintaining the Cold War paradigm.

South Korea missed an opportunity to deal with North Korea over *Cheonan* on its own terms by seeking an unlikely Security Council resolution and partnering with the United States in pressuring the North through joint military drills which it also did in response to the North's attack on Yeonpyeong. To regain the initiative, the South Korean government should have put a halt to its policy and find ways to resolve the conflict over the sinking of *Cheonan* and the shelling of Yeonpyeong on the basis of understanding the complex nature of inter-Korean relations. Simply put, South Korea should not have treated *Cheonan* and Yeonpyeong as international legal issues that pit one sovereign state against another and making use of hegemonic forces. By doing so, South Korea further complicated an already complex relationship and lost the chance to constructively resolve the issue on a bilateral basis.

The Lee administration should have focused on developing its policies over these issues with an aim to deal with the North directly as opposed to the strategy it adopted which has sought to increase pressure on the North through the international community and the United States as proxies. That policy failed and only emboldened the North. Instead, the South Korean government should have been more willing to exercise the leverage it had over North Korea. In 2009, inter-Korean trade amounted to $1.6 billion USD which represents 32.8% of North Korea's total trade volume and only 0.24% for South Korea. The Kaesong Industrial Complex situated in North Korea where South Korean companies have established industries employing North Korean workers accounted for 75.5% of inter-Korean trade in 2010. Clearly, North Korea needs Kaesong more than the South. The South Korean government could have severely restricted South Korea business activities at Kaesong thereby reducing the amount of foreign capital available to the North. In his address to the South Korean people on May 24, 2010, President Lee hinted to that possibility when he indicated that "Matters pertaining to the Kaesong Industrial Complex will be duly considered, taking its unique characteristics into consideration." However, the only South Korean action that has been taken regarding Kaesong was to prevent new South Korean investments from entering and reducing the number of South Korean employees at the site. The Lee administration should have given serious weight to shutting down Kaesong in response to the violent North Korean attacks.

VI. Conclusion

South Korea must be able to deal with North Korea on its own terms given the unique relationship that exists between the two countries. By placing its bet on the passage of a Security Council resolution that it ultimately failed to secure in regards to the *Cheonan* incident and ratcheting up the military pressure on North Korea in response to Yeonpyeong, the South's ability to find ways to seek justice for the innocents who lost their lives in both attacks was compromised. The vague wording of the presidential statement from the Security Council and the uncertain legal status of the statement itself left no international legal basis upon which South Korean could have taken further actions against the North. Indeed, the silence of the statement as to state responsibility created the impression that the international community took no stance as to North Korea's culpability. To further complicate the matter, the involvement of the United States brought about concern and skepticism from China which is widely recognized to have the most leverage over North Korea. The Lee administration needed to have abandoned its course of merely declaring stern words and conducting joint naval drills with the US and should have seized the opportunity to play a more active in role in settling the NLL issue on a bilateral basis. The future of inter-Korean relations and justice for those who perished was and continues to be at stake.

CHAPTER TEN

NORTH KOREAN HUMAN RIGHTS AND THE FAILURE OF PROTECTION: THE PLIGHT OF NORTH KOREANS IN FLIGHT

Jae-Chun Won*

I. Introduction

The plight of North Koreans at home and abroad is becoming an international concern. Ever since the terrible food shortage in the mid-1990s, millions of North Koreans either have suffered malnutrition or died from starvation. Although the international community has been providing humanitarian aid to North Korea, the majority of North Koreans still fight for basic survival. They still die from hunger and easily treatable diseases.[1] In addition, in most areas of their lives, basic human rights are not realized. They have little freedom of thought, conscience, and religion.[2] There is no independent mechanism in North Korea to advocate or address the concerns of the weak.[3] Except for those who belong to a privileged

* Professor of Law, Handong International Law School; Former Director-General, National Human Rights Commission of Korea. The author expresses his gratitude to Professor Vitit Muntarbhorn, former UN Special *Rapporteur* on North Korea, for his guidance on this chapter and to Ann Buwalda, Esq. and Professor Tarik Radwan for introducing him to refugee issues. The author expresses his indebtedness to his mentor, Reverend Benjamin Yoon, founder of Citizens' Alliance for North Korean Human Rights, for exemplifying integrity and his unceasing efforts to shine light on the democracy movement in South Korea and on the human rights issues in North Korea. I would also like to give special thanks to Helen Hyun Jin Lee and Daniel Yun Seong Chun for their outstanding research assistance.

1 Human Rights Watch, *World Report 2006 (Events of 2005)*, 292–93 (2006), *available at* http://hrw.org/wr2k6/wr2006.pdf [hereinafter *WR 2006*]; *see also* H. Comm. on Foreign Affairs, North Korean Human Rights Reauthorization Act of 2008, H.R. Rep. No. 110–628, at 5 (2008) [hereinafter 2008 Reauthorization Act Report].

2 *Id.* at 291–92; *see also* Amnesty Int'l, *2004 UN Commission on Human Rights—Mission: To Promote and Protect Human Rights*, AI Index IOR 41/001/2004, Jan. 1, 2004, *available at* http://web.amnesty.org/library/pdf/IOR410012004ENGLISH/$File/IOR4100104.pdf. [hereinafter Amnesty Int'l, *Mission*]

3 *WR 2006*, *supra* note 1; Kay Seok, *Put Human Rights First in North Korea*, The Observer, Sept. 11, 2004, *available at* http://hrw.org/english/docs/2004/09/20/nkorea9354.htm.

class, North Koreans spend their lives struggling to find basic necessities for survival, with little hope for future prospects.

That explains why hundreds of thousands of North Korean refugees, including women and children, have already crossed the border into neighboring countries, risking their own lives.[4] Even after they make a successful border crossing, these North Koreans face other kinds of human rights violations since they do not receive any kind of protection from host countries. They are becoming a growing concern in Northeast Asia, and something tangible needs to be done in order to alleviate the current pain and suffering of people who have rights under international law.

This chapter intends to address the legal points that surround the issue of national and international protection for North Koreans in flight. In Part II, the human rights situations in North Korea and China will be discussed in order to develop an understanding of why the issues of North Korean refugees must be dealt with urgently. In Part III, the possibility of national protection will be explored by examining relevant domestic laws of South Korea and their implementation. The limitations and passivity of the South Korean government in protecting North Koreans will also be addressed, and it will show that the international assumption about the possibility of national protection for North Koreans by South Korea is unfounded. In Part IV, the importance of fully utilizing existing international protection systems will be emphasized and recommendations will be provided to encourage all the players, national or international, and stakeholders to work together to provide tangible protection to North Koreans in flight.

II. The North Koreans' Egregious Situation

A. *Human Rights Violation in North Korea*

North Korean authorities continue to restrict information about, and access to North Korea to any entities or individuals who might expose the realities of

---

4 CRS Report for Congress, North Korean Refugees in China and Human Rights Issues: International Response and U.S. Policy Options (2007), Order Code RL 34189 (2007), *available at* http://www.fas.org/sgp/crs/row/RL34189.pdf; *see also* U.S. Comm. for Refugees and Immigrants ("USCRI"), World Refugee Survey 2003: Country Report—North Korea 129 (2003) [hereinafter WRS 2003]; the term "refugee" is defined by Convention relating to the Status of Refugees, July 28, 1951, 189 U.N.T.S. 150 (entered into force Apr. 22, 1954 [hereinafter 1951 Refugee Convention] and Protocol relating to the Status of Refugees, Jan. 31, 1967, 19 U.S.T. 6223, 606 U.N.T.S. 267 (entered into force Oct. 4, 1967) [hereinafter 1967 Protocol]; Accordingly, "refugee" is defined as person who owing to a well-founded fear of being persecuted for reasons of race, religion, nationality, membership or a particular social group or political opinion, is outside the country of his nationality and is unable or owing to such fear, is unwilling to avail himself of the protection of the country.

the North to the world.[5] North Korea has repeatedly prohibited the UN Special *Rapporteur* on human rights and the UN Special *Rapporteur* on the right to food from entering North Korea.[6] North Korea also turned down the requests of international NGOs and other independent human rights groups to visit the country.[7]

Despite North Korea's unwillingness to provide information, there are already more than twenty-five thousand North Korean refugees that have found freedom in South Korea, and their testimonies have been collected and analyzed by credible experts, including Amnesty International, Citizens' Alliance for North Korean Human Rights, and the UN Special *Rapporteur* on North Korea. Based on their reports, the UN Commission on Human Rights and UN Human Rights Council adopted resolutions "calling on North Korea to respect basic human rights."[8] Since November 2005, every year the UN General Assembly passes a resolution against North Korea, citing "systemic, widespread and grave violations of human rights."[9] Furthermore, testimonies by North Korean defectors from various social statuses in the North, and by visitors who were exceptionally permitted to enter North Korea, support the conclusion that there are serious patterns of grievous human rights violations. Also, many of the violations are the result of intentional action or inaction by all concerned states, causing even more serious concerns for systematically persecuted North Koreans.

1. Intense Personality Cult Forced by the State

In the 1950s and 1960s, the North Korean regime constructed and implemented an obscure belief system replacing existing Korean thought and belief systems.[10] North Koreans refer to this unique belief system as "the *Juche* idea," "Kim Il Sung Revolutionary Thought," "Kimilsungism," "the monolithic ideology system," and the like.[11] These terms are used synonymously. "Kimilsungism, the monolithic,

---

5 Amnesty Int'l, *North Korea: Briefing on Present Situation*, AI Index ASA 24/002/2005, July 28, 2005, *available at* http://www.amnesty.org/en/library/asset/ASA24/002/2005/en/dom-ASA240022005en.pdf. [hereinafter Amnesty Int'l, *North Korea*]; Amnesty Int'l, *Mission, supra* note 2.

6 Amnesty Int'l, *North Korea, supra* note 5.

7 *Id.*; Amnesty Int'l, *Mission, supra* note 2; Human Rights Watch, *World Report 2005 (events of 2004)*, 309 (2005), *available at* http://hrw.org/wr2k5/wr2005.pdf.

8 *WR 2006, supra* note 1, at 295.

9 *Id.*

10 Press Conference on North Korea Report by David Hawk & Jae Chun Won, U.S. Comm'n on Int'l Religious Freedom, Thank You Father Kim Il Sung 78 (Nov. 15, 2005) (on file with U.S. Comm. on Int'l Religious Freedom), *available at* http://www.uscirf.gov/index.php?option=com_content&task=view&id=2227&Itemid=1.

11 *Id. Juche* means "self-reliance" and/or "self-sufficiency" in Korean; *see also* BRADLEY K. MARTIN, UNDER THE LOVING CARE OF THE FATHERLY LEADER: NORTH KOREA AND THE KIM DYNASTY 111 (2004); *see also* THOMAS J. BELKE, JUCHE: A CHRISTIAN STUDY OF NORTH KOREA'S STATE RELIGION (1999).

the one and only ideological system based on *Juche*" remained at the level of the secular or mundane when it was first introduced in the 1960s and 1970s.[12] However, in the hands of Kim Jung Il, the late Kim Il Sung's son and anointed heir, Kimilsungism "acquired a patina of philosophic universalism, and an exceedingly heavy gloss of ethnocentrically Korean messianic religiosity."[13]

Despite its Constitution and comprehensive range of statutes, the state systematically forces the personality cult through the "Ten Great Principles of the Unitary Ideology System"[14] which illustrates with precision the harsh reality of people's lives in North Korea. It may resemble the Ten Commandments of Christianity, but here it functions as the most important legal and cultural document of North Korea, which is more powerful than North Korea's Constitution. The Ten Great Principles of the Unitary Ideology System is de facto supreme and compulsory.[15] What is worse is that this personality cult leads to strong control over people's minds and justifies horrible violations of human rights in almost all aspects of their lives.[16]

---

[12] *Id.* at 79.

[13] *Id.*

[14] Joanna Hosaniak, *Prisoners of Their Own Country: North Korea in the Eyes of the Witnesses* 58–64 (Citizens' Alliance for North Korean Human Rights 2005), *available at* http://eng.nkhumanrights.or.kr/bbs/bbs/board.php?bo_table=report&wr_id=4&page=2:

1. Struggle with all your life to paint the entire society with the one color of the Great Leader Kim Il Sung's revolutionary thought.
2. Respect and revere highly and with loyalty the Great Leader Kim Il Sung.
3. Make absolute the authority of the Great Leader Kim Il Sung.
4. Accept the Great Leader Kim Il Sung's revolutionary thought as your belief and take the Great Leader's instructions as your creed.
5. Observe absolutely the principle of unconditional execution in carrying out the instructions of the Great Leader Kim Il Sung.
6. Rally the unity of ideological intellect and revolutionary solidarity around the Great Leader Kim Il Sung.
7. Learn from the Great Leader Kim Il Sung and master communist dignity, the methods of revolutionary projects, and the people's work styles.
8. Preserve dearly the political life the Great Leader Kim Il Sung has bestowed upon you, and repay loyally for the Great Leader's boundless political trust and considerations with high political awareness and skill.
9. Establish a strong organizational discipline so that the entire Party, the entire people, and the entire military will operate uniformly under the sole leadership of the Great Leader Kim Il Sung.
10. The great revolutionary accomplishments pioneered by the Great Leader Kim Il Sung must be succeeded and perfected by hereditary successions until the end.

[15] *Id.* at 57.

[16] *Id.* at 18, 57.

2. Extensive Discrimination and Violation of Human Rights

North Korea is party to four of the key international human rights treaties: International Covenants on Civil and Political Rights and on Economic, Social, and Cultural Rights; the Convention on the Rights of the Child; and the Convention on the Elimination of All Forms of Discrimination against Women.[17] However, it routinely and egregiously violates nearly all international human rights standards.[18] North Korea recognizes only few civil and political rights.[19] The ruling Workers' Party "controls the Parliament, which has only symbolic authority, and all other smaller parties are pro-Government and State-controlled."[20] Although elections are held periodically, all candidates must be state-approved.[21] Furthermore, voting results in almost "100 percent turnout and approval rate" because state officials openly monitor the voting process.[22] Expression of dissent against government policy or doctrines is considered a serious offence against the state.[23] For political crimes, whether actual or perceived, collective punishment of the entire family is the norm and guilt-by-association is widely practiced.[24]

Offenses related to the personality cults of Kim Jung Il and Kim Il Sung are subject to cruel punishment.[25] Even when family members of political offenders are not sent to prison, their choice of schools, residence, and jobs becomes severely restricted, potentially for generations.[26] There is no organized political opposition in North Korea.[27] Also, no independent nongovernmental organizations can exist.[28] The state manages all media and censors all publications.[29] The simple act of watching or listening to the foreign press or tampering with televisions or radios is a crime that carries harsh punishment.[30]

---

17 *See* United Nations Treaty Collection databases, *available at* http://treaties.un.org/Pages/ViewDetails.aspx?src=UNTSONLINE&tabid=1&id=321&chapter=4&lang=en#Participants.

18 *WR 2006, supra* note 1, at 291.

19 *Id.* at 292.

20 *Id.*

21 *Id.*

22 *Id.*

23 Amnesty Int'l, *North Korea, supra* note 5; Amnesty Int'l, *Mission, supra* note 2.

24 Amnesty Int'l, *North Korea, supra* note 5; *WR 2006, supra* note 1; Amnesty Int'l, *Mission, supra* note 2.

25 *WR 2006, supra* note 1.

26 *Id.*; *see also* Kang Cho-Hwan & Pierre Rigoulot, The Aquariums of Pyongyang (2005).

27 *WR 2006, supra* note 1.

28 *Id.*

29 *Id.*; Amnesty Int'l, *North Korea, supra* note 5.

30 Amnesty Int'l, *North Korea, supra* note 5; *WR 2006, supra* note 1; Amnesty Int'l, *Mission, supra* note 2.

Quality of education, employment opportunities, and access to health care in North Korea are governed by the politically determined classification system.[31] One's political background restricts membership in the Workers' Party, "which is imperative to one's professional success."[32] Generally, college education and prominent job opportunities are only available to children of the elite.[33] Medical treatment is also subject to discrimination based upon social background.[34] This prohibits the majority of North Koreans from receiving treatment of easily curable diseases.[35] The state controls all trade unions in all industries.[36] Strikes and collective bargaining as well as independently organized labor activities are banned.[37]

There is no freedom of religion.[38] Prayer and religious studies are supervised by the state, and often used for state propaganda.[39] Independent worship is not allowed[40] and, if caught, worshippers are severely punished, which may include public executions.[41]

3. Lack of Due Process of Law: Arbitrary Detention, Torture and Summary Execution

North Koreans are deprived of due process; no legal counsel is available to criminal suspects and many are tortured or mistreated during the interrogation process.[42] All prisoners are subjected to "forced labor and face cruel, inhuman, and degrading treatment."[43] Many of the prisoners die in prison from mistreatment, malnutrition, and lack of medical care.[44] In a Human Rights Watch report released in 2002, a former detainee in a North Korean logging camp gave an account of how prisoners survive, "catching rats by using shoes as traps, then roasting, and eating them secretly."[45]

---

31 *WR 2006, supra* note 1.
32 *Id.*
33 *Id.*
34 *Id.*
35 *Id.*
36 *Id.* at 293.
37 *Id.*; Amnesty Int'l, *North Korea, supra* note 5.
38 Won, Jae-Chun, *Religious Persecution in North Korea*, 4 Int'l J. for Religious Freedom, Issue 1, 87 (2011); *see also WR 2006, supra* note 1, at 292; Amnesty Int'l, *North Korea, supra* note 5; U.S. Comm'n of Int'l Religious Freedom, A Prison Without Bars 19 (2008).
39 *WR 2006, supra* note 1, at 292.
40 *Id.*
41 Amnesty Int'l, *North Korea, supra* note 5; Amnesty Int'l, *Mission, supra* note 2.
42 Amnesty Int'l, *North Korea, supra* note 5; *WR 2006, supra* note 1, at 293.
43 *WR 2006, supra* note 1, at 293; Amnesty Int'l, *Mission, supra* note 2, at 60–61.
44 Amnesty Int'l, *North Korea, supra* note 5; *WR 2006, supra* note 1, at 293.
45 Mike Jendrzejczyk, Human Rights Watch, *From Eating Rats in North Korea to Sex Abuse in China: A Refugee Travesty*, Int'l Herald Trib., Nov. 19, 2002, *available at* http://hrw.org/editorials/2002/nkorea-refugees.htm.

Torture is pervasive in North Korea.[46] For example, communication between prisoners is strictly prohibited and, if caught, they are "beaten with wooden sticks or iron bars."[47] Some report that after beatings, "cold water was poured over the bodies even in the middle of winter."[48] In some cases, prisoners are subjected to "water torture," the forcible consumption of large quantities of water.[49] Numerous eyewitness accounts by North Korean escapees detail how executions are carried out in public, "often at crowded marketplaces, and in the presence of children."[50] During the food crisis in the 1990s, North Korea began executing people accused of crimes caused by economic hardships, such as stealing grain or cattle.[51]

North Koreans who return from China can face detention, torture, and execution.[52] If they are found to be repeat offenders or have had contact with westerners or South Koreans while in China, especially missionaries, they are subject to harsh punishments, sometimes in the presence of their own families, including public execution by hanging or firing squad.[53] A large number of North Koreans, who had been repatriated and punished during interrogation and post-interrogation detention, have testified that they are discriminated by the North Korean authorities and society, and have concluded that they have no future in North Korea.[54]

In an unprecedented move, two members of the Committee on the Rights of the Child were able to visit North Korea in 2004.[55] During their visit, they highlighted the mistreatment of children who returned from China, as well as economic exploitation, trafficking, juvenile justice, and cases of torture.[56]

---

46 Amnesty Int'l, *North Korea, supra* note 5; *WR 2006, supra* note 1, at 293.

47 Amnesty Int'l, *North Korea, supra* note 5.

48 *Id.*

49 *Id.*

50 *WR 2006, supra* note 1, at 293.

51 Amnesty Int'l, *North Korea, supra* note 5; *WR 2006, supra* note 1.

52 U.N. Comm. for Refugees and Immigrants (USCRI), *World Refugee Survey 2005: Country Reports—China (2005)* [hereinafter *WRS 2005*]; *see also* Vitit Muntarbhorn, Situation of Human Rights in the Democratic People's Republic of Korea, G.A. Res. 60/150, U.N. Doc. RES/A/60/150 (Aug. 2005).

53 *Id.*; It should be noted that returning people who might face torture is a violation of the UN Convention Against Torture and Other Cruel, Inhumane and or Degrading Treatment or Punishment. Art. 3(1), Dec. 9, 1975, S. Treaty Doc. No. 100 20 (1988), 145 U.N.T.S. 85. "No State Party shall expel, return ("refouler") or extradite a person to another State where there are substantial grounds for believing that he would be in danger of being subjected to torture."

54 Seok, *supra* note 3.

55 Amnesty Int'l, *North Korea, supra* note 5.

56 *Id.*

B. *Human Rights Situation of North Koreans in China*

The actual number of North Koreans in China remains unknown. NGOs estimate the number ranges between 200,000 and 300,000.[57] Although China has forcibly repatriated tens of thousands of North Koreans throughout the years,[58] defectors continue to cross into China.[59] Since the 2008 Beijing Olympic Games, the Chinese government expanded its efforts to repatriate North Koreans back to their home country to minimize international attention on North Korean refugees.[60] Therefore, unless there is tangible international pressure, aid from the Chinese government to improve the North Koreans' human rights situation should not be expected for now.[61]

1. Human Trafficking and Exploitation

Acute food shortages and ample violations of human rights in North Korea have forced tens of thousands of people to flee across the border into China's northeastern provinces and many illegally remain in border areas enduring appalling conditions.[62] They receive no support or protection from any entities except certain humanitarian NGOs and religious groups, and are vulnerable to physical, emotional, and sexual exploitation.[63] A typical example of exploitation is when an undocumented woman worker demands her paycheck at the end of the month, the employer threatens to report her to the authorities.[64] The victim cannot seek justice through the legal system due to her illegal status.[65]

As a result of industrialization in China, Chinese women are less attracted to the hardships of rural and village life, bringing about the development of a market for rural brides.[66] Humanitarian groups in China report that there has been a great increase in the number of women crossing the border since 1998, most

---

57 U.N. Comm. for Refugees and Immigrants (USCRI), *World Refugee Survey 2001: Country Reports—North Korea (2001).*

58 U.N. Comm. for Refugees and Immigrants (USCRI), *World Refugee Survey 2004: Country Reports—China (2004).*

59 *WRS 2005*, *supra* note 52.

60 Mahn-Seop Huh, *An Exclusive: Confidential Report of National Human Rights Commission on the Situation of North Korean Escapees in China*, SHINDONGA, Jan. 1, 2005, *available at* http://www.minjukorea.com/cgi-local/note/read.cgi?board=nor_relate&y_number=47.

61 *Id.*

62 Amnesty Int'l, *North Korea*, *supra* note 5.

63 HUMAN RIGHTS WATCH, THE INVISIBLE EXODUS: NORTH KOREANS IN THE PEOPLE'S REPUBLIC OF CHINA 11 (2002), *available at* http://www.hrw.org/reports/2002/north korea/norkor1102.pdf. [hereinafter THE INVISIBLE EXODUS].

64 Huh, *supra* note 60.

65 *Id.*; Seok, *supra* note 3.

66 THE INVISIBLE EXODUS, *supra* note 63, at 12; Huh, *supra* note 60.

of them looking for opportunities to make money to send back to families in North Korea.[67] These "opportunities" involve the sale of sexual services in the form of prostitution or arranged marriage, sometimes voluntarily but often forced through third party agencies.[68] North Korean women married to Chinese men are often exposed to domestic violence.[69]

Children fleeing the border are affected by factors similar to those of adults, with the additional elements of a disorganized school system and absenteeism in provinces most affected by food shortages.[70] Most of these children have lost their parents, or their parents are incapable of taking care of them, and cross the border unaccompanied.[71] Most appear to be ten years old or older.[72] In the late 1990s, they were visibly present as beggars in public areas, and sometimes in karaoke bars and restaurants that cater to foreigners.[73] Typically, the children frequently cross the border to engage in trade and bring their small earnings back to their families in North Korea.[74] Humanitarian and missionary groups shelter some of the children; other children sleep on the streets.[75] Chinese authorities conduct periodic crackdowns to round up street children.[76] Although a few children are fortunate enough to make it to a third country, their previous life of wandering between China and North Korea and the "survival skills" learned in flight hinder their ability to integrate into society.[77]

Those who arrive in South Korea suffer from serious psychological trauma as a result of rape, confinement, or physical abuse in China.[78] These children are effectively deprived of their right to an education. In South Korea, they face the pressure of adapting to an organized school system, often accompanied by the challenges of cultural and age differences.[79] They tend to think little of life,[80] and say they are not afraid of death.[81]

---

67 The Invisible Exodus, *supra* note 63, at 12.
68 *Id.*
69 Jendrzejczyk, *supra* note 45.
70 *Id.* at 15.
71 *Id.*
72 The Invisible Exodus, *supra* note 63, at 15.
73 *Id.*
74 *Id.*
75 *Id.*
76 *Id.*
77 *Id.* at 15–16.
78 *Id.* at 16.
79 *Id.*
80 Huh, *supra* note 60.
81 *Id.*

2. Arbitrary Detention and Mistreatment

In an interview conducted by Human Rights Watch, seven refugees shared their experience of being arrested by the Chinese authorities.[82] Some attested to reasonable treatment and prison conditions, but others reported abuse.[83]

Mr. Cho D., a former high-ranking military official, shared the situation surrounding his May 1998 arrest.[84] "At the time I was arrested, I was in a small shop, eating. Five guys in civilian clothing attacked me, grabbed me, and threw me to the floor, and tied me with rope all around my body from my chest down. It was terrible."[85] After spending forty days in the Shenyang security office, he was sent to the Dandong border facility, where he escaped by removing a window bar and jumping out.[86] During his detention, he learned that the North Korean consulate sent a document to the Chinese authorities accusing him of being a murderer, explaining the excessive force used during his arrest.[87] He denied this accusation, but the Korean-Chinese interpreter at the police station explained to him that such accusations served as a way for North Korea to request the arrest and extradition of North Koreans in China.[88] In an incident at the Mongolian border in July 1988, Yong Kim reported being beaten with clubs by the Chinese border guards after stating that he was not a North Korean migrant.[89]

Chinese authorities no longer exempt humanitarian NGOs and independent individuals who help North Koreans from arbitrary detention and mistreatment.[90] In May 2001, the Chinese Public Security arrested four workers from the South Korean Buddhist organization, Good Friends,[91] for allegedly violating a statute entitled Support of Illegal Migrants' Entry to or Departure from China.[92] In

---

82 The Invisible Exodus, *supra* note 63, at 16.

83 *Id.*

84 *Id.*

85 The Invisible Exodus, *supra* note 63, at 16.

86 *Id.*

87 *Id.*

88 *Id.*

89 *Id.*

90 *WRS 2005, supra* note 52; Amnesty Int'l, *People's Republic of China: Serious Human Rights Violations and the Crackdown on Dissent Continue*, AI Index ASA 17/047/2002, Sept. 2002, *available at* http://web.amnesty.org/library/pdf/ASA170472002ENGLISH/$File/ASA1704702.pdf. [hereinafter Amnesty Int'l, *China*]; The Invisible Exodus, *supra* note 63, at 16.

91 The Invisible Exodus, *supra* note 63, at 18.

92 Article 318 stipulates that anyone who makes arrangements for another person to cross a national border illegally shall be sentenced to fixed-term imprisonment of two to seven years and be fined. In any of the following cases, (s)he will be sentenced to no less than 7 years imprisonment (up to life), and may be fined or have property confiscated:

(1) Being a ringleader of a group that makes arrangements;

(2) Repeatedly making such arrangements for a large number of persons;

most situations, China expels religious and aid workers assisting North Koreans, but "this time the four were detained for fifty days, accused of espionage, and, maltreated prior to their expulsion."[93] One writer reported, "Sometimes they screamed and caught us by the front of our shirts and forced us to talk."[94] Several were systematically ill-treated, including sleep deprivation and physical disciplinary punishment for extended periods of time.[95] Another worker related, "They handcuffed me by one of my hands and hung me on a high wall. I had to stand on my tiptoes."[96] This sort of inhumane treatment is borderline torture and is strictly banned under international law.[97]

3. Refoulement

China is a signatory to the 1951 Refugee Convention, the 1967 Refugee Protocol, and the Convention Against Torture, which prohibit their signatories from forcibly returning people who fear persecution in their home countries.[98] Since it is a long-recognized customary international law, all nations are bound not to forcibly repatriate those who are subject to persecution in their country of origin.[99]

In January 2005, a South Korean National Human Rights Commission report stated that the Chinese authorities repatriate around 300 North Korean detainees

---

(3) Causing serious injury or death to persons for whom he makes arrangements;
(4) Depriving or restricting personal freedom of the persons for whom he makes arrangements;
(5) Resisting inspection by means of violence or threat;
(6) Gaining illegally form such enterprise; or
(7) Being involved in other exceptionally serious circumstances.

Criminal Law, part two, chapter VI, art. 318, § 3 (1997) (P.R.C.).

93 THE INVISIBLE EXODUS, *supra* note 63, at 18.

94 *Id.*

95 *Id.*

96 *Id.*

97 *Id.*

98 NORMA KANG MUICO, AN ABSENCE OF CHOICE: THE SEXUAL EXPLOITATION OF NORTH KOREAN WOMEN IN CHINA 12 (Anti-Slavery International 2005); *see* United Nations, *Final Act of the United Nations Conference of Plenipotentiaries on the Status of Refugees and Stateless Persons*, July 25, 1951, United Nations, Treaty Series, vol. 189, at 137, *available at* http://www.unhcr.org/refworld/docid/3e2becbb4.html [hereinafter Treat Series, vol. 189]; JAE CHUN WON, RESOLVING NORTH KOREAN HUMAN RIGHT ISSUES THROUGH INTERNATIONAL ORGANIZATIONS AND LAWSUITS (2002), *reprinted in* THE 6TH INTERNATIONAL CONFERENCE ON NORTH KOREAN HUMAN RIGHTS & REFUGEES 71 (Citizens' Alliance for North Korean Human Right 2005).

99 *See* ERIKA FELLER, VOLKER TURK, & FRANCES NICHOLSON, REFUGEE PROTECTION IN INTERNATIONAL LAW: UNHCR'S GLOBAL CONSULTATIONS ON INTERNATIONAL PROTECTION (2003); *see also* The UN Handbook on Procedures and Criteria for Determining Refugees Status under the 1951 Convention and the 1967 Protocol relating to the Status of Refugees.

weekly from detention camps in the northeast provinces of China.[100] The detainees and returnees are denied domestic asylum procedure or access to UNHCR.[101] According to this report, it is suspected that the increased military force in border cities is intended not only to tighten the security of the border, but also to arrest and repatriate North Koreans who have illegally crossed the border and are in hiding.[102] The report confirms that *refoulement* camps are maintained in military units and isolated from the outside world.[103]

The Chinese government maintains that no North Koreans in China are refugees and that its primary obligation lies under a 1986 agreement on the repatriation of migrants with North Korea.[104] Accordingly, China arrests and expels North Koreans without affording them the opportunity to seek asylum, violating customary international law and its duty under the conventions to which it is a state party.[105] Professor Vitit Muntarbhorn, former UN Special Rapporteur on North Korea, expressed serious concern of *refoulement* in his 2005 UN General Assembly report stating that many North Koreans are in fact *refugee sur place* since they face criminal prosecution and possible persecution upon their return even though some of the North Koreans were not refugees when they left their country of origin.[106]

III. National Protection

A. *Domestic Laws of South Korea Concerning North Koreans' Nationality*

Though criticized for its passive and ineffective action, the South Korean government is trying to protect North Korean asylum seekers in third countries and support their resettlement in South Korea. Actions taken by South Korea are based on its legal duties stipulated by its domestic laws, such as its Constitution and other relevant statutes. This chapter will review the Korean Constitution, the Nationality Act, and the Protection Act to see on what basis North Koreans are entitled to South Korean nationality and, therefore, protection by the South Korean government.

---

100 Huh, *supra* note 60.

101 Amnesty Int'l, *China, supra* note 90; Huh, *supra* note 60.

102 *Id.*

103 *Id.*

104 U.N. Comm. for Refugees and Immigrants (USCRI), *World Refugee Survey 2000: Country Reports—China (2000)* [hereinafter *WRS 2000*].

105 Huh, *supra* note 60.

106 Special Rapporteur of the Commission on Human Rights, *Situation of human rights in the Democratic People's Republic of Korea,* ¶¶ 27, 64, U.N. Doc. A/60/306 (Aug. 29, 2005) (by Vitit Muntarbhorn).

1. Constitution

The founding Constitution of South Korea was established in 1948, after the Korean peninsula was divided.[107] Article 2 of the Constitution stipulates nationality as "Nationality in the Republic of Korea shall be prescribed by the Act."[108] Nevertheless, Article 3 of the Constitution implicitly answers the question on North Koreans' eligibility for South Korean nationality in that: "The territory of the Republic of Korea shall consist of the Korean peninsula and its adjacent islands."[109] As to the meaning of this article, the Supreme Court,[110] the Constitutional Court,[111] and the majority of Korean Constitutional legal scholars[112] suggest the opinion that: (a) under Article 3 of the Constitution the northern region of the Korean peninsula is part of the South Korean territory; (b) it should be under South Korean sovereignty; and (c) the North Korean regime is merely a hostile entity rather than a sovereign state.[113]

Accordingly, South Korean authorities derive a conclusion from the interpretation of Article 3 that a North Korean, as does a South Korean, acquires South Korean nationality at birth.[114] Practically speaking, it is impossible for a North Korean to exercise any rights as a South Korean national as she resides in North Korea. Likewise, it is highly unlikely that a North Korean may exercise such rights even in a third country. Therefore, it seems that a North Korean who fled to South Korea, who has South Korean nationality *de jure* by birth, may enjoy full legal rights as a South Korean national *de facto* when she finishes the adaptation process in South Korea.

2. Nationality Act

The Nationality Act, enacted on December 20, 1948 and revised five times since then, provides the requirements for a foreigner to become a South Korean national. In granting nationality, South Korea principally follows the personal

---

107 HEONBEOB [CONST.] (S. Korea).

108 *Id.* art. 2.

109 *Id.* art. 3.

110 1996 Nu 1221 Verdict [Pangyeol] (S.C. Nov. 12, 1996) (S. Korea) [hereinafter Verdict 1221].

111 1997 Heonka 12 (Const. Ct., Aug. 31, 2000) (S. Korea); 1992 Heonba 78 (Const. Ct., June 30, 2005) (S. Korea) [hereinafter Heonba 78].

112 HEE-YUL KYE, THE CONSTITUTIONAL LAW I 163 (1995); Interestingly, South Korea's position on North Korea is very similar to West Germany's official position towards East Germany before unification.

113 *Id.*

114 *Id.*; Verdict 1221, *supra* note 110; Heonba 78, *supra* note 111; *see generally* Gukjeok Beob [Nationality Act (N.A.)] of 2008, L. No. 8892, art. 2, para. 1 (S. Korea) (establishing the acquisition of South Korean nationality by birth).

principle (the bloodline doctrine), and applies the territorial principle (the place of birth doctrine) in a supplemental manner.

Under Article 2 of the Nationality Act, a person becomes a South Korean national if either parent is a South Korean national or the person is born in South Korea and both parents are unknown or have no nationality.[115] Although there is ambiguity about how a person's mother or father born before the Nationality Act's enactment acquired South Korean nationality, a person born after the enactment of the Nationality Act in December 1948 and whose father or mother is a South Korean national, acquires South Korean nationality under the meaning of Article 2, Section 1, Subsection 1.[116]

The important point to note is that North Koreans fleeing and arriving in South Korea to resettle there are not subject to a naturalization process in acquiring South Korean nationality.[117] During their adaptation process, the authorities, without any additional administrative or judicial procedure, confirm their nationality as a South Korean, and are permitted to register or create a family registration.[118] The Nationality Act is silent on the question of North Koreans' nationality as South Koreans. The Ministry of Justice, which worked on the revision of the Nationality Act in 1997, stated that a provision on North Koreans' nationality was deliberately excluded from the proposal because it would not have made sense if the Nationality Act, which regulated the requirements and procedures for a non-South Korean national to acquire South Korean nationality, had a special provision concerning the nationality of North Koreans who are already South Korean nationals under its laws.[119]

3. Protection Act

a. *Clear Purpose but Timid Application*

In 1997, South Korea enacted the Act on the Protection and Settlement Support of Residents Escaping from North Korea ("Protection Act").[120] Article 1 of the Act provides:

---

115 N.A. art. 2(3)-1. It provides "A person who is born in the Republic of Korea, where both of parents are unknown or have no nationality." *Id.*

116 Doo-Hoon Choi, *Several Problems of Nationality Act of South Korea: North Korean Residents and South Korean Nationals Residing Abroad,* 35 L. & PUB. ADMIN. REV. 74–76 (2000).

117 Dong-Hyun Seok, *Revision of Korean Nationality Law: The Direction of Revising the Korean Nationality Law,* 4 SEOUL INT'L L. RES. 25 (1997).

118 *Id.*

119 *Id.*

120 Bukhan Ital Jumin Ui Boho Mit Jeongchak Jiwone Kwanhan Beoblyul [Act on the Protection and Settlement Support of Residents Support of Residents Escaping from North Korea (P.A.)] of 2008, L. No. 8852 (S. Korea).

> The purpose of this Act is to provide such matters relating to protection and support as are necessary to help North Korean residents escaping from the area north of the Military Demarcation Line (hereinafter referred to as "North Korea") and desiring protection from the Republic of Korea, as quickly as possible to adapt themselves to, and settle down in, all spheres of their lives, including political, economic, social and cultural spheres.[121]

Under the Protection Act, the South Korean government may provide protection over externally displaced North Koreans asking for protection.[122]

It is not clear, however, from the language of the Protection Act whether such protection is based on the constitutional duty provided by in Article 2, Section 2 of the Constitution of South Korea to protect its nationals residing abroad[123] and the perspective that a North Korean is also a South Korean national residing abroad.[124] Article 4, Section 1 of the Protection Act merely provides, "The Republic of Korea shall provide persons subject to protection with special protection on the principle of humanitarianism."[125] It is also silent on North Koreans' acquisition of South Korean nationality, but it has a provision on the procedure of application for family registration.[126] Article 19 provides that a person who does not have original family registration in South Korea may decide to create one

---

121 *Id.* art. 1.

122 *Id.*

123 Const., *supra* note 107, art. 2, para. 2. It provides "It shall be the duty of the State to protect citizens residing abroad as prescribed by Act." *Id.*

124 *See generally* N.A. art. 2. South Korean courts and law scholars agree that the northern region of the Korean peninsula is part of South Korean territory, and therefore, N.A. art. 2 grants South Korean nationality to those born on the Korean peninsula.

125 P.A. art. 4, para. 1.

126 Choi, *supra* note 116. Explaining the difference between nationality and family registration, Choi writes:

> Nationality should be distinguished from family registration. As mentioned above, nationality is a legal link which makes an individual pertain to a state and a premise of which is a state structure since it defines the status of a national, one of the elements of a state. On the contrary, family registration is distinguished from nationality in that its premise is the family system. It is based on a concept of civil law (private law), which defines the family unit. Therefore, these two are totally different legal concepts in terms of legal theory or founding statutes. However, it is apparent that in fact family registration provides significant evidence for determining a genuine link of nationality. This is supported by the fact that each state's nationality act has an organic relationship with the identity-registration system such as a census registration. The Korean family registration system provides that only a person who has acquired South Korean nationality is qualified for putting his/her name in the family register and requires all the people who have South Korean nationality to be registered. Therefore, it could be a kind of national registration system. Accordingly, it should be clearly noted that family registration functions as evidence proving acquisition or existence of nationality, but it in itself by no means creates the legal effect of acquisition or loss of nationality. *Id.*

and file for a family register to the Seoul Family Court.[127] Accordingly, one could conclude that "family registration" can be evidence of nationality, but may not create or grant nationality.

b. *Inclusion, Exclusion, and Cessation Clauses*

Under the Protection Act there is a set of criteria for providing North Koreans with protection.[128] The Protection Act provides protection only for people who meet all of the following requirements: North Korean residents (a) who have escaped from North Korea; (b) who have their residence, lineal ascendants and descendants, spouses, workplaces, and so on in North Korea; (c) who have not acquired any foreign nationality after escaping from North Korea; and (d) who have expressed their intention to be protected by South Korea.[129]

In determining whether or not protection should be provided for an applicant pursuant to Article 8, Section 1 and Article 9 of the Protection Act, the Minister of Unification may not grant protection to such persons as prescribed as follows:

> (i) international criminal offenders involved in aircraft hijacking, drug trafficking, terrorism or genocide, etc.; (ii) offenders of nonpolitical, serious crimes such as murder, etc.; (iii) suspects of disguised escape; (iv) persons who have for a considerable period earned their living in their respective countries of sojourn;[130] or (v) such persons as prescribed by the Presidential Decree as unfit for the designation as persons subject to protection.[131]

"Such persons as prescribed by the Presidential Decree as unfit for the designation as persons subject to protection" refers to persons who are expected to bring about serious political and diplomatic difficulty for South Korea if protection is granted.[132]

---

127 P.A. art. 19, para. 1. It provides:

The Minister of Unification shall, in respect of a person subject to protection who has no permanent domicile in the area south of the Military Demarcation Line (hereinafter referred to as "South Korea"), help him determine a permanent domicile having a regard for his intention, and file to the Seoul Family Court an application form for permission to acquire a permanent domicile. *Id.*

128 However, it may be a right view that such procedure to decide to grant protection is the *de facto* procedure to grant South Korean nationality in that the way to live as a real South Korean national is opened to only the North Korean escapees who are granted such protection.

129 P.A. arts. 2, paras. 1, 3.

130 Tae-Chun Kim, *The Responses to Situations of a Mass influx of Residents Escaping from North Korea in the Context of International Law*, 2 Korean Y.B. Int'l L. (1998). Some critics argue that among the criteria for granting protection, the subsection 4 of article 9 should be abolished because, in reality, it may perfectly block entrance of North Korean escapees who are staying in third countries for a considerable period, only waiting for the chance to go to South Korea.

131 P.A. art. 8, paras. 1, 9.

132 *Bukhan Ital Jumin Ui Boho Mit Jeongchak Jiwone Kwanhan Beoblyul Sihaenglyeong* [Enforcement Decree of Protection Act] of 2008, Presidential Decree No. 21087, art. 16 [hereinafter Protection Act].

Article 8 of the Protection Act provides, "In the case of a person who is likely to affect national security to a considerable extent, the Director-General of the National Intelligence Service shall decide on the admissibility of the application."[133] Here, "a person who is likely to affect national security to a considerable extent" means:

> (i) a person who committed or attempted to commit crimes such as rebellion, assistance to a foreign enemy or violations of the National Security Act, and etc.; (ii) a person who actively worked for the Workers' Party of North Korea, the Ministry, the Armed Forces, or the National Security Agency to defend or uphold the North Korean political system; (iii) a spouse or relative of the head of North Korea; or (iv) a person who has high technology or high level of intelligence closely related with national security.[134]

When the person granted protection is involved in the activities listed above, the Minister of Unification may suspend or terminate protection and settlement support subject to the deliberations of the Consultative Council on Residents Escaping from North Korea ("Consultative Council"):[135]

> (i) when he is sentenced to imprisonment with or without prison labor for not less than one year and his sentence is made irrevocable; (ii) when he intentionally provides false information contrary to the interest of South Korea; (iii) when he is judicially declared dead or missing; (iv) when he attempts to go back to North Korea; (v) when he violates the Protection Act or an order issued thereunder; or (vi) when he comes under such grounds prescribed by the Presidential Decree.[136]

c. *Procedure of Application for Protection*

First, any North Korean escapee who desires to be protected under the Protection Act "shall apply for protection to the head of an overseas diplomatic or consular mission, or the head of any administrative agency (including the commander of a military unit of various levels; hereinafter referred to as the 'head of an overseas diplomatic or consular mission.')."[137] A North Korean shall apply for protection for himself, unless one of his family members applies on behalf of the rest of his family or there are emergency reasons.[138]

Second, "the head of the overseas diplomatic or consular mission who receives an application for protection shall without delay inform the Minister of Unification and the Director-General of the National Intelligence Service via the head of the central administrative agency to which he belongs."[139]

---

133 P.A. art. 8, para. 1.
134 Protection Act, art. 14.
135 *Id.* art. 2; P.A. art. 6, paras. 1–3.
136 P.A. art. 27, paras. 1–16.
137 *Id.* art. 7, para. 1.
138 Protection Act, art. 10.
139 P.A. art. 7, para. 2.

Third, the Director-General of the National Intelligence Service, once notified, shall take provisional protective measures or other necessary steps.[140] In practice, this step includes a brief interview to determine whether the applicant genuinely originates from North Korea.[141] As long as they successfully enter the compound of the foreign mission of South Korea, almost all are brought to South Korea.[142] When they enter South Korea, they are subject to interviews by the Joint Investigative Agency consisting of the Police, the National Intelligence Service, the Defense Intelligence Command and so on, to find out whether the applicant qualifies under the requirements enumerated in the previous paragraph.[143]

Fourth, if no problem is found, the Minister of Unification shall, when he receives such notice,[144] decide on the admissibility of the application for protection following the deliberations of the Consultative Council.[145] The Director-General of the National Intelligence Service shall decide on admissibility in the case of a person who is likely to considerably affect national security.[146] Those who have exhausted the investigative process are then accommodated in settlement support facilities for North Korean escapees[147] referred to as *Hanawon*.[148]

Once the South Korean government has decided that a North Korean escapee is entitled to protection, that escapee faces no further legal discrimination or limited status.[149] The escapee is awarded legal rights equivalent to those of native South Koreans, and those rights are upheld and respected by the South Korean government.[150] In the past, former North Koreans had been discriminated against when seeking passports, but a complaint filed with the National Human Rights Commission resulted in a correction of this form of discrimination.[151] Absent any unusual circumstances, a passport may be issued to an escapee three months from the point of entry into South Korea.[152]

---

140 *Id.* art. 7, para. 3.

141 Interview with Dae-Jung Kwak, Editor, DailyNK.Com (Apr. 20, 2005) (on file with author).

142 *Id.*

143 *Id.* Explaining in his e-mail: "This step of investigation was newly made after a North Korean spy who had disguised himself as a North Korean escapee and successfully entered South Korea was arrested. However, it is not clear that such investigation has a statutory basis." *Id.*

144 P.A. art. 7, para. 3.

145 *Id.* art. 8, para. 1.

146 *Id.*

147 After they are transferred to a settlement support facility, they are called "*Saetermin*," which means "new settlers."

148 Interview with Dae-Jung Kwak, *supra* note 141.

149 *Id.*

150 Interview with Young-Ja Kim, Dir. Gen., Citizens' Alliance for North Korean Human Rights (Apr. 25, 2005) (on file with author).

151 *Id.*

152 *Id.*

B. *Limitation Faced by South Korea: The Reality of National Protection*

1. Diplomatic Limitation

According to an NGO, before the plight of North Koreans became an international issue, the South Korean government did not have a clear policy of bringing those North Korean escapees to the South who entered South Korean foreign missions in China.[153] The government simply refused to grant protection despite its legal duties towards them.[154] There are a number of reported cases where applications were refused for protection of North Koreans who entered either a South Korean embassy or a consular office in China.[155] Those who could not enter the embassy sought protection outside the embassy by phone but those requests were also denied.[156]

However, in 2002, the South Korean government implemented an internal policy regarding North Koreans who enter a South Korean foreign mission and hope to resettle in South Korea. The South Korean foreign mission is now obliged to accept North Korean escapees and negotiate with the host state in a humanitarian way to resolve the case.[157] The South Korean government delivered this policy to each foreign mission in the relevant countries.[158] A government officer in a relevant agency explained, "Now there is a so-called 'designed asylum project' through a foreign mission systematically led by NGOs in third countries.[159] Since the number of escapees seeking protection is rapidly increasing, it is our natural obligation to accept all the North Korean escapees who enter our missions."[160] He continued by stating that, "The [South Korean] Government transmitted the internal instructions to foreign missions in order to cope with this problem."[161]

Nevertheless, whether South Korea may actually provide protection for North Koreans escapees mainly depends on the respective relationships between the state of sojourn and South and North Korea.[162] In order to bring North Korean escapees into South Korea, the South Korean government issues temporary passports. Then negotiations with the host state become critical in determining the

153 *Id.*
154 *Id.*
155 Interview with Young-Ja Kim, Dir. Gen., Citizens' Alliance for North Korean Human Rights (Oct. 27, 2008) (on file with author).
156 *Id.*
157 Jae-Hoon Ryu, *Acceptance of North Korean Escapees Who Enter Foreign Mission Compound of South Korea*, INTERNET HANKYOREH, May 24, 2002, *available at* http://www.hani.co.kr/section-003100000/2002/05/003100000200205241852084.html.
158 *Id.*
159 *Id.*
160 *Id.*
161 *Id.*
162 Interview with Dae-Jung Kwak, *supra* note 141.

fate of North Korean escapees.[163] For example, if the host state has diplomatic relations with North Korea, it cannot resolve the matter with the South Korean government alone.[164] If that state disapproves of the North Koreans' departure for South Korea, the South Korean government has no way to bring them to South Korea, even though North Korean escapees have temporary South Korean passports. On the other hand, if the state voluntarily accepts South Korea's request and chooses to ignore its relations with North Korea, then the host state would allow South Korean foreign missions to take the escapees to South Korea. Here, the host state's decision could be arbitrary. However, action should be based on clear legal principles.[165]

There are few favorable host countries for North Korean escapees. Thailand is the only country listed in the UNHCR Statistical Yearbook 2003 as having assisted the UNHCR with its repatriation of more than 100 North Korean asylum-seekers to South Korea.[166] Although it is not a state party to either the 1951 Convention or to the 1967 Protocol, Thailand deserves international recognition for its humanitarian gesture for North Korean asylum-seekers in that it abides by the customary international law of *non-refoulement.* This is in contrast to other state parties that often ignore their duties they are bound to observe.

Mongolia openly declared that it would not expel North Korean escapees who have entered it, even though it has retained diplomatic relations with North Korea.[167] South Korean foreign missions in Mongolia have reportedly reimbursed the Mongolian government for the expenditures incurred for transportation, food, and accommodation of North Korean escapees from the China-Mongolia border to Ulaanbaatar while they temporarily stay at refugee camps before being transferred to a South Korean foreign mission.[168] Mongolia is unique in the sense that it maintains a favorable relationship with South Korea,[169] while also maintaining relatively friendly diplomatic relations with North Korea.

China is the least cooperative country when it comes to dealing with North Korean refugees. Vietnam, Laos, and Cambodia are more responsive, but they also fall short of international refugee protection standards. The applicable practice and laws of these three countries are explained below in succession.

---

163 *Id.*

164 *Id.*

165 *Id.*

166 U.N. High Comm'r for Refugees [UNHCR], *Statistical Yearbook 2003, Thailand, available at* http://www.unhcr.org/cgi-bin/texis/vtx/statistics/open doc.pdf.

167 *Id.*

168 *Id.*

169 Interview with Sahm-Hyun Song, Prosecutor, Ministry of Justice of Republic of Korea, in Seoul, S. Korea (May 4, 2005).

a. *China*

Although China, as a state party to the 1951 Convention and the 1967 Protocol, is obligated not to send back asylum-seekers in danger of persecution, it has ignored its obligations.[170] Chinese authorities have arrested and repatriated North Korean asylum-seekers to North Korea.[171] Upon their return, many of these asylum-seekers have become subject to prolonged prison terms or even the death penalty.[172] China maintains the position that it is faithfully complying with its "Illegal Immigrants Repatriation Agreement" with North Korea.[173] The agreement, entered into in the early 1960s, stipulates that China return North Korean defectors.[174] The agreement was later amended in 1986, but the content of the amendment remains confidential.[175]

In the last few years, the rush of North Koreans into diplomatic compounds in China drew the world's attention and embarrassed Chinese authorities. In turn, China tightened its border security to search for North Koreans in hiding and demanded that foreign embassies turn over North Koreans. China also started to crack down on human right activists who were allegedly helping North Korean escapees in China.[176] China reportedly fines those who harbor North Koreans and financially rewards those who turn in North Koreans.[177] It is also reported that foreign nationals in China who help North Koreans escape into or out of China face fines, imprisonment, and deportation.[178] China does not acknowledge South Korea's position that it has a right to protect North Koreans based on the foundational premise in the South Korean Constitution that North Korea is not a sovereign state.

Recently, however, the Chinese government seems to have slightly changed its position. China now tacitly permits a small number of North Koreans who enter South Korean foreign missions to go to South Korea by means of expelling them to a third country.[179] Nevertheless, China still argues that the issue of North Korean escapees is a matter to be dealt with exclusively by China and

---

170 *See* Treaty Series, vol. 189, *supra* note 99 and UN General Assembly, *Protocol Relating to the Status of Refugees*, Jan. 31, 1967, United Nations, Treaty Series, vol. 606, at 267, *available at* http://www.unhcr.org/refworld/docid/3ae6b3ae4.html (Feb. 5, 2013); Jendrzejczyk, *supra* note 46.

171 The Invisible Exodus, *supra* note 64, at 2.

172 *Id.* at 4.

173 *Id.* at 11.

174 *Id.*

175 *Id.*

176 Jendrzejczyk, *supra* note 46.

177 U.N. Comm. for Refugees and Immigrants (USCRI), *World Refugee Survey 2003: Country Reports—China (2003)*.

178 U.N. Comm. for Refugees and Immigrants (USCRI), *World Refugee Survey 2004: Country Reports—China (2004)*.

179 Ryu, *supra* note 157.

North Korea.[180] It should concern the international community that China has reportedly built several new North Korean defector *refoulement* camps in its military installations near its borders and is sending hundreds of North Koreans back to North Korea almost every week.[181]

It is China's position to disregard the possibility that North Korean escapees may have a valid claim as refugees. China neither accepts North Korean escapees as refugees nor grants legal status to them to live in China, and continues to hinder North Koreans from leaving for third-party countries, including South Korea.[182] On December 5, 2002, Chinese and North Korean security forces jointly started a hundred-day campaign in an effort to find North Korean escapees.[183] According to NGOs, China returned up to one thousand North Koreans everyday from the initiation of the campaign to the end of the year.[184]

In May 2002, dozens of North Korean escapees entered the Spanish Embassy and the German School in Beijing and sought South Korea's protection. The South Korean foreign mission in China decided to accept all North Koreans who entered the foreign missions of South Korea and have expressed their desire for protection.[185] Since then, it has been the practice of the South Korean foreign missions to accommodate all North Koreans who successfully enter South Korea foreign missions in China.[186] Once a North Korean submits a protection application, the South Korean embassy begins to negotiate with the Chinese government.[187] Normally, North Korean applicants are able to go to South Korea by way of expulsion to a third country.[188]

It has been reported that some of the major transit states are Mongolia, Vietnam, Burma, Laos, Cambodia, and Thailand.[189] During this negotiation, which usually takes several months, North Korean escapees are lodged in a temporary camp inside the embassy.[190] However, it should be noted that due to Chinese security sealing off of South Korean missions,[191] it is extremely difficult for North Korean escapees to enter the missions to apply for protection. So far, the South

---

180 Huh, *supra* note 61.

181 *Id.*

182 Interview with Sahm-Hyun Song, *supra* note 169.

183 *WRS 2003*, *supra* note 4.

184 *Id.*

185 Interview with Dae-Jung Kwak, *supra* note 141.

186 *Id.*

187 *Id.*

188 *Id.*

189 The Invisible Exodus, *supra* note 64, at 6.

190 Interview with Sahm-Hyun Song, *supra* note 169. He further testified that North Korean asylum-seekers had a hard time there due to the poor condition of the facilities but the current circumstances did not allow expansion or improvement of the camp. *Id.*

191 The Invisible Exodus, *supra* note 64, at 3.

Korean government has not made public claims that North Koreans in China are entitled to diplomatic protection under South Korea's domestic law.

A report by the South Korean National Human Rights Commission explains the South Korean government's difficulties and limitations in protecting or supporting North Koreans.[192] It states that under international law and in reality, North Korea is a sovereign state, which seems to contradict the South Korean position that North Korea is not a sovereign state.[193] The reality of North Korea being a functioning nation-state limits South Korea's exercise of its right of diplomatic protection over North Koreans in third-party countries, especially in a country like China, which has a close relationship with North Korea. China does not consider North Korean escapees as South Korean nationals but rather treats them as illegal economic migrants from North Korea.[194]

b. *Vietnam*

As to the matter of North Korean escapees staying in Southeast Asian countries, the South Korean government cannot disclose any information about the diplomatic channels through which they are transferred to South Korea. While there is a possibility that South Korea is exercising the right to protect North Korean refugees, the countries concerned are not open about on what legal basis they are cooperating with South Korean authorities to channel North Koreans to South Korea. In this context, when 468 North Koreans entered South Korea in 2004, a South Korean government officer stated that "The entrance channel and the arrival time cannot be disclosed due to the diplomatic promise with the concerned state," and that "It is our policy that any matter concerning North Korean escapees will not be open to the public."[195]

Before October 2004, the South Korean foreign missions in Southeast Asian countries had accepted North Korean applications for protection.[196] However, North Korea made a strong protest to Vietnam for the channeling of 468 North Koreans to South Korea, and since then, the Vietnamese government has limited cooperation with South Korea on the issue of North Korean refugees.[197] Now, Vietnam strictly controls North Korean escapees and even punishes any person

---

192 Huh, *supra* note 61.

193 *Id.*; *see also* ANTHONY AUST, HANBOOK OF INTERNATIONAL LAW 189 (2007), economic migrants generally does not qualify for the refugee status.

194 Muico, *supra* note 103, at 7; Vitit Muntarbhorn, *Situation of Human Rights in the Democratic People's Republic of Korea* 10 (July 29, 2005).

195 In-Goo Kim, *Arrival of 200 North Korean Defectors*, CHOSUN.COM, July 27, 2004, *available at* http://www.chosun.com/national/news/200407/20040720020.html.

196 Interview with Dae-Jung Kwak, *supra* note 141.

197 *Id.*

who assists them.[198] Accordingly, the South Korean foreign missions in Vietnam can no longer process protection applications.

c. *Cambodia*

According to an official in charge of North Korean escapee matters in the Ministry of Justice, the King of Cambodia used to favor South Korea, but the opposition party objected to the idea of Cambodia becoming a transit state for North Koreans to South Korea.[199] Thus, Cambodia does not allow North Korean escapees to come to its territory and leave for South Korea.[200] Human Rights Watch refers to this practice in its assertion that the Cambodian government should turn over North Korean asylum-seekers it detained to South Korea.[201] Human Rights Watch further maintains that Cambodia should fulfill the obligations under the 1951 Convention and the 1967 Protocol, to both of which it is a state party.[202] It is unclear whether Cambodia will comply with international refugee protection standards.

2. Passive and Selective Protection

As indicated by the South Korean National Human Rights Commission in explaining the reasons for South Korea's limitations in protecting North Koreans,[203] there is the perspective under international law that North Korea is a sovereign state.[204] This limits South Korea's exercise of its right of diplomatic protection on behalf of North Koreans in third-party countries. This is especially true in a country like China, which views North Koreans as North Korean nationals and does not recognize their "semi-dual" status as South Korean. For China, they are mere illegal economic migrants, not refugees.[205] Second, North Koreans in third countries are in hiding, making it more difficult to have access to them and provide any kind of assistance through appropriate entities.[206] Last, there are allegedly false

---

198 Interview with Sahm-Hyun Song, *supra* note 169. He further testified that after this occurrence, North Korea has strongly criticized South Korea for "kidnapping" (forcibly taking) its nationals, which finally became one of the factors to cause the cease of talks between South and North Korea for a couple of months. *Id.*

199 *Id.*

200 *Id.*

201 Human Rights Watch, *Cambodia: Protect North Korean Asylum Seekers* (2004), *available at* http://hrw.org/english/docs/2004/09/24/cambod9386.htm.

202 *Id.*

203 Huh, *supra* note 61.

204 *Id.*

205 *Id.*

206 *Id.*

refugee protection cases fabricated by secret agents of North Korea which have undermined the credibility of North Korean escapees applying for protection.[207]

First, regarding North Korean sovereignty, while it is understandable that there is a gap between South Korean domestic law and international law on North Korea's status as a sovereign state, it is not legally sound to say that it is difficult to exercise the right of diplomatic protection in a country that does not recognize North Koreans as refugees. Under South Korean law, there is no distinction between North Koreans and South Koreans.[208] North Koreans are entitled to the same national protection as South Koreans, regardless of whether a third country recognizes them as illegal migrants.[209] While the previous statement is legally correct, in actual practice, the South Korean government has never explicitly claimed its right of diplomatic protection over North Koreans abroad. Second, North Korean escapees in China or other countries who crossed the border have no other choice than to stay in hiding. Only a few escapees have risked their lives to seek asylum.[210] It is simply difficult to extend any kind of protection to those who are in hiding or otherwise inaccessible. Lastly, the South Korean government should be aware that the existence of fabricated cases is an unavoidable problem in any asylum process.

Concerned human rights activists heavily criticize South Korea's inaction and discriminatory selection of whom to protect. Although South Korean missions had officially announced that it would not provide protection if applications were made outside the embassy, the government has secretly brought some North Koreans to South Korea who possessed information of high value through the maneuvering of the South Korean Intelligence Agency.[211]

Additionally, one of the NGOs for North Korean human rights complained that embassy officials did not properly carry out temporary protection measures.[212] In-Goo Kang, the Research Director of the Headquarter of the Campaign for Protecting North Korean Refugees, testified that South Korean officers permitted Chinese officers to interrogate the North Korean escapees who have already entered South Korean foreign missions.[213] According to his testimony, the Chinese government asks for permission from the South Korean government to

---

207 *Id.*

208 *See generally* Nu 1221, *supra* note 110; Heonba 78, *supra* note 115; Kye, *supra* note 116. South Korean courts and law scholars stating that the northern region of the Korean peninsula is part of the South Korean territory; *see also* N.A art. 2(1) (nationality is attributed at the time of birth on the Korean peninsula). *Id.*

209 Interview with Dae-Jung Kwak, *supra* note 141.

210 Amnesty Int'l, *China*, *supra* note 95, at 10.

211 Interview with Dae-Jung Kwak, *supra* note 141.

212 Interview with In-Goo Kang, Research Dir., Comm'n to Help North Korean Refugees (Apr. 14, 2005) (on file with author).

213 *Id.*

interview North Korean escapees in order to find out who assisted them to enter the embassy.[214] The South Korean authority permits the interviews and strongly recommends that escapees cooperate with Chinese security officers.[215] Scared of being taken to the Chinese government during the interrogation, the North Korean refugees usually provide Chinese officials with the information of the organizations or individuals that helped them out, thus putting the safety of human rights workers in jeopardy.[216]

The report by the National Human Rights Commission says that the South Korean government is being pressured to reduce the mass movement of North Koreans, to lessen protection of North Koreans in China, and not to support their entry into South Korea.[217] The Korean Consul at Shenyang, China also expressed his view that there is little possibility for China to recognize North Koreans as refugees.[218]

The report concludes that South Korea should instead ask China to provide aid to North Koreans rather than forcibly repatriate them unless they have criminal records in China.[219] This conclusion may be interpreted to suggest the dim prospect that the South Korean government would assert its right of diplomatic protection over North Koreans as its nationals.[220]

IV. International Protection

A. *Failure of International Protection*

Concerned international organizations face the same diplomatic limitations that the South Korean government faces in third-party countries like China. The Chinese government has not allowed any involvement of UNHCR with North Koreans since 1999 when UNHCR visited the China-North Korea border and determined that some North Koreans were refugees.[221] International organizations generally have no police power and normally do not offer any political or economic incentives for cooperation.[222] Therefore, a request for cooperation by international organizations has no effect on third-party countries that are in zealous pursuit of political or economic gains. The UNHCR has continuously voiced its concern

---

214 *Id.*
215 *Id.*
216 *Id.*
217 Huh, *supra* note 61.
218 *Id.*
219 *Id.*
220 *Id.*
221 *WRS 2000*, *supra* note 105.
222 U.S. Comm. for Human Rights in N. Korea: Failure to Protect A Call for the UN Security Council to Act in North Korea 70 (2006) [hereinafter Failure to Protect].

over North Koreans in flight, particularly in China,[223] but it has been plagued by the same limitations.[224]

In this regard, the international community maintains the view that North Korean asylum-seekers may not be entitled to international protection within its mandate because North Koreans are also South Korean nationals under South Korean domestic law. Article 1(A)(2) of the 1951 Refugee Convention stipulates:

> In the case of a person who has more than one nationality, the term "the country of his nationality" shall mean each of the countries of which he is a national, and a person shall not be deemed to be lacking the protection of the country of his nationality if, without any valid reason based on well-founded fear, he has not availed himself of the protection of one of the countries of which he is a national.[225]

Clearly, the recognition of North Koreans as South Korean nationals under South Korean law is based on the non-recognition of North Korea as a sovereign state.[226]

While South Korea is reluctant to apply its national law beyond its border, the South Korean government's domestic practice has consistently treated North Koreans as South Korean nationals. This practice refers to the protection and recognition of North Korean escapees as South Korean nationals without a naturalization process once they reach South Korean soil.[227]

As discussed previously, national protection by the South Korean government of North Korean escapees is ineffective. It appears that only a few countries are aware of South Korean law dealing with North Koreans abroad. UNHCR is, or should be, aware of the ineffectiveness and inadequacy of national protection by the South Korean government. The Handbook on Procedures and Criteria for Determining Refugee Status under the 1951 Convention and the 1967 Protocol relating to the Status of Refugees, in Paragraph 97, explains the phrase "and is unable or, owing to such fear, is unwilling to avail himself of the protection of that country" as the following: "... the present phrase relates to persons who have

---

223 *WRS 2000*, *supra* note 105.

224 FAILURE TO PROTECT, *supra* note 222.

225 Convention Relating to the Status of Refugees art. 1(A)(2), April 22, 1954, 189 U.N.T.S. 137.

226 Nu 1221, *supra* note 110; Heonba 78, *supra* note 111; Kye, *supra* note 112; *see also* N.A art. 2(1)(3). Nationality is attributed to an individual at the time of birth on the Korean peninsula.

227 *See generally* Dong-Hyun Seok, *supra* note 117. Given that a North Korean is attributed with South Korean nationality, it would defeat the purpose of the Nationality Act to stipulate naturalization procedures for North Korean who enters into South Korean territory. *Id.*

a nationality. Whether unable or unwilling to avail himself of the protection of his Government, a refugee is always a person who does not enjoy such protection."[228]

In many cases, North Korean asylum-seekers are unable to avail themselves of the protection by the South Korean government due to its substantially passive and ineffective protection of its "semi-dual" citizens abroad. Once China sealed off the South Korean missions, any application of protection became very limited, if not impossible.[229] While there are reports that these refugees are being arrested, detained, deported, tortured, or even executed after forceful repatriation to North Korea,[230] South Korea has never openly claimed or is not willing to claim its right of diplomatic protection over North Koreans in third-party countries. This deficient provision of national protection makes it impossible for North Koreans to avail themselves of the protection they are entitled to.

In regard to international protection of North Koreans in China, *The Global Appeal*, published by the UNHCR, has reported over a six year period (2002–2007) as follows:

(1) 2007: "UNHCR continues to seek durable solutions for individuals refugees in China, principally through resettlement, where protection concerns include the lack of appropriate national refugee regulations, and the legal status of North Koreans; in particular the need to prevent forced deportation and to create humanitarian space."[231]
(2) 2006: "UNHCR continues to call... for increased access to North Korean asylum-seekers who may be in need of international protection."[232]
(3) 2005: "The [UNHCR] Office will pursue practical approaches with the [Chinese] Government to provide protection and facilitate durable solutions for North Koreans of concern to UNHCR."[233]

---

228 UNHCR, Handbook on Procedures and Criteria for Determining Refugee Status under the 1951 Convention and the 1967 Protocol relating to the Status of Refugees ¶ 97 (1979).

229 Interview with Dae-Jung Kwak, *supra* note 141. South Korean embassy officials may not go out and physically bring North Koreans requesting protection into the embassy due to the anticipated diplomatic conflict with the concerned government. The South Korean Embassy in Beijing has officially announced that they would not provide this kind of assistance. In sum, if a North Korean physically enters an embassy or a foreign mission compound, his application for protection shall be accepted, but if he asks for protection by phone or other means outside the embassy, it will be rejected. *Id.*

230 *WRS 2000*, *supra* note 109; The Invisible Exodus, *supra* note 64.

231 UNHCR, Global Appeals 2007, Fundraising Reports (Dec. 31, 2006) 273 (Nov. 2008), *available at* http://www.unhcr.org/static/publ/ga2007/ga2007toc.htm.

232 UNHCR, Global Appeals 2006, Fundraising Reports (Dec. 31, 2005) 281 (Nov. 2007), *available at* http://www.unhcr.org/static/publ/ga2006/ga2006toc.htm.

233 UNHCR, Global Appeals 2005, Fundraising Reports (Dec. 31, 2004) 254 (Dec. 2006), *available at* http://www.unhcr.org/static/publ/ga2005/ga2005toc.htm.

(4) 2004: "UNHCR remains concerned about the plight of North Koreans in China... Based on available information, North Koreans who left their country illegally fall within the criteria of persons considered to be of concern to UNHCR."[234]
(5) 2003: "UNHCR remains concerned about the situation of North Koreans in China, some of whom may be in need of international protection."[235]
(6) 2002: "UNHCR remains concerned about the risk of deportation of North Koreans elsewhere in China. UNHCR continues to seek access to these people in order to ascertain asylum claims, as among these individuals there may be persons in need of international protection."[236]

These reports demonstrate that UNHCR has shown concern for the North Koreans in China for years. While acknowledging them as "people who may be in need of international protection," UNHCR has been largely unsuccessful in their attempt to gain access to the North Koreans.[237]

Further, the Country Operations Plan for China also reveals that the Beijing Representation of UNHCR has shown concerns about North Korean asylum-seekers and has struggled to improve the situation. The relevant excerpts out of each year's Country Operations Plan for six years are as follows:

(1) 2007: Differences between UNHCR and the government on the status, situation and treatment of North Korean in China, continue to restrict the scope of UNHCR's protection activities beyond monitoring and advocacy. Thus, UNHCR's main objectives for 2007 are to maintain an accurate understanding of the situation and treatment of North Koreans in China; the prevention of forced deportation; and the creation of a humanitarian space in China for this beneficiary population. Building on the outcome of the visit of the High Commissioner to China in March 2006, and the meetings he held with Chinese interlocutors on that issue, UNHCR will also engage in further expert discussions between UNHCR and Chinese counterparts on the legal status of this population.[238]

---

234 UNHCR, Global Appeals 2004, Fundraising Reports (Dec. 31, 2006) 386 (June 2005), *available at* http://www.unhcr.org/static/publ/gr2004/gr2004toc.htm.

235 UNHCR, Global Appeals 2003, Fundraising Reports (Dec. 31, 2002) 214 (June 2004), *available at* http://www.unhcr.org/static/publ/gr2003/gr2003toc.htm.

236 UNHCR, Global Appeals 2002, Fundraising Reports (Dec. 31, 2001) 341 (June 2003), *available at* http://www.unhcr.org/static/publ/gr2002/gr2002toc.htm.

237 Failure to Protect, *supra* note 224.

238 UNHCR, Country Operations Plan 2007—People's Republic of China (Mainland China, Hong Kong SAR, Macao SAR and Mongolia) 2 (Sept. 1, 2006), *available at* http://www.unhcr.org/refworld/country,,,COP,CHN,,450e588a2,0.html.

(2) 2006: North East of China, a region where most North Koreans are believed to live and work, remains inaccessible for UNHCR. While the Chinese government claims that all the North Koreans in China are illegal economic migrants, due to excessive punishment they often face if (forcibly) returned to North Korea because of their illegal departure, UNHCR believes that they are persons of concern. Nevertheless, it is assumed that some common ground can be found in addressing the root-causes that compel North Koreans to leave their country, the problems faced by those North Koreans already living in China, and the situation of (forced) returns to the Democratic People's Republic of North Korea. In addition, UNHCR will continue to intervene in the cases of individual asylum-seekers approaching the office. UNHCR will continue to monitor the situation of North Korean asylum-seekers and related developments within and beyond the sub-region, through various sources, including UNHCR's representative offices and non-governmental organizations in asylum countries, and relevant advocacy constituencies.[239]

(3) 2005: UNHCR has not been granted access to North Korean asylum-seekers in China and substantive progress has not been made in seeking arrangements that would provide protection and solutions for them. In light of these unsatisfactory circumstances, the High Commissioner concluded in September 2003, that in view of their international protection needs, North Koreans in China were considered to be, as a group, persons of concern to his Office. UNHCR will continue to seek a meaningful dialogue with the Chinese authorities towards harmonizing approaches to promote asylum, prevent *refoulement* and facilitate solutions for North Korean asylum-seekers.[240]

(4) 2004: The situation of North Korean asylum-seekers remains of particular concern due to lack of access. UNHCR will pursue practical approaches with the Government to provide protection and facilitate durable solutions for North Koreans.[241]

(5) 2003: UNHCR will continue to pursue ways and means of harmonizing approaches with the concerned governments to promote asylum, prevent *refoulement* and facilitate durable solutions for all asylum-seekers in the sub-region.[242]

(6) 2002: UNHCR's goal is to improve international protection for, and provide essential assistance to, refugees and asylum-seekers, and to seek durable

---

[239] UNHCR, COUNTRY OPERATIONS PLAN 2006—CHINA, HONG KONG SAR, MACAO SAR AND MONGOLIA 1 (Sept. 1, 2005), *available at* http://www.unhcr.org/refworld/country,,,COP,CHN,,4332c4e32,0.html.

[240] UNHCR, Country Operations Plan 2005—China 2 (Sept. 1, 2004), *available at* http://www.unhcr.org/refworld/docid/4180ea894.html.

[241] UNHCR, Country Operations Plan 2004—China 2 (Sept. 1, 2003), *available at* http://www.unhcr.org/refworld/country,,,COP,CHN,,3f8138314,0.html.

[242] UNHCR, Country Operations Plan 2003—China 2 (Sept. 1, 2002), *available at* http://www.unhcr.org/refworld/country,,,COP,CHN,,3d941f510,0.html.

> solutions for refugees in Mainland China, Hong Kong SAR, Macau SAR, and Mongolia... The situation of North Korean asylum-seekers remains of particular concern... Concerning North Korean asylum-seekers, a constructive dialogue with the Chinese authorities and other concerned governments will be further pursued, to establish closer understanding and co-operation towards approaches that would address issues such as *refoulement* and the provision of international protection to genuine asylum-seekers.[243]

However, the statistics in *2004 Global Refugee Trends* do not reflect concern over North Koreans which is evidence of UNHCR's failure to provide effective international protection. For example, the population of North Korean refugees throughout the world identified by UNHCR was 304 at the start of 2004 and 343 at the end.[244] Also, the total number of North Korean asylum-seekers worldwide identified by UNHCR in the same year was 44 at the start of the year and 69 at the end.[245] UNHCR has been blocked from access to North Koreans detained by various local authorities. However, the tally of 304 refugees and 187 asylum-seekers demonstrates that UNHCR should become more active and improve its effectiveness in assisting those in need of international protection.

More surprisingly, none of the North Korean refugees in 2004 received assistance from UNHCR.[246] Likewise, none of the asylum-seekers in 2004 received assistance from UNHCR.[247] In China, 91 mandate refugees received UNHCR's protection,[248] and 10,812 Vietnamese refugees are also being assisted by UNHCR.[249] While UNHCR faces many barriers in executing and implementing its missions, the fact that no North Korean asylum-seeker received assistance from UNHCR in 2004 reflects the total failure of international protection.

Even though China is a state party to a number of human rights treaties, including the 1951 Refugee Convention, the 1967 Protocol, and the Convention Against Torture, China has exempted itself from the clause which grants the International Court of Justice jurisdiction over disputes arising under those treaties.[250] Therefore, unless China voluntarily submits itself to the jurisdiction of

---

243 UNHCR, Country Operations Plan 2002—China 2 (July 1, 2001), *available at* http://www.unhcr.org/refworld/country,,,COP,CHN,,3b666cd31,0.html.

244 UNHCR, Population and Geographical Data Section, Division of Operational Support, *2004 Global Refugee Trends: Overview of Refugee Populations, New Arrivals, Durable Solutions, Asylum-Seekers, Stateless and Other Persons of Concern to UNHCR*, Geneva, 20 (June 17, 2005).

245 *Id.* at 42.

246 *Id.*

247 *Id.*

248 *Id.* at 60.

249 *Id.* at 32.

250 Interview by ChosunJournal.Com with Tarik M. Radwan, Assistant Professor of Law, Handong Int'l Law School, in Seoul, S. Korea (Jan. 21, 2003), *available at* http://www.chosunjournal.com/radwaninterview.html.

the International Court of Justice, which is highly unlikely, there is no other way to compel its jurisdiction over China.[251] Hence, China maintains the illegitimate position that illegal North Korean escapees cannot apply for asylum.[252]

The one exception is found in the 1995 Agreement, whereby the UNHCR maintains an office in China and sets forth how the UNHCR will conduct itself there.[253] However, the Agreement does not replace the 1961 Convention and the 1967 Protocol.[254]

Under the terms of the Agreement, the UNHCR, with the cooperation of the government, is to have "unimpeded access to refugees" in the country.[255] Disputes between the two parties are, if necessary, to be resolved through binding arbitration.[256] UNHCR, however, has not invoked this provision, saying "the primary purpose of the agreement was to ensure the appropriate status and treatment of the UNHCR office, staff, and property, with binding arbitration available to resolve disputes over such matters."[257] It continues to say that "China's obligations toward refugees and its duty to cooperate with UNHCR, while noted in the agreement, are enshrined in the Convention itself and should be governed by the Convention."[258] Like the South Korean government, UNHCR appears to be very cautious in providing protection to people of its particular concern.

B. *U.S. North Korean Human Rights Act: Desirable Alternative*

The U.S. North Korean Human Rights Act[259] should be considered a desirable model that may encourage the international community to expand protection for those in needs. However, this Act has been criticized by many interested groups as exceeding its authority.[260] The Act illustrates a uniquely abnormal situation in North Korea that its people are forced to endure in Section 3(1)–(15), (20).

These illustrations are summarized in Section 308(a)(1), which reads: "In general—For purposes of section 244(b)(1)(C) of the Immigration and Nationality Act (8 U.S.C. § 1254a(b)(1)(C)), extraordinary and temporary conditions shall be considered to exist in North Korea that prevent aliens who are natives or citizens

---

251 *Id.*

252 *Id.*

253 *Id.*

254 *Id.*

255 *Id.*

256 *Id.*

257 U.N. Comm. for Refugees and Immigrants (USCRI), *World Refugee Survey 2003: Country Reports—China (2003)*.

258 *Id.*

259 North Korean Human Rights Act of 2004, Pub. L. 108–333, 118 Stat. 1287, codified in 22 U.S.C. § 7842 (2004).

260 Se-Moon Chang, *North Korean Human Rights Act*, KOREA TIMES, Dec. 31, 2004, at 6.

of North Korea from returning to North Korea in safety."[261] These findings are not only authoritative, but also similar to what others have found in North Korea as mentioned earlier.

Furthermore, this Act accurately depicts the reality of North Koreans in flight and hiding, particularly in China. It is enumerated in Section 3, Subsections 16 to 19. These Subsections allude to human trafficking, sexual exploitation, *refoulement*, and the Chinese government's breach of its obligations under the 1951 Convention and the 1967 Protocol. They are the same issues that international organizations and domestic and international NGOs have repeatedly recognized and reported.

Although the U.S. recognizes that South Korea will play a principal role in rescuing North Koreans, Section 3(24) of the U.S. North Korean Human Rights Act encourages the U.S. to take the lead role when dealing with North Korean refugee issues.[262] It states:

> Although the principal responsibility for North Korean refugee resettlement naturally falls to the Government of South Korea, the United States should play a leadership role in focusing international attention on the plight of these refugees, formulating international solutions to that profound humanitarian dilemma, and making prudent arrangements to accept a credible number of refugees for domestic resettlement.[263]

Although the major political party and NGOs in South Korea expressed concerns about the possibility of the U.S. interfering with the sovereignty of South Korea,[264] domestic groups did not contend that they could have done more to save their brethren had the U.S. not taken action to rescue the North Korean refugees.

The key idea of this Act that may help the concerned international organizations overcome the most critical legal obstacle is laid out in Section 302 as follows:

> (a) Purpose—The purpose of this section is to ensure that North Koreans are not barred from eligibility for refugee status or asylum in the United States on account of any legal right to citizenship they may enjoy under the Constitution of the Republic of Korea. It is not intended in any way to prejudice whatever rights to citizenship North Koreans may enjoy under the Constitution of the Republic of Korea.
> (b) Treatment of Nationals of North Korea—For purposes of eligibility for refugee status under section 207 of the Immigration and Nationality Act (8 U.S.C. § 1157), or for asylum under section 208 of such Act (8 U.S.C. § 1158), a national of the Democratic People's Republic of Korea shall not be considered a national of the Republic of Korea.[265]

---

261 U.S. North Korean Human Rights Act of 2004, *supra* note 259.

262 *Id.* § 3(24).

263 *Id.*

264 Chang, *supra* note 260.

265 U.S. North Korean Human Rights Act, *supra* note 259, § 302(a)–(b); Since the passage of the North Korean Human Rights Act in 2004 to early 2011 approximately 130 North

Subsection (b) provides that a North Korean shall not be considered a national of South Korea, which allows North Koreans to be eligible for refugee status. This legal fiction is intended only to grant protection to those who need it in the context of asylum and immigration, and it appears to be more efficient than any other legal means designed to protect them.

C. *Role of International Protection: Safety Net*

International protection is called for when national protection fails to function properly. While the two key players on whom North Korean refugees lay their hope repeat the same justification for their failure of providing adequate protection, North Korean refugees are being abused in their host countries or deported back to the North where they are tortured and may face execution. Providing protection for the voiceless, who are being abused and who are at risk of persecution upon deportation, is not a political issue, but rather a humanitarian and legal matter. If the problem could be resolved by political power or mechanisms, international organizations with humanitarian mandates would be rendered moot. Only action can save the lives of the most vulnerable who despair in silence. Then, who should take action?

All governments or international organizations engaged in bilateral human rights dialogues with China, including the U.S., Japan, the European Union, U.K., Canada, and Australia, should ensure that the specific recommendations regarding North Korean migrants and asylum-seekers are prominent on the agenda for all dialogue meetings, and also meetings between foreign ministers and heads of state and senior Chinese officials.[266] Members of parliament should also be active. Resolutions adopted by parliaments are also helpful to increase the pressure on China to comply with its international refugee obligations.[267]

Countries affected by North Korean migrant flows, including Russia, Mongolia, Vietnam, Burma, Laos, Cambodia, and Thailand, should grant asylum. They should also ensure that North Korean migrants are not prevented from seeking permanent asylum in third countries.[268] North Korea's neighbors should refuse any requests by North Korea to arrest asylum-seekers or forcibly return them to North Korea where they would be at serious risk of torture, ill-treatment, arbitrary detention, or execution.[269]

Korean refugees have settled in the United States; between 1994 and 2012, more than 23,000 have settled in South Korea; between 1994 to 2008, approximately 2,900 have settled in Europe.

[266] The Invisible Exodus, *supra* note 64, at 11.

[267] *Id.*

[268] *Id.*

[269] *Id.*

V. Conclusion

North Korean refugee issues deserve immediate attention. All the measures offered above by various groups concerning North Koreans in-flight would help to improve the situation. However, they require that the governments of concerned countries act to find collective solutions for the problem. Unfortunately, governments, including parliaments, are preoccupied with their own political interests. In 1951, the signatories of the Refugee Convention recognized that nations are not willing to take care of asylum-seekers without entering into a binding treaty and created an international organization to address the matter. The core nature of governments is self-serving and will not change any time soon. That is why international organizations have been established, and why they are playing such a critical role as a minimum safety net. Now is the time for international organizations to exercise their mandate, stand strong, and use all possible means to assist North Koreans in flight.

CHAPTER ELEVEN

INTERNATIONAL LEGAL EDUCATION UNDER KOREA'S NEW LAW SCHOOL SYSTEM

Hee Moon Jo*

I. Introduction

International legal education in Korea witnessed a major shift with the implementation of the law school system in 2007,[1] admitting its first students in 2009.[2] Under the new system, students are required to complete the professional graduate program at a law school to be qualified to take the new bar examination. The purpose of this new education system is "to train lawyers with sophisticated culture, deep understandings in humanity and society and to aim for healthy professional ethics based on liberty, equality, justice. . . ."[3]

Changes in society have led to complicated legal problems, requiring sound ethics and professionalism, seemingly unobtainable from the existing legal education system.[4] The existing system allowed anyone to sit for the bar examination as long as the candidate had a minimum number of law course credits.[5] This caused too many candidates to unsuccessfully toil year after year in an attempt

---

* Professor of Law, Hankuk University of Foreign Studies Law School.

1 Graduate Law School Establishment and Management Law (GLSL) of 2008, L. No. 8852.

2 While 2000 students have been admitted to 25 law schools, there is still much debate about the ideal number of law school admittees.

3 GLSL, *supra* note 1, art. 2 (Educational Ideal): "The educational ideal of law schools is to train lawyers with sophisticated culture, deep understandings in humanity and society and to aim for healthy professional ethics based on liberty, equality, justice, and the ability to solve complex legal disputes professionally and efficiently, thus to provide quality legal services to the public."

4 Ahn, Hyung Jun, *The ongoing direction of the Korean Bar Exam System*, Int'l Symposium on the Bar Exam Systems in the United States of America and Japan and Korea's Task 144 (Nov. 17, 2008).

5 Anyone, including foreigners, with more than 35 credits in law courses can take the bar examination.

to pass the bar exam. Therefore, the government adopted the new law school system to meet social demands and to strictly regulate the education system, school facilities, and the process for entering the legal profession.[6] For example, the universities that established law schools must eliminate their existing undergraduate legal education courses.[7] The law school faculty-student ratio must be 1 to 15,[8] with at least 20 full-time instructors.[9] These changes greatly reduce the number of law students compared to the previous system. Moreover, at least 20% of the law school faculty should be licensed lawyers, local or foreign, with at least 5 years experience.[10] Overall, the new law school system emphasizes practical education.

The purpose of law school is to train lawyers in various fields of expertise. Thus, each law school must offer specialized programs. To obtain diversity and expertise, students are required to take courses that meet their aptitudes and fields, thus de-emphasizing preparing for the bar exam during the three years of law school. For this, the most important factor is the bar exam pass rate. In the United States (US) and Japan, the two systems on which the Korean system is based, the concept of the bar exam is different. The bar exam in the US merely verifies the exam-taker's minimal competence as lawyer.[11] It has a relative evaluation system that determines the pass rate every year and gives the examinee a standardized score. Thus, a pass rate of over 70% for first time exam-takers is usually achieved.[12]

On the other hand, Japan's bar exam pass rate remains at approximately 30%. Japan's new bar examination was adopted in 2006 with the goal of accomplishing a 70–80% pass rate. However, the first pass rate was 48% and the numbers dropped 5–8% every year, with the fourth exam in 2009 having a passage rate of only 27.6%. Some critics argue that the government manipulates the bar examination to admit only those who meet the requirements of a lawyer and that the low pass rates means that there is a lack of students who are qualified.[13] Thus, the Japanese expect one to be fully qualified as a lawyer to pass the bar exam. Unlike the US, the Japanese bar exam is an absolute evaluation system, so the difficulty and content of the exam differ greatly between the two countries. Japan has three compulsory subjects (public law, civil law, and criminal law) and one elective

---

6 GLSL, *supra* note 1, arts. 4–7.

7 *Id.* art. 8.

8 *Id.* art. 16, para. 1.

9 *Id.* para. 3.

10 *Id.* para. 4.

11 David Lee Mundy, *Yes Graduation Licensure, No Korean Bar Examination?*, Int'l Symposium on the Bar Exam Systems in the United States of America and Japan and Korea's Task 47 (Nov. 17, 2008).

12 *Id.* at 54.

13 Goto Akira, *Japan's Bar Exam System*, Int'l Symposium on the Bar Exam Systems in the United States of America and Japan and Korea's Task 10, 13 (Nov. 17, 2008).

subject, and the exam is comprised of short answer questions (40%) and essays (25%). Short answer questions and essays have a minimum score requirement, while examinees must also pass an overall score limit set by the bar examination committee.[14] The minimum score for the fourth bar exam was 785 points (50%).

Korea's new legal education system follows the US system for law school management but the Japanese system for bar exams. Judging from Japan's recent experience, Korea's pass rates will also likely drop each year; and may result in law school education becoming heavily dependent on the bar exam passage rate, which contradicts the establishment objectives. Korea's first bar exam pass rate under the new system in 2012 was 87.15% and 75.2% for the second bar examination in 2013; quite high compared to the initial pass rate in Japan after the implementation of the law school system. If legal education and training is to keep up with Korea's globalization, the bar exam should not test one's full qualifications as a lawyer, but rather, verify one's minimal qualifications. Otherwise, the education process will become driven by preparing for bar exam subjects.

The biggest change with the introduction of the law school system is that sitting for the bar exam is now limited to those who have graduated from law school.[15] The previous bar exam was a civil service examination; those who passed had to also undergo two years of training at the Judicial Research and Training Institute (JRTI) in order to become a judge, prosecutor, or lawyer. With the new system, however, one must graduate from a law school to take the test; the bar exam therefore becomes a qualification test rather than a civil service exam. To meet the law school establishment purposes, some prerequisite issues must be resolved.

First of all, is the new system more efficient than the system it is replacing? Under the new system one has to spend four years in university and three years in law school, so there should be an alternative option for those who fail the exam. The crucial point is whether the test is a simple qualification exam or one that requires extensive legal knowledge. Currently, concerns for the pass rate are high because the bar exam follows the Japanese exam model, and the level of knowledge necessary for passing the exam is expected to be similar to the knowledge required of first year JRTI trainees. In other words, students have to undergo the pressure of passing the exam, which in turn makes them focus more on the exam subjects while in law school.[16]

Furthermore, it is necessary to evaluate what law firms, businesses, or even the government itself expect from lawyers who graduate from these law schools. Currently, each law school must decide its specialized legal area, limit the number

---

14 *Id.* at 18–19.

15 Bar Examination Law of 2009, art. 5, L. No. 9747.

16 Ahn, *supra* note 4, at 150 (arguing that the new bar exam will be operating as simple qualification test as shown in art. 10, para. 1 of the Bill (art. 9, para. 3) contrary to the Japanese testing system).

of students, and regulate facilities and full time faculty. Undoubtedly, it is very important to forecast the potential demands.

Additionally, students will come to law school with more specific and determined goals than ever before. It will be necessary to establish educational systems to satisfy their needs beyond the bar exam. Law schools have to find a way to satisfy the school-student-business relationship. Nevertheless, it is the government that holds the key variable for law school—student enrollment and bar exam pass rates.

The following sections will evaluate the efforts to teach international law in the past three years at Korean law schools, noting that its success or failure will only be fully determinable after analyzing the bar exam results. Thus, this evaluation will be limited to the international law curriculum and lecture methods. This chapter will discuss the fundamental limits of the new bar exam, the specific areas of international law taught in each school, lecture methods, and conclude with a general evaluation.

II. Reflection upon Existing Education Methods

There are various reasons for restricting the scope and methods of teaching international law in law classes, but there are two that have the strongest influence. First is that international law is being considered for inclusion in the Civil Service Examination. Because Korean students grow up in an educational system based on harsh competition and exam scores, disciplines that are not exam subjects do not receive much attention. Even exam subjects that are perceived to be difficult or broad in scope tend to be avoided by students. International law is no exception.

The second reason is Korea's position in international society. When Korea was economically underdeveloped, international law had limited practical use. International law was treated as an idealistic study on world peace, war, international organizations, and human rights in pursuit of international diplomacy. However, the establishment of diplomatic relations with Russia in 1990, membership in the UN along with North Korea in 1991, the establishment of diplomatic relations with China in 1992, the founding of the WTO in 1995, and OECD membership in 1996 triggered social interest in international law. Globalization raised many international legal issues for domestic businesses. Thus, within the last 20 years, the perception of international law has changed in many ways.

Although the curriculum or teaching methods cannot be modified quickly, many younger scholars are rethinking these aspects of international legal education. While questions on international law exams have become longer and more complex, the challenge remains in ensuring that the level of difficulty will not lead to the problem of losing student interest in these courses.

Interest in international economic law and trade law grew greatly with the growth of the economy, and with that, there was an awareness of the importance of English. It was thought that the study of international law required proficiency in English. However, although many international law scholars have studied in English speaking countries, most of them are not able to teach international law in English. Moreover, its inclusion as a bar exam subject makes it counterproductive to conduct such courses in English.

Another interesting factor is the convergence of domestic and international law. Because international legal issues also arise domestically, domestic legal scholars are taking an interest in international law, and international legal scholars in domestic law. Interest in interdisciplinary approaches is increasing as well.

III. International Legal Education under the Law School System

Established in 2009, the law school system is distinct from the former legal education curriculum. The 25 law schools reflect Korea's globalized society by focusing on international law. The number of international law courses offered at each law school (public and private international law), as surveyed by Professor Ki-Gab Park of Korea University, is shown in Table 1.[17]

Professor Park states that among international law courses, English lectures and practical courses (e.g., business, human rights, dispute resolution, especially those in the field of international trade) increased in number, whereas it was difficult to find traditional international legal courses such as maritime law, armed conflict, and humanitarian law. As shown in the above research, the current law school curriculum shows some distinct differences from the former legal educational system.

Table 1. Number of international law courses at Korean law schools.

Number of international law courses	Number of law schools
1–5	5
6–10	14
11–15	3
16–20	3

[17] Ki-Gab Park, Current Status and Analysis of International Law Courses in Law Schools (unpublished paper presented at the Korean Society of International Law Conference) (July 17, 2009) (on file with author).

A. *The Preference of Globalization is Strong as a Specialized Field of Law Schools*

When they were established, each of the 25 law schools selected its own specialized field of law as shown below. As Table 2 shows, 10 out of 25 law schools use the terms "international" or "global," although all of the law schools have some connection to global topics as evident in the number of international law courses and their contents. However, as also shown in the table below, the number of full-time faculty for specialized field is limited, so the effectiveness of the specialization system needs to be further evaluated.

Table 2. Specialized fields and number of full-time instructors.

Law school	Specialized field	Number of full-time instructors
Kangwon	Environmental Law	3
Konkuk	Real Estate Law	3
Kyonpook	IT Law	1
Kyunghee	Global Business Law	3
Korea	International Law	7
Dong-A	International Commercial Law	2
Pusan	Finance. Maritime Trade	3
Sogang	Business Law	2
Seoul National	International Law, Public Rights, Corporate Finance	3
University of Seoul	Tax Law	2
SungKyunKwan	Business Law	4
Ajou	Small-Medium Business Law	2
Yonsei	Public Governance, Global Business, Medical Science Technology	5
Yeungnam	Public Interest, Human Rights	1
Wonkwang	Biomedical Science	7
Ewha	Biomedical Law	3
Inha	Intellectual Property Rights, Logistics	7
Chonnam	Public Interest, Human Rights	2
Chonbuk	Northeast Asia Law	2
Cheju	International Law	2
Chungang	Culture Law	3
Chungnam	Intellectual Property Rights	4
Chungbuk	Science Technology Law	3
Hankuk University of Foreign Studies	International & Regional Law	3
Hanyang	International Litigation, Cultural Knowledge Business, Public Minority Rights	No data available

Source: Soon-hyun Im, *Shunning Specialized Courses*, Law Times (May 29, 2010) (revised by author).

B. *Increasing Views of International Law as a Practical Study*

The law school curriculum regards international law as a practical field of study, which is also reflected in the requirement to have 20% of the faculty who are licensed lawyers with five years of experience.[18] Consequently, legal education is intended to be practical. The law schools have a variety of international law courses that are categorized in different disciplines which are practical and specialized. The number of courses that are conducted in English demonstrates a desire to globalize legal education.

Table 3. Types of International law courses at Korean law schools.

Course	Law schools	Course taught in English
State Jurisdiction and Exemptions	Hanyang, Yonsei	
International Trade Law	All	
International Law (International Trade Law, WTO Law)	All	Korea, Yonsei, Kyunghee, University of Seoul, Hankuk University of Foreign Studies (HUFS)
International (Public) Law	All	Kyunghee, Korea, Ewha, University of Seoul, Chungang
International Relations Law	Kangwon	
International Disarmament Law	Yeungnam	
International Organization Law	Sungkyunkwan, Yonsei, Ewha, Chonnam, Cheju, University of Seoul, HUFS	Korea, Kyunghee
International Trade and Environment	Korea	
International Distribution Dispute Resolution Law	Inha	
International Civil Litigation Law	Seoul National	
International and Domestic Law	Pusan, Yonsei	
International Law Mock Trial	Korea	
International Law Case Study	Konkuk, Dong-A, Chonbuk, Korea, University of Seoul	
International Law Seminar	Sogang, Yeungnam, Inha, Chungbuk, Kyongbuk	
International Dispute Resolution	Konkuk, Kyongbuk, Korea, Pusan, Seoul National, Yonsei, Chungang, Hanyang, Ajou	
International Jurisdiction	Seoul National, Inha, HUFS	

[18] GLSL, *supra* note 1, art. 16, para. 4.

Table 3 (*cont.*)

Course	Law schools	Course taught in English
International Litigation and Arbitration	Seoul National, Hanyang	HUFS
International Export Regulation Law		Kyonghee
International Human Rights Law	Kangwon, Konkuk, Kyongbuk, Korea, Pusan, Sogang, Seoul National, Sungkyunkwan, Yonsei, Yeungnam, Ewha, Inha, Cheju, Chungang, University of Seoul, Chonbuk, HUFS	University of Seoul (Japanese), Chonnam
International Humanitarian Law	Yeungnam, Ewha	
International Treaty Law	Konkuk, Pusan, Seoul National	
International Tax Law	Inha	
International Intellectual Property Law	Korea, Inha, Chungnam	
International Trade Law Seminar	Sogang, Hantang	Ewha, Chungang
International Trade Dispute	Korea, Dong-A, Yonsei, Yeungnam, Inha, Hanyang	Seoul National, University of Seoul, Ewha, Chungang
International Investment Law	Korea, Seoul National, Cheju	Korea, HUFS
International Maritime Law	Pusan, Inha, Cheju, Chungnam, University of Seoul	University of Seoul
International Criminal Law	Sogang, Yonsei, Hanyang	Kangwon, Ewha
International Environment Law	Kangwon, Konkuk, Dong-A, Seoul National, Sungkyunkwan, Yonsei, Inha, Chungnam, Ajou, HUFS	Seoul National
Global Governance and International Law	Cheju, Yonsei	
Foreign Public Law	Korea, Ajou	
Northeast Asia and Human Rights	Chonbuk	
East Asia International Law	Seoul National	
Trade Relief Business	Seoul National, Ajou	
US and EU Trade Law	Yeungnam, University of Seoul	
Antidumping Law	Korea	
Bioengineer and International Law		Kyonghee
Asian Law	Inha	
UK and US Law	Inha	HUFS
Diplomacy and International Law Business	Inha	
Space Development Law	Chungbuk	
FTA	Korea, Songkyunkwan	Chungang, Ewha
Aerospace Law		Kangwon

Table 3 (*cont.*)

Course	Law schools	Course taught in English
EU Law	Korea, Yonsei, Inha, Kyungbuk, Chonnam	Chungang
GATS & TRIPS	Yonsei, University of Seoul	
International Taxation	Seoul National	
WTO and Northeast Asia	Chonbuk	

Source: Ki-Gab Park, Current Status and Analysis of International Law Courses in Law Schools (unpublished paper presented at the Korean Society of International Law Conference) (July 17, 2009) (table revised by author).

A notable point is that many law school students wish to increase their studies more in the field of international law. In the case of HUFS, more than half of the students in the second year, 26 out of 50, showed an interest in international law related work.[19] Because HUFS students are more fluent in English than students from other Korean law schools, they are willing to attend English lectures despite the challenges of the bar examination.

Also, students voluntarily create study groups and academic societies to research certain specialized areas. For example, HUFS has student groups that are focused on international law, international law research (an English debating group), carbon emission trading schemes, etc.[20] These students have a specific preference for their future careers. Another notable phenomenon is the creation of student run journals at law schools which started with the publication of *Chungbuk Law Journal* by the students of Chungbuk Law School in May 2009.[21]

Due to the complexity and variety of the new courses being offered at Korean law schools, it is difficult to lecture with existing textbooks. Thus, many lecturers are producing their own textbooks even though it is burdensome. New textbooks are being created to satisfy both the theoretical and practical demands of

19 The author conducted this survey in May 2010 for reporting in the Expertise Road Map for HUFS Law School internal use.

20 It should be emphasized that students run academic associations at most law schools reflecting their own specialized areas, e.g., Carbon Emission Law Association at HUFS, Japanese Law Association at Dong-A University, Anglo-Saxon Law Association at Yeungnam University, Human Rights Law Association at Cheju National University, Economic Law Association at Seoul National University, etc.

21 Examples include: ANIMA (Kangwon, Apr. 2010), Law Review (Kyungpook, Dec. 2009), Middle and Small Enterprises and Law (Ajou, Sept. 2009), Chonnam Law Journal (Chonnam, Mar. 2010), VOR-JURIST (Chungnam, Mar. 2010), Bupdo (Cheju, Sept. 2009), Lawwave (Pusan, Mar. 2010), Yonsei Global Business Law Review (Yonsei, Dec. 2009), Global Law Review (HUFS, Jan. 2010), etc.

legal education. It is likely that lecturers will collaborate with their peers who are teaching the same subjects to produce more new textbooks.[22]

IV. International Law Lecture Methods

The biggest issue with the establishment of the law school system was choosing the lecture methods to be utilized for international law courses. It is generally thought that because Korean law schools adopted the US law school system, international law courses would follow the Socratic method in class. The problem was that most international law lecturers were not familiar with the Socratic teaching method.[23]

Legal education is a practical field of study. Thus, it should satisfy the demand of the society in which international law applies. It is necessary to show students how international law can be applied so that students can understand the operation of international law in society and take a greater interest in such issues. Therefore, in developing teaching methods, it is essential to know the demands of the society and the expectations of students.

Each law school should consider its limitations with respect to teaching international law including language, faculty experience, bar exam preparation pressure, and budget in order to optimize their resources to meet educational purposes and goals. Law schools need to produce lawyers, not theorists, so goals for a law school class must be more specific and practical than they were in the past. Also, it is crucial to consider carefully whether students in international law classes are willing to pursue careers in the field.

International law teaching methods can be categorized into the theory-based lecturing method, case method, problem solving method, and seminar. The theory-based lecture method has traditionally been used in Korea; a method where professors systematically explain abstract theories of law in Civil Law countries. The case method allows students to debate in class over international legal jurisprudence issues that the lecturer provides in advance.[24] In the problem

---

22 The Korean Association of Law Schools (KALS) which represents the interests of law schools has been promoting collaboration among professors for the development of textbooks since 2008. Until now, more than 30 textbooks have been published in the areas of constitutional law, civil law, administrative law, entertainment law, EU law, corporate law, economic law, IP law, social security law, etc. These publications can be downloaded for academic purposes on KALS's website.

23 There has been no research done on the progress thus far with respect to teaching methodologies to measure their outcomes, but since law schools have recently begun to produce graduates, it will be worth researching after a few more years. Nevertheless, many lecturers agree that a new teaching method is required.

24 The Socratic method can be applied in this type of case method. Robert Perry Barnidge, *The Socratic Method in the Teaching of International Law*, CAN. LEG. ED. ANN. REV./

solving method, hypothetical cases are provided to students who must find solutions by studying precedents[25] which can enhance their analytical abilities. The seminar method is used predominantly in graduate school and involves the assignment of readings in advance and extensive in-class discussion of these readings moderated by a member of the faculty.

In law school, it is up to the lecturer to choose the method of teaching. Generally, they have departed from simple lectures and have sought to apply the case study and problem solving methods; sometimes even creating their own teaching methods. Lecturers have also translated international case precedents into Korean[26] because they recognized the need for case studies. This is because they now see international law as a practical field of study. Even the civil service examinations tend to include more case analysis questions, so the interpretation and application of international law is becoming more important. This too has changed the method of teaching in law schools.

Traditional methods force the lecturers to teach from textbooks, whereas law schools require students to read the assigned material beforehand so that during class, they can analyze hypothetical cases and determine which international law principles or theories should be applied. Therefore, it is difficult for students to follow the lecture unless they prepare for class beforehand. Law school lecturers provide a list of references for students to research and also provide a list of experts in each field so that they can interact with them.[27]

Revue de l'Enseignement du Droit au Canada (2010) (arguing that the Socratic method as dominant teaching tool in American legal education could be effectively used in teaching of international law in any jurisdiction).

25 Kim, Young Suk, Teaching Methods of International Law in Law School 9–10 (unpublished paper presented at 2009 International Lawyers Conference, Seoul) (on file with author).

26 In fact, a good number of international law related publications have been published since 2008 just before the start of the law school system in 2009. These publications are different from previous ones as they analyze more cases and legal issues involving Korea.

27 An interesting point here is that some lecturers discuss with their students about what they wish to learn about. In the case of this author, an attempt was made to use a new method in an international trade law class. In this new method, referred to as the Team Based Learning method (TBL), students were put into groups and were allowed to choose their own topics and cases for presentation. They researched international law and chose a topic through group discussion, after which they sought approval from me regarding their chosen topic. The groups analyzed chosen cases to explain which principle or theory of international trade law could be applied, and they also created hypothetical cases. The analyzed case was then presented before the class to stimulate debates and discussions which I moderated. Through this method, I not only helped students find cases but also heightened their practical abilities by creating hypothetical cases. Through TBL, students learned to critically read international legal theories, precedents, and treaties.

International law professors are experimenting and developing new teaching methods. Whatever the method, the important point is to allow students to utilize and strengthen their practical abilities.[28] Students must be able to analyze and judge international legal issues on their own. Generally, Korean students are reticent in the classroom and do not like to articulate their opinions. Professors have the duty to break this habit, yet many fail to fully understand how heavily young students utilize different means of digital communication, including email, text messaging, and social networks. Therefore, professors should embrace technology to develop new methods such as educational blogs for interacting with their students.

There are some promising developments for the future of law schools in Korea. They include a growing interest in the legal profession to participate in legal education. The judiciary and the prosecutor's office have created a system to dispatch working judges and prosecutors to conduct classes when appropriate.[29] Law schools welcome this initiative because they can be utilized for practical lectures or participating in international law moots which allow students to gain international legal skills and knowledge.

Law firms are providing more internship opportunities. Some have developed their own training facilities to educate lawyers and provide practical knowledge that students cannot learn in the classroom. Many law firm lawyers also give lectures at law schools. It has become a new trend for lawyers to participate in team-taught courses.[30]

Meanwhile, the importance of a "hands-on" approach has been steadily gaining popularity. This method allows students to learn from participating in clinics or field trips. For example, students are dispatched to participate in institutions such as human rights committees, NGOs, international relief groups, National Assembly committees, and even international law firms to learn what the practice is like in the field. The opportunity to participate in these institutions allows

---

28 Matthew J. Wilson, *U.S. Legal Education Methods and Ideals: Application to the Japanese and Korean Systems*, 18 CARDOZO J. INT'L & COMP. L. 295 (2010).

29 Since the fall semester of 2010, 19 Judges and 10 prosecutors were dispatched to law schools. Second year students attended lectures. 19 law schools requested lecturers who are judges, while prosecutors lectured in all 25 law schools. Judges lectured on criminal court practices and prosecutors about their practices. This public-private academic cooperation was expanded to all 25 law schools in 2011. Jie-hae Park, *Contrasting Practical Lectures in Law School by Courts and Prosecutors*, LAW TIMES, Jan. 7, 2011.

30 A very striking phenomenon is occurring in law firms. Big law firms are actively participating in law school internship programs as a way to recruit good students. The internship program during the winter vacation for second year students was used as a way to recruit future lawyers. Bae, Kim & Lee and Shin & Kim are most active in this kind of recruitment. Kim & Chang and Yulchon also are following this trend. Law school students with foreign language skills and specialized areas such as IT, IP, and CPAs are strongly preferred by law firms. LAW TIMES, Nov. 26, 2010.

students to understand the benefits and challenges of international law practice in real life. While the best form of clinical education is for law schools to establish and essentially operate their own law offices, this is currently against the regulations and should be resolved in the near future.

Lastly, an interest in continuing legal education (CLE) is increasing. Some lecturers and professionals in the field agree that while international law has its limits as a bar exam topic, its practice requires practical continuing legal education for young lawyers.[31] These CLE courses will likely evolve into study courses such as in LL.M. and S.J.D. programs. For this to be successful, it will require the education of domestic lawyers, but also with globalization and the influx of foreign students, a joint collaboration and cooperation with foreign law schools as well.[32] In fact, law schools are developing interactive methods with foreign law schools such as credit exchanges and dual degree programs.

V. Law School's Achilles' Heel—Bar Examination

As mentioned above, the success of law schools will be judged by the bar passage rate.[33] No matter how great a new system may be, the supreme task of the law school system is to produce qualified lawyers. As the government holds on to the

---

31 This lack of interest in international law caused by the bar exam was one of the factors for legal education reform. For example, Simon Spencer Reyner Lee argues that "Even if universities and cram schools offered students a wider selection of subjects, students are only interested in domestic matters that may be examined on the Bar Examination. Accordingly, the legal syllabus fails to promote the notion of foreign and international law, which are important for Korea as a trading nation. Consequently, the majority of Korean legal officers who have completed the two compulsory years of practical legal training are not well-equipped when foreign jurisdictional work is involved. Therefore, for example, when Korea is involved in international trade negotiations, Korean public officers are forced to conduct negotiations with the help of a translator, neither of whom are licensed legal practitioners, although the public officers may have graduated from an undergraduate law course." Simon Spencer Reyner Lee, *Legal Education in Korea, in* Legal Education in Asia 172–73 (Stacy Steele & Kathryn Taylor, eds., 2010).

32 Professor Brostoff shares her experience on applying comparative cultural learning method as an American law professor. This experience will be helpful when Korean law schools accept foreign students in international exchange programs. Teresa Kissane Brostoff, *Using Culture in the Classroom: Enhancing Learning for International Law Students*, 15 Mich. State J. Int'l L. 557–75 (2007).

33 Actually, there are two major obstacles for the law schools' short-term development—the bar passage rate and the entrance quota. The Ministry of Justice decided that bar pass rate for 2012 was to be 75% of students enrolled in December 2010. However, there is nothing set for after 2010. In fact, the quota of students is tied to the traditional bar exam which will continue until 2017. Until then, it will be unrealistic to guarantee the "normal" functioning of the law school system. There have also been discussions in the political arena about permitting non-law school graduates to take the bar exam, thus threatening the firm establishment of the new system.

power to accredit law schools, their future will depend greatly on their bar passage rate. Under this system, a student's academic path is tied to the bar exam. Similarly, teaching will also be restricted by the bar exam as long as the subject remains a bar examination topic. If the examination is broad in scope and the questions difficult, students will most certainly choose to take international law not as a bar exam subject, but as an elective course in law school.

Under this paradigm, international law related topics are divided into two categories: those that are tested and not tested on the bar exam. For example, courses that cover bar exam topics are public international law and international economic law. These courses require lecturers to employ teaching methods to adequately prepare students for success on the bar exam. On the other hand, students choose courses that do not cover bar exam topics to build their personal expertise in international law. These courses allow the lecturers more freedom to decide upon teaching methods.

According to the Bar Examination Law, only law school graduates are qualified to sit for the exam[34] with attempts limited to five times within five years of graduation.[35] The bar exam consists of a mixture of multiple choice questions and essays.[36] Compulsory subjects include public law (constitutional law & administrative law), civil law (civil law, commercial law & civil procedure law) and criminal law (criminal law & criminal procedure law), in addition to legal ethics (pass/fail at 70% score) and an elective (specialized legal subject). International law is one of the seven elective subjects, which also includes international trade law, labor law, tax law, intellectual property law, economic law, and environmental law.

The Korean Society of International Law has been making an effort to narrow the range of the international law section of the bar exam in order to encourage more students to take international law as one of their elective bar examination subjects. Fortunately, exam takers are allowed to consult conventions and treaties. If conventions were not utilized as a reference, it would be extremely difficult not only to answer the questions, but it would also burden exam takers by requiring them to memorize the relevant international rules.

Even with these limits, the variety of international law related courses being offered gives some hope for international legal education. Students are taking these international law courses on their own initiative. Though the bar exam may be the law school's Achilles' heel, this will be resolved in time. Eventually, the system will shift from the cumbersome Japanese method to the internationally proven US method.

---

34 Bar Examination Law, *supra* note 15, art. 5, para. 1.
35 *Id.* art. 7.
36 *Id.* art. 8.

V. Conclusion

International legal education should be based on a critical analysis of social problems and their solutions. The lectures themselves should not be the goal, but rather they should focus on resolving international legal problems. Law is a social system and acts as a framework for the analysis and resolution of problems occurring within society. Finding solutions to these problems with this tool is to achieve the ultimate goal of social justice in the international and domestic community. International law lecturers should convey to students the significance of international law within domestic law, and also explain why domestic laws are necessary for a nation to fulfill its duty as a member of the international community.

Korea's new law school system was established to break away from the outdated view of international law and to focus on its realistic application and mechanisms. However, the bar exam is still a limiting factor, and the government is the source of both the problem and the solution. Regardless, Korean society's understanding of international law has grown positively within a short period of time. Those that are the source of the demand for future lawyers are interested in the process of supplying these lawyers; that is, the education process itself. They wish to train the students they want, in the way they want in cooperation with law schools. These changes have closed the gap between universities, the Korean Bar Association, law firms, and businesses.

At the center of the matter are the students. This new generation has come to law school with specific goals and convictions to be lawyers and to become specialized in a particular field. Their needs are more specific and determined than what was expected in the past. Although some lecturers doubt the quantity of knowledge the students possess, it is more important from now on to test their potential to become lawyers and increase their capacity for acquiring knowledge.

The conclusion is clear and the means are obvious. The method and content of international legal education should no longer remain just an academic discipline. Rather, practitioners should come to law schools to lecture and contribute their practical knowledge. However, the bar exam will be a critical limiting factor in determining the methods and contents of law school lectures. The actual bar exam system is distinctively characteristic of the Korean legal education system and must be dealt with in an appropriate fashion.

INDEX